Design for Aging Review 12

AIA Design for Aging Knowledge Community

Design for Aging Review

AIA Design for Aging Knowledge Community

THE AMERICAN INSTITUTE OF ARCHITECTS

Published in Australia in 2014 by
The Images Publishing Group Pty Ltd
ABN 89 059 734 431
6 Bastow Place, Mulgrave, Victoria 3170, Australia
Tel: +61 3 9561 5544 Fax: +61 3 9561 4860
books@imagespublishing.com
www.imagespublishing.com

Copyright © The Images Publishing Group Pty Ltd 2014
The Images Publishing Group Reference Number: 1135

National Library of Australia Cataloguing-in-Publication entry

Title:	Design for aging review : AIA design for aging knowledge community / The American Institute of Architects (AIA).
Edition:	12th edition
ISBN:	9781864705850 (hardback)
Subjects:	Older people—Dwellings—United States—Design and construction.
	Old age homes—United States—Design and construction.
	Barrier-free design for older people—United States.
	Architecture—Awards—United States.
Other Authors/Contributors:	American Institute of Architects Design for Aging Center.
Dewey Number:	725.56022273

Executive editor: Virginia Ebbert
Edited by Gina Tsarouhas and Sabita Naheswaran

Designed by Ryan Marshall, The Graphic Image Studio Pty Ltd, Mulgrave, Australia
www.tgis.com.au

Pre-publishing services by Mission Productions Limited, Hong Kong
Printed on 150gsm Quatro Silk by Everbest Printing Co. Ltd., in Hong Kong/China

Contents

M   Merit recipient
S   Special Recognition recipient

AIA Foreword

About ten years ago, Charlie (not his real name) made what was for him a difficult decision. Although he was in good health and still very much active in his community, he sold his single-family bungalow and moved out of state into a senior living facility. His was not a snap decision, but the outcome of months, indeed years of careful research that involved considering a number of factors: affordability, the ease with which friends and relatives could visit, the aesthetics and reputation of the facility, as well as the perceived commitment to a mission over penny pinching at the expense of the residents. Most important, however, Charlie knew that his health—both physical and mental—depended on being engaged; engaged not only with the other residents, but with the community beyond the facility's front door.

The checklist Charlie went through that shaped his decision—which, by the way, has been vindicated handsomely—reflects many of the findings of this, the 12th edition of the AIA's invaluable "Design for Aging Review." I say "invaluable" for at least two reasons.

First, the jury that examined the projects submitted for this review encouraged research. The increasing importance of evidence-based and replicable data is an important and welcome trend within the architectural profession. This includes, thankfully, getting out of the office and talking to those most affected by the design of these facilities—seniors. Having these data helps architects make the argument to those who invest in these projects to factor in the kinds of amenities that allow the elderly, like Charlie, to enjoy a high quality of life, often well into their 90s.

In Charlie's case, he chose to live in a high-rise whose internal layout facilitates easy contact with the other residents. High ceilings and large windows in the dining room afford wonderfully expansive views of water and gardens. Yes, transportation is provided for those who want to participate in the community's lively cultural scene, but it's also possible to walk to nearby coffee shops, libraries, clothing stores, and restaurants. Residents are not marooned in an attractive but remote facility in the middle of nowhere.

This connectivity engenders a welcome sense of freedom and the opportunity to engage with people of different ages.

The second reason for calling this report "invaluable" is, quite frankly, selfish. I'm a member of the Baby Boom generation whose leading edge is (even now) confronting the prospect of making decisions that will determine how we'll live the rest of our lives. This is an awesome prospect for future residents and a huge challenge for those who design senior facilities. The creativity and sensitivity demonstrated by projects documented in this report give hope that these years, if not golden, can be lived with dignity, allowing us to continue to be contributing and valued members of society.

Read and be inspired.

Helene Combs Dreiling, FAIA
2014 AIA President

LeadingAge Foreword

The 12th edition of the *Design for Aging Review* showcases state-of-the-art senior housing and services. It also reflects the realities of our recent economic downturn with the addition of the new Small Projects category. Although the need for housing and services increased as our population aged, many providers and older consumers alike had less to spend and invest. And, as is often the case when we are forced to be more thoughtful and resourceful during leaner times, quality and innovation flourished, as witnessed by the captivating projects featured in this publication!

We know that a majority of older people today express the desire to age in their communities, if not in the actual house they have called home for decades. Yet, a subset of the population is proactively moving to more accessible housing and amenity-rich, walkable communities. While some of these environments may be purpose-built senior housing, others exist within a broader spectrum of community-integrated options and settings.

Providers and designers are especially challenged to respond to the great variety of needs presented by our diverse older population—these include disparate financial status, functional abilities and social supports. And, while very much focused on meeting current consumer needs, aging services organizations are also positioning themselves for the anticipated preferences of emerging and future cohorts of older consumers.

Our jury found a number of significant trends and innovations as they studied this cycle's submissions. The jury-recognized projects in the following pages feature design approaches that address and support the physical, psychological, and cultural needs of older persons in skilled nursing, hospice, special care units, assisted living, independent housing, adult day care, and wellness centers. They demonstrate planning strategies that connect senior living and care environments to the larger community, and enhance the organizations' roles as community centers for successful aging.

Within this context, the 12th cycle of the *Design for Aging Review* identified a number of important themes and trends that enhance senior housing and services including: linking to nature and accessing natural light; connecting to other residents, as well as to the great community; designing to a residential scale, along with reducing walking distances; and improving the resident experience while also responding to cultural needs and preferences.

Ultimately, the jury evaluated the success and appeal of these projects and communities based on the age-old question: "Is this a place in which we would want to live?"

William L. (Larry) Minnix, Jr.
President and Chief Executive Officer
LeadingAge

Jury Statement

One is filled with a sense of honor, humility, and responsibility when offered a seat on a six-person national jury of one's peers, when the better part of one's career has been devoted to a particular industry. Our group consisted of three prominent members invited by LeadingAge for their expertise on the operational side of senior living facilities, two national architects, and one leading interior design professional. This jury statement has had the benefit of the input of this entire group, and attempts to represent the unified opinion of all its members.

Coming together for the common goal of evaluating the wide array of submissions from across the nation to identify the most progressive ideas in seniors' environments and experience was an exciting and complex undertaking. The projects selected for awards and subsequent publication represent the most innovative, creative, and socially responsive solutions that will enhance the life experience for our seniors both today, and for years to come. They also represent the utilization of efficient design—from an operational perspective—to optimize staffing, allowing the highest level of care and services. A noticeable impact of the recent recession was the interest in bringing *value* to the forefront from among the many desirable underlying features needed to attract today's seniors. This was evident in the large number of renovation and repositioning projects that were included in the submissions compared to new projects. At least for now, gone are the overly extravagant, and those that need to be "large for the sake of being large." Another important underlying theme was providing *choice*, something we all have in our everyday lives, but that has not always been made available to residents in seniors' communities of yesterday.

Successful solutions quite often involved transforming "ordinary" tasks like eating, bathing, grooming, and socializing into the extra-ordinary: by incorporating a variety of thematic restaurants and spa-type experiences, for example, and embedding these daily tasks into social opportunities. Our jury was partial to solutions that encouraged "Design for Aging" which can be manifested in many ways. Regardless of the financial and spatial challenges encountered in the renovation projects, we felt these solutions would improve the quality of life of the residents.

As one jury member pointed out, "If some of the same design solutions [were] submitted as part of a new construction project, we would have not seen them as favorably."

The jury appreciated the variety of projects submitted, from high-end luxury to the more challenging affordable housing and community-based. It was gratifying to see the renewed sense of responsibility and cultural sensitivity displayed in serving all markets, including the homeless, lower income, varied religious denominations, and affinity groups like Native Americans, as well as those with special needs like memory care and developmentally disabled.

The small projects category (i.e., where construction cost $3 million or less) displayed great examples of urban and community-based services, including senior cafes, adult day care services, respite, and PACE programs. Continued emphasis on wellness and fitness was also evident in many submissions and manifested itself in a variety of elaborate spas and fitness centers.

Our jury went through a rigorous process of separating the outstanding submissions from a very superior palette of entries. The successful projects exemplified many of the following criteria:

- **Engagement with the outdoors and natural surroundings.** The importance of making the built environment fit in with the rural, urban, or suburban surroundings was evident in many of the successful submissions, as was an emphasis on the ability to access and enjoy the outdoors. Enhancing the overall living experience on a macro level outside of one's private space and on a micro level within one's immediate living unit was successfully achieved in many submissions.

- **Connectivity to the greater community.**
  We felt that the project's integration with the neighboring and greater community was essential to providing a complete and whole life experience for our seniors.

- **Nesting / residential scale neighborhoods.**
  Avoiding a commercial / medical feel in favor of a residential and more intimate scale was successfully achieved in many instances by the use of small clusters of rooms that avoided the use of corridors and grouped rooms around living and activity areas, much like one's home. At the same time, this afforded great lines of sight for staffing supervision with minimal barriers. This was especially evident in a number of the innovative solutions in Memory Support units.

- **Shorter walking distances.** Successful entries were also able to cut down walking distances to dining and other essential amenities by optimizing adjacencies and using neighborhood-scale pods. This had the effect of minimizing (or completely avoiding) long hallways in spite of the large numbers served.

- **Emphasis on natural light.** Many designs incorporated clerestories, large bay and corner windows to take advantage of different views and exposures. Smaller living units dictated by cost considerations were enhanced by large windows, which give the impression of a larger room.

- **Innovative repositioning of existing facilities.**
  This resulted in the dramatic transformation of aging campuses and facilities.

If we can someday successfully solve the contrarian (but simultaneous) objectives of being able to provide all the choices and variety that one experiences and takes for granted in one's daily life *before* entering a seniors' community, and *also* provide all the economies and efficiencies of scale that are offered *within* a seniors' community, we will come a long way in providing what many of us are truly looking for and need.

This is a daunting objective because it means being able to afford all the stimulation of interaction with children and young adults, the ability to go to the street corner bakery, access a wide variety of thematic restaurants, sporting events, and travel. Ideally, we would be able to provide this without sacrificing security, with the only limitation being one's physical ability and doing this efficiently and economically to still be affordable. This may take the form of "seniors' communities without walls" or other future solutions, but only time will tell. Our industry is still relatively young with many new innovative ideas coming to the forefront every day – we are getting ever closer to a Utopia for our seniors of tomorrow.

On behalf of the DFAR12 Jury,
Shekhar Bhushan, AIA
Jury Chair

The Jury

Andrew Lee Alden, Assoc. AIA

Andrew Lee Alden, Assoc. AIA, is the Living Environments Studio Director for Eppstein Uhen Architects (EUA) in Milwaukee, Wisconsin, and leads the firm's design for projects with an aging focus. Andrew's passion and design expertise extends through the full continuum of care environments. As a respected member in the design for aging community, his thoughtful design solutions and forward thinking ideas make him a sought after resource. As a believer in the value of bridging the gap between research and practice, he engages in applied research, publishes articles, and presents at regional and national conferences. He is an active committee member for regional and national organizations including the Shorewood Elder Services Advisory Board (ESAB), the Society for the Advancement of Gerontological Environments (SAGE), and the American Society on Aging (ASA).

Shekhar Bhushan, AIA

Shekhar Bhushan, AIA, has been associated with the senior industry for the last 30 years and has focused entirely on the field for the last 15. As the director of design at one of the nationally known firms in senior living from the mid-1980s through 2003, he was heavily involved in the assisted living prototypes for Marriott Senior Living, Manor Care, Sun Health, and many others across the country. In 2003, Shekhar opened his own firm, SB Architecture PC, Inc., specializing in senior living environments and housing as a design consultant. His primary role is working with operators and providers in senior living facilities in the master planning, repositioning, and programming of their campuses across the country. He also specializes in feasibility and yield analysis reports. He has written papers in *Long-Term Living* and conducted research in a number of related fields.

Linford Good

Linford Good has expertise in planning, leading design efforts, organizing construction, and operating continuing care retirement communities. His primary interest is the atmosphere and feel of the built environment and how the attitudes and activities of occupants can influence that atmosphere. Currently serving as vice president of planning and marketing at Landis Homes in Lititz, Pennsylvania, Linford has 28 years of experience in continuing care retirement communities. Prior to joining Landis Homes in 1998, he spent 13 years in planning and marketing at Messiah Village located in Mechanicsburg, Pennsylvania. Linford's career has focused on improving the physical environment within retirement communities to encourage resident and staff growth, fulfillment, and wellness.

Renee Anderson

Renee Anderson has been associated with Saint John's Communities, Inc., a Milwaukee CCRC, since September 1996. She began her Saint John's career as director of finance, was named vice president in 2001 and was promoted to president and CEO in 2011. Prior to Saint John's, Renee was the controller for MJ Care, Inc., a regional provider of physical, occupational and speech therapy; an analyst for Extendicare, one of the nation's largest providers of skilled nursing services; and an auditor with Arthur Young. She is a CPA and a Certified Nursing Assistant.

Ingrid Fraley, ASID

Ingrid Fraley has been active in the design of interior environments for over 30 years, and is the President of Design Services, Inc., which she formed in 1984 to provide turn-key services to clients involved in new construction, remodeling, and / or the renovation of senior living environments nationwide. Ingrid co-authored the results of post-occupancy evaluation data from award-winning senior housing projects. She received support from the Rothschild Foundation to form a task force to begin discussions with the United States Access Board and ANSI to modify regulations that are in conflict with best practices for elder care. In 2009, she participated in a congressional briefing on older Americans. Ingrid is chair emeritus for the AIA Design for Aging Knowledge Community and co-chair of the Design for Aging Washington, DC chapter. She has served on the ASID Council on Aging and the Revision Committee for the Facilities Guidelines Institute. Her public speaking engagements include the national conferences of LeadingAge and AIA.

C. William (Bill) Trawick, CASP

Bill Trawick is President and CEO of Bishop Gadsden, a life care retirement community affiliated with The Episcopal Church and located in Charleston, South Carolina. In this position since 1985, he has overseen the development of the 70-acre, 435-resident community from its beginning. Bishop Gadsden has been recognized twice by the *Design for Aging Review*: in 2001 for the quality of architecture of its $60 million expansion and in 2007 for its chapel. Bill has been a licensed nursing home administrator and residential care administrator for 25 years and has his Aging Services Professional Certification. He has been active in LeadingAge South Carolina, having served as its president; LeadingAge National, having served in the House of Delegates; and, the White House Conference on Aging, having served as a delegate. Bill is active in local civic affairs, including the Rotary Club, the Preservation Society of Charleston, and Charleston Area Senior Services.

Projects and Awards

Small // Building // Planning / Concept Design

GMPA Architects, Inc.

Brandman Centers for Senior Care

Reseda, California // Los Angeles Jewish Home

Facility type: CCRC or part of a CCRC
Target market: Low income / subsidized
Site location: Urban; greyfield
Project site area (square feet): 9,400
Gross square footage of the renovation / modernization involved in the project: 9,400

Purpose of the renovation / modernization:
Repositioning
This site is within 1,000 feet of public transportation.
Provider type: Faith-based non-profit

Below: Expansive windows provide a vibrant inside / outside connection.
Opposite: The reception area radiates hospitality, with wood / ceiling details and ample daylighting.

Overall Project Description

A non-profit organization, dedicated to improving the lives of vulnerable and low income seniors, expended its services by adding a Program of All-inclusive Care for the Elderly (PACE). This nationally recognized program offers nursing home eligible, low income seniors the option of remaining in their own homes, thereby enhancing the quality of their lives as well as lowering the cost of medical expenses. PACE participants are not on-campus residents; they are brought to and from their homes to the PACE building for healthcare and social services, with 95 percent of the participants at this particular campus relying upon Medicaid or Medicare payment.

The PACE facility is located on the ground floor of an existing office building within a campus that houses skilled nursing homes, assisted living, and administrative offices. This PACE was envisioned as a flagship destination—the first of a multi-site regional healthcare network for the non-profit

organization. Although the tight footprint of the existing building remains unchanged, the floor plan was transformed dramatically into a contemporary, upbeat, light-filled space that is integrated with the campus, the community at large, and the existing administrative offices on the second and third levels.

The comprehensive program includes medical clinics, nurses' station, exam rooms, dental treatment rooms, preventative care, social services, dining, hygienic services such as bathing and grooming, an outdoor courtyard, a state-of-the-art physical therapy center, a kitchen, multipurpose room, offices, a quiet room, and group therapy and activity rooms. The design solution encourages seniors to frequent the facility for physical, mental, and social needs, and to look forward to their visits in an environment that is comfortable, friendly, modern, and oriented towards the community.

Project Goals

What were the major goals?

- A main project goal was to fit all of the complex program requirements into an existing building that was significantly smaller than a typical PACE center. To maximize square footage, the upstairs offices for marketing and campus management were left intact, allowing more space on the lower level for participants in the PACE program. A new lobby and an elevator link the upper and ground floor levels, bridging the connection between old and new. The new reception area allows direct access to multipurpose spaces, the clinic, personal care, physical therapy, and administration. Clusters of similar services are grouped together: the medical cluster is accessed directly from the lobby eliminating the need to go through the multipurpose area; the transportation coordinator's and administrator's offices face the drop off area and are sited adjacent to one another to facilitate communication, and the physical therapy room is away from the main entrance. From the multipurpose room, patients can safely wander out to the courtyard. Generous corridors accommodate wheelchairs and create an open feel. Multiple bathrooms placed throughout can be accessed from all main spaces. The multipurpose room accommodates dining, computers, library, arts and crafts, meetings, and socializing.

- A second goal was to create an individual identity for the PACE Center, yet at the same time link it to the community. Originally, access to the building was via the main gated entry, and the administrative building had an inward focus, isolated from the street by high windows. To address this, the side wall at the ground floor was transformed into an inviting open lobby—a pedestrian-friendly space now faces the community. Outside, a welcoming entry court with a large stone patio and long canopy creates a strong connection to the street. Prior to the renovation, small, high windows along the perimeter visually separated the facility from the street. Newly enlarged windows connect to the community, while landscaping and modern signage add visibility from the street.

- Another goal was to create opportunities for donor recognition while maintaining the names of original donors. Since funding for capital improvements relies on donations, the creation of meaningful venues for donor recognition was critical. An upscale donor display area was created, combining new and old names in a tribute that can be easily updated.

Challenges: What were the greatest design challenges?

Renovating an existing building in a tight, infill location with ongoing services: the project is located in a tight space on a campus that annually serves more than 1,700 seniors, renovation of the existing office floor required close daily coordination to maintain ongoing operations. Since the second and third levels —which

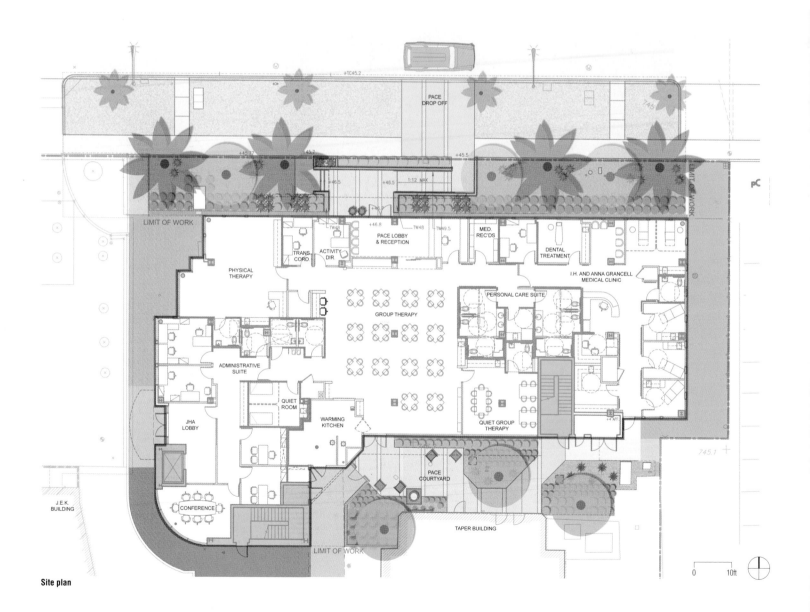

Site plan

house the marketing department and office space for overall non-profit management—remained fully active, careful staging coordination was required, particularly during the work week. As walls were demolished, structural and mechanical problems were unveiled, necessitating further design changes, and further stretching the available budget. Significant portions of the building required updating, a new HVAC system was necessary, a communication system was added, and an elevator was replaced. Despite these coordination challenges, the daily operation of the two upper floors and overall administration for the campus functioned smoothly with minimal disruption.

Designing an attractive, stylish, and functional, yet cost effective facility that conforms to the strict government-regulated PACE requirements, and within a budget funded solely by philanthropic support, was also a challenge. An unusual color scheme, luxurious fabrics, and natural finishes were chosen; sophisticated lighting added casual elegance to the facility. The most dramatic interior detail is rounded soffits at the ceiling, punctuated with special lighting. The design inspiration is an adaptation of mid-century modern style with features that include clean lines, repetition of a circle motif (used in the chair upholstery, lighting fixtures, the design on the frosted glass panel dividers,

and the interior of the elevator), drought tolerant landscaping, glass tile accents in the bathrooms, a bamboo finish on the doors, and a color palette of warm beige tones with soft red accents.

Below: The multipurpose room serves as a hub of interaction and connects to all major cluster areas, including the outdoor garden.

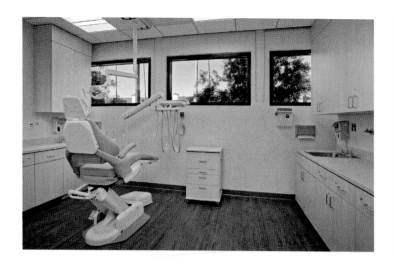

Innovations: What innovations or unique features were incorporated into the design of the project?

Architecturally, the design for the PACE Center offers a welcoming, upscale environment, unlike typical medical facilities of this type. Elaborate lighting fixtures, carefully selected and placed, accentuate and define spaces and unify the interior. Details include round-cornered ceiling coffers punctuated with dramatic lighting and specially chosen lighting suspended over the reception desk and nursing station. Multiple wood textures and patterns further refine the spaces and help identify different areas. Even though the building is a clinic, it has a warm, residential feel. Daylight filters throughout, creating an uplifting participant experience and allowing open views and connections to nature. Given the constraints of the existing structure and the strict regulations for PACE centers, the design creates a sense of comfort and calmn, bringing an unexpected, refined sense of style to a tightly regulated facility of this type.

Transportation to and from the center is via vans. This unique approach maximizes land usage because it requires no additional parking space on the existing campus, with the exception of a loading / unloading area for the vans. This green design solution minimizes gas usage, and also enhances the safety of seniors, especially those with poor eyesight, physical limitations, and those with no driving license, car, or friend to drive them. From an architectural standpoint, transportation coordination was an important design consideration. Van pick up and drop off is safely near the front entrance, while the transportation coordinator's and office administrator's offices are adjacent.

Personal grooming services are another unique feature. At the Center, seniors can shower, leave their clothes to be laundered, and return home wearing fresh, clean clothing. To accommodate this, spacious upscale men's and women's showers with ADA compliant features were added, as well as a laundry room.

Marketing / Occupancy: What issues were encountered regarding marketing and / or achieving full occupancy?

Marketing projections were made to determine the number of potential seniors interested in receiving healthcare and preventable services while living at home. Due to the dense elderly population donations were sought, fundraising events were held, and the project was described in newsletters and on the non-profit's website. Since it is located on a busy existing campus, the building will be operating at high occupancy relatively soon. Plans are underway for an additional PACE facility nearby. Marketing efforts emphasize high quality all-inclusive care (including comprehensive primary, specialty medicine, prescription medications, adult day care, fitness, and social opportunities) for nursing-home eligible seniors who prefer to remain in their own homes. Key selling points include the non-profit's legacy, enhancing the quality of life, and cost savings.

Data / Research: What innovative or unique data collection and / or research was applied during the planning and / or design process?

At the outset of the project, the architectural firm conducted extensive research to review the strict regulations of the government-sponsored PACE program and to analyze built PACE projects in California. Afterwards, both the managing principal and the design principal traveled throughout California (along with the vice president of planning and community-based programs) touring and studying multiple PACE site design and operations. They interviewed staff, doctors, and visiting seniors to determine what works best and what improvements might be suggested.

Collaboration: How did stakeholders, occupants, the design team, and / or others collaborate during the planning and / or design process?

After touring other PACE facilities and interviewing stakeholders, the architects participated in the site selection process along with the non-profit's leadership committees, visiting several potential sites and commenting on each. Working with the organization, its committees, board members and stakeholders, a decision was made to use the main existing campus as the prototype rather than purchase or rent a new parcel. Advantages for doing so included financial considerations and speed of delivery, as well as the ability to showcase the new center on a fully operational campus. Once the location was determined, the architects studied the regulations governing the site and worked with the organization to carefully coordinate all construction activities around an active, functioning campus. Prior to the design work, the existing structure was analyzed by the architect and consultant team to identify any potential issues.

Outreach: What off-site outreach services are offered to the greater community?

The program's target market is skilled nursing home–eligible seniors who prefer to live in their own homes. Outreach services offered to the community include medical and dental services, preventative healthcare, physical therapy, social events, speaking events, personal care, dining, computers, and arts and crafts. The facility, which opened at the beginning of 2013, is anticipated to serve hundreds of seniors each month.

Green / Sustainable Features: What green / sustainable features had the greatest impact on the project's design?

Site selection, maximized daylighting, and reuse of existing building structure and / or materials.

What were the primary motivations for including green / sustainable design features in the project?

Support the mission / values of the client / provider and the design team, and make a contribution to the greater community.

What challenges did the project face when trying to incorporate green / sustainable design features?

Actual first cost premium.

Common Spaces: What senior-friendly common spaces are included in the project?

Bistro / casual dining; dedicated fitness equipment room; dedicated rehabilitation / therapy gym; large multipurpose room; dedicated conference / meeting space; library / information resource center; art studio / craft room; and outdoor courtyard.

Jury Comments

This creative renovation project is a great example of providing maximum benefit within a limited budget under the PACE Program, without appearing to be frugal. With 95 percent of its residents dependent on Medicaid, the program succeeds in providing most of the vital everyday amenities necessary for a fulfilling life for these seniors in an inviting and cozy atmosphere. The changes to the physical environment started with the desire for an adaptive reuse of a former greyfield (under-utilized) office building. The experience of the PACE client was considered with renovations occurring at the entry of the building and continuing through the program/ activity spaces, including the service areas. Attention was given to the interior finishes to create an ambiance that is light-filled, contemporary, and warm.

Opposite top left: Medical and dental services are offered as well as preventative healthcare and social services.
Opposite top right: Spa-like bathrooms have upscale surroundings.
Left: The nurses station is open yet functional with extra space located underneath the desk area.
Photography: Adrian Tiemans Photography

THW Design

Cosby Spear Highrise

Atlanta, Georgia // Atlanta Housing Authority

Facility type (date of initial occupancy): Independent Living (October 2011)
Target market: Low income / subsidized
Site location: Urban
Project site area (square feet): 16,750
Gross square footage of the renovation / modernization involved in the project: 16,750

Purpose of the renovation / modernization: Repositioning
Ratio of parking spaces to residents: 1:0.35
This site is within 1,000 feet of public transportation, and within 1,000 feet of at least 10 basic services with pedestrian access to those services.
Provider type: Governmental

Below: Lobby
Opposite: Community room

Overall Project Description

When the owner received stimulus funding, the team determined programming and design that would result in maximum impact for the seniors and disabled residents of the two highrise buildings on a prominent north avenue site along the edge of the city. The design style for the property was focused on providing light and open spaces which promote socially interactive programs. By providing open spaces, residents are constantly exposed to the activities taking place. Whereas the original design put everything behind closed doors, the new design invited residents to join in. The use of a more contemporary style was fitting to the newness of the repositioning. A liveliness is achieved through lighting, materials, and color which give the spaces a warm and inviting style.

This project is a successful transformation from "housing of last resort" to a living well residential development. Residents are now proud of their home resulting in increased interaction with family,

friends, and service providers. Now fully operational, the new open social spaces and programming are bringing residents out of their units and allowing them to engage as never before. With the stimulation of mind and body, the buildings are contributing to a healthy, more meaningful lifestyle for the residents, visitors, and staff.

Project Goals

What were the major goals?

The goal was established to create social spaces that would be able to compete with the private sector. The improvements would provide residents with indoor and outdoor spaces for meeting, entertainment, arts and crafts, wellness, dining, developing computing skills, and recreation. Though the buildings posed many challenges, such as structural shear walls and security concerns, the new open spaces created an inviting flow. Such openness increased social interaction among residents and adds to the value of the programming.

Challenges: What were the greatest design challenges?

All work had to be performed whilst the building was occupied. Coordinated by management and the contractor, the design had to allow access to the building, to the elevators, and to the egress stairs at all times during construction. The design incorporated a plan that included phasing to provide continuous function for vehicle and pedestrian circulation, life safety, and essential building functions. The impact on residents' daily lives was minimized.

Another difficult design challenge was to open spaces and create inviting environments in an existing concrete frame highrise building that required shear walls at the ground floor, dividing it into segments approximately every 20 feet. As structural elements, there were few apparent options as they could not be eliminated. Where inexpensive solutions could not be found, these walls were selectively provided with reinforced punched openings to give the feel of openness and transition from one space to another.

Innovations: What innovations or unique features were incorporated into the design of the project?

With the senior population of the building, security was a top priority. The design team was striving for openness and an ease of interior to exterior circulation. While the two goals seemed incompatible, both were achieved through thoughtful planning. By moving the main security line to the property line, access control allowed passage to only residents and authorized guests. Once inside this line, a lesser degree of security allowed residents to enter and exit the building at multiple points. The security officer became the concierge, greeting all residents and visitors. Perimeter cameras were provided and monitored, though the monitors were concealed from public view. Thus, security was provided, but did not compromise the resort-like feel.

Marketing / Occupancy: What issues were encountered regarding marketing and / or achieving full occupancy?

The community is currently operating at full occupancy and has an extensive waiting list.

Data / Research: What innovative or unique data collection and / or research was applied during the planning and / or design process?

A complete physical needs assessment was performed to make sure that the life safety and viability needs of the property were met. When

Top left: Social cafe
Top right: Community media room
Photography: Jonathan Hillyer

all of this input had been detailed, budgets were reviewed and priorities set. Two themes were emphasized: the monies spent touch all the residents, and the result has maximum impact in an effort to totally transform and reposition the property.

Collaboration: How did stakeholders, occupants, the design team, and / or others collaborate during the planning and / or design process?

Prior to drawing the first line, all stakeholders were engaged in a series of planning sessions. Resident input was obtained through focus groups. Management staff were queried to make sure that facilities properly serve the efficiency of staff and the needs of residents.

Outreach: What off-site outreach services are offered to the greater community?

The community provides residents with outreach services. These services vary from computer training to visiting nurses.

Green / Sustainable Features: What green / sustainable features had the greatest impact on the project's design?

Energy efficiency and water efficiency.

What were the primary motivations for including green / sustainable design features in the project?

Support the mission /'values of the client / provider and the design team, and lower operational costs.

Common Spaces: What senior-friendly common spaces are included in the project?

Bistro / casual dining; coffee shop / grab-and-go; dedicated fitness equipment room; large multipurpose room; library / information resource center; and an art studio / craft room.

Jury Comments

This HUD/low-income, urban high-rise for seniors received stimulus funding. The goal was to achieve maximum impact to transform / reposition the project with limited funds (less than $3 million). The contemporary design provides light and open spaces, which promote socially interactive programs. The sheer walls, which had divided the community space and served as barriers, were opened to create visual connectedness and better circulation. While the original design put everything behind closed doors, new design invites residents to join in. A lively, inviting environment is achieved through attention to contemporary lighting, varied textures and a warm color palate. Being urban and serving a senior population, the new "openness" brought with it security concerns. These were overcome by moving the security access to the property line with cameras monitored at the concierge desk, thereby enabling residents / guests to enter / exit the building at multiple points; thus allowing for greater connectedness between interior / exterior spaces. The building entrance has an updated identity by the use of contemporary lighting, canopy and seating. The feeling is as if one is arriving at a resort, which is a source of pride for the residents.

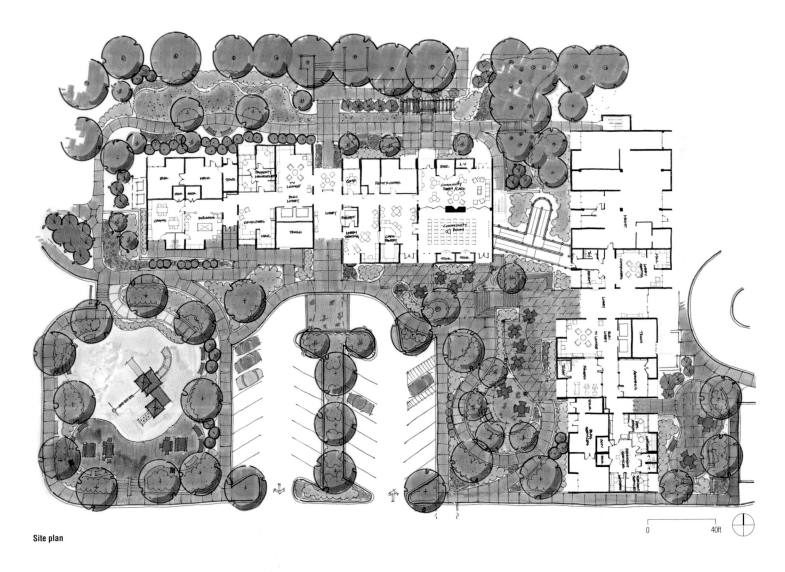

Site plan

0   40ft

Perkins Eastman

Marian's House
Rochester, New York // Jewish Senior Life

Facility type (date of initial occupancy): Assisted Living—dementia / memory support (April 2013); CCRC or part of a CCRC
Target market: Middle / upper middle
Site location: Urban; greyfield

Project site area (square feet): 239,561
Gross square footage of the new construction involved in the project: 5,323
Provider type: Faith-based non-profit

Below: Outdoor dining area in the courtyard
Opposite: Casual seating in the courtyard patio

Photography: courtesy Perkins Eastman

Overall Project Description

Marian's House provides adult day care—for people with early to mid-stage Alzheimer's and other related dementias—in a contemporary setting that offers a retreat for those with memory impairment and a respite for caregivers. Located within a residential neighborhood off campus, Marian's House offers meals, activities, supervision, and specialized programming in a warm, residential facility. An enhanced respite program is possible; a caregiver lives on the premises in a one bedroom apartment. In partnership with the Alzheimer's Association and other senior care agencies, Marian's House is also a resource center and provides training and support for family caregivers.

The house is specially designed for both one-on-one interaction and group activities:

- Large, open kitchen and eating area enable participants to be part of meal preparation.
- Great room provides ample space for activities, movies, and relaxation.
- Dining room is for shared meals or family caregiver support meetings.
- Den offers an alternative get-away with a soothing, calm environment.
- Screened porch provides a safe overlook to the public street and front yard.
- Fenced-in garden with an abundance of plants, flowers, and shrubs allows for safe outdoor walking.
- Two guest rooms are available for occasional overnight respite stays.
- On-site 24-hour caregiver has a one-bedroom apartment.

Project Goals

What were the major goals?

The owner wanted a day care center and respite for families that have a relative with dementia who may need care during the day or on occasional weekends.

- Create a daytime home for people with dementia that fits into the surrounding community and does not stand out. The house's narrow side was turned to the street to visually reduce its larger size for passersby; it also sits back from the street, abiding by the neighborhood's setback restrictions. The residential scale of materials, massing, and roofs allow this large house to feel homelike. The single drive leads to a parking area hidden from the street.

- Create a house with a secure setting, without having a locked-in character. The front door is not visible or prominent from most rooms to reduce resident elopement or anxiety from family / visitor comings and goings. The majority of views from the house are into the secure main garden. The house has sight lines that allow the caregiver to see residents in many rooms simultaneously, as well as the main garden area and paths.

- Design a house reflecting homes that are familiar to the typical resident. The house has a contemporary character with typical residential size rooms: a kitchen, breakfast nook, dining and living room with library alcove, and family room that serves as a place to watch television or host educational meetings for families learning about living with a family member with early dementia. The garden is residential in character and offers a terrace directly off the living room.

- Provide a flexible respite program with an on-site 24-hour caregiver. The design provides a separate apartment and garage for the caregiver, so that their home is not accessible to residents. There is flexibility in the use of two respite bedrooms, which can be open to the caregiver as private guest rooms, or to the day care portion of the home when residents stay over.

- Provide family caregiver support by using Marian's House as a resource center. All day care spaces are designed for double use as an evening resource center for classes and

discussion groups. Media and technology has been integrated for participant use, for evening presentations, and training videos / presentations.

Challenges: What were the greatest design challenges?

The greatest challenges were the narrow site, designing two houses in one, and creating a secure place for people with memory support needs. Marian's House is, in essence, two interconnected residences on one site: the day care house and the caregivers' suite. The narrow lot presented both site and design challenges

resulting in an L-shaped house; designers turned the narrow side of the house to the street and created a private parking court with a less visible entry for residents and family to come and go. This L-shaped design created courtyard space for the day care house, and provided the caregivers with a backyard. It also created an interstitial, flexible space with an office and two respite rooms between the residences, serving as a buffer. Great attention was given to being welcoming and open, and encouraging residents to explore while using design tools as the mechanism to create safety.

Marian's House is not a licensed day care program for seniors, nor is it a residence for older adults, nor is it a single-family residence; however, it has components of all three. This created design, building code, and zoning ambiguities around how to approach a unique solution, yet meet the highest levels of fire safety. Careful work with public officials, neighbors, and the building department resulted in a building that maintains its residential appeal, while respecting building code standards for adult day care, local zoning setbacks for residential structures, and high quality housing standards for the caregiver apartment.

Innovations: What innovations or unique features were incorporated into the design of the project?

The most innovative feature is the arrangement of the rooms to allow for flexible uses by daily participants, on-site caregivers, and families. Subtle changes in door arrangements allow for areas to be closed or extended as needs dictate throughout the day and evening. In addition, sight lines that allow caregivers to see residents as they move from room to room help create a secure environment. The front door has a vestibule with an interior door that is hidden from the living room by a fireplace; it is around the corner from the dining room so residents do not see other

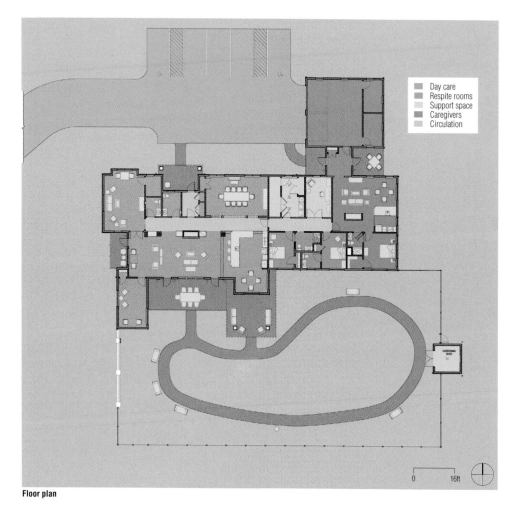

■	Day care
■	Respite rooms
■	Support space
■	Caregivers
■	Circulation

0   16ft

Floor plan

residents or guests coming and going, reducing the temptation to wander out. The higher ceilings and large windows in the main rooms open to the garden, directing resident attention away from the entry and into the garden area where a looped path leads into and out of the house.

Additionally, the house includes two respite rooms that were designed with dual functions: a place for residents to rest during the day or for an occasional overnight respite stay, and as a private guest room space for the caregiver that can be locked off from the day care facility.

Marketing / Occupancy: What issues were encountered regarding marketing and / or achieving full occupancy?

The owner's target is families or couples who are caring for people with early onset dementia at home. One of the key factors in offering this service to these family members is to allay their concerns about taking a family member to a strange location and allowing others to care for this individual. Once the day care house was open, anecdotal stories confirmed the owner's selling point that most residents do better in Marian's House due to increased social interaction and caregiver attention.

Data / Research: What innovative or unique data collection and / or research was applied during the planning and / or design process?

The project commenced with a community needs assessment. Focus groups were held with community organizations providing senior services, family caregivers, and potential participants in the early stages of dementia. These discussions led

Below: The living room is open and engaging, allowing guests and caregivers to connect.
Photography: John Smillie

to crafting Marian House's unique program with respite services and on-site, live-in caregivers. Program components also evolved with interest in tapping a large pool of volunteers to provide focused activities that would build continuity between participants and their former community roles as teachers, bankers, or craftsmen. The resource center grew out of discussions with families who felt strongly about their caregiving role at home but wanted to be able to do it better by managing behaviors, anticipating safety issues, and meeting a wide range of psychosocial needs.

The designers combined 25 years of experience designing special care environments with a recently completed post-occupancy evaluation of five buildings built over a 20 year period. Re-visiting these residences many years after completion (and their initial post-occupancy evaluations) confirmed many crucial findings about the role of outdoor space, the central image of the kitchen, and the importance of sight lines for unobtrusive surveillance of the environment. Just as powerful was seeing how innovative concepts from 20 years ago were often still relevant and how new needs adapted spaces as programs evolved.

Collaboration: How did stakeholders, occupants, the design team, and / or others collaborate during the planning and / or design process?

The sponsor included their senior management team in the entire design process, bringing a wide range of perspectives to this unique model. They also integrated expertise from community organizations such as the Alzheimer's Association, who in turn brought insights from family caregivers.

Outreach: What off-site outreach services are offered to the greater community?

The outreach includes:

- Local primary doctors (internal medicine), geriatricians, and memory-specific doctors.
- Social workers at hospitals and transitional care social workers.
- Geriatric care managers.
- Organizations: Lifespan, Eldersource, Alzheimer's Association, Senior Options for Independence (SOFI), Greater Rochester Area Partnership for the Elderly (GRAPE), AARP, YMCA, Jewish Family Services, Jewish Community Center, Catholic Family Services, Senior Centers.

- Companion care service providers in Rochester.
- Home care agencies: VNS, HCR, Lifetime, Interim Health.
- Board members / volunteers.
- Other local senior living communities and other adult day care programs.
- Memory care facilities in Rochester.

Green / Sustainable Features: What green / sustainable features had the greatest impact on the project's design?

Site design considerations, energy efficiency, and maximized daylighting.

What were the primary motivations for including green / sustainable design features in the project?

Support the mission / values of the client / provider, lower operational costs, and resident health.

What challenges did the project face when trying to incorporate green / sustainable design features?

Perceived first cost premium, and lack of support / encouragement from contractor.

For a project with a residential component, what was critical to the success of the project?

Improving common spaces / amenities.

Common Spaces: What senior-friendly common spaces are included in the project?

Large open kitchen, great room, dining room, and den.

Jury Comments

Marian's House provides memory-based services away from senior campus and which are embedded in the community to support caregivers and provide social and engaging activities for those with early to mid-stage dementia still residing at home. The home fits into the surrounding community and does not stand out. The "L" shaped design places the narrow end of the house to the street, visually reducing the perception of its size. It also creates a courtyard space, with an abundance of plants, flowers and paved walks for the day care clients, and a less visible parking court and entry for residents and families to come and go. The house design is welcoming and open with a variety of areas for both one-on-one and large group activities: an open kitchen enables participants to be part of meal preparation; a great room provides space for activities, movies and relaxation; a den offers an alternative calm space; and a screened porch overlooks the courtyard and street activity. Occasional overnight respite stays are made possible due to the availability of two guest rooms and an on-site 24-hour resident caregiver, who is provided their own apartment with separate entrance.

Opposite top left: The dining room is used by guests during the day and for training video presentations at night.
Opposite top right: Multiple sight lines from the kitchen promotes safety and encourages residents to explore.
Top: The contemporary kitchen is a typical residential size.
Bottom: The lounge doubles as an evening resource center for classes and discussion groups.

Photography: John Smillie

DiMella Shaffer

Orchard Cove

Canton, Massachusetts // Hebrew Senior Life

Facility type: Independent Living; CCRC
Target market: Upper
Site location: Suburban
Project site area (square feet): 1,655,280; 9 acres developed

Gross square footage of the renovation / modernization involved in the project: 36,000
Purpose of the renovation / modernization: Repositioning
Ratio of parking spaces to residents: 1:1
Provider type: Faith-based non-profit

Below: Courtyard between wings
Opposite: An aerial rendering of the entire Orchard Cove community, as viewed from the southwest pond side

Photography: DiMella Shaffer

Overall Project Description

Orchard Cove is a continuing care retirement community (CCRC) that was designed 20 years ago in a modern architectural vocabulary that has enabled it to stand apart from the more traditional senior environments of its day. Administration and marketing staff began to realize that the lifestyles and interests of their potential new residents had drifted from those of the original residents. In particular, they were interested in having access to fitness / wellness facilities similar to those they had routinely utilized in their independent lives. With this in mind, Orchard Cove embarked on a repositioning and renovation project of the building's existing common spaces to update their high-end image and better promote their strategic business model for wellness and healthy living.

The project objectives included a redesigned and expanded health and wellness area to complement and support their Vitality 360 program,

improvements and finish upgrades to the pavilion and garden dining rooms, the introduction of a new all-day casual dining concept at the Pequit, an expanded commons area and activity rooms, and an updated and expanded library.

Project Goals

What were the major goals?

- A new fitness / wellness center—to complement and support the Vitality 360 program—was created by enlarging the existing fitness area, carved out from under-utilized offices and institutional rehabilitation rooms that had occupied a critical central location within the building. This allowed for an open studio with ample natural light, exercise equipment, integrated therapy rooms, a juice bar overlooking the pool, a spa, hair and nail salon, and several flexible program / amenity spaces. The fitness / wellness center has become one of the new hubs of the community.

- The project had several technical challenges that required combined engineering and architecture design studies. The issue of an unacceptable ambient noise level within the two major dining rooms, and the air flow and noise from HVAC vents that rendered the dining experience unpleasant to seniors. Working with acoustical engineers, the design team studied how to efficiently integrate new acoustical materials within the surface treatments of the walls, ceilings, and floors, and add the appropriate window treatments to correct the reverberation of sound within these highly utilized social spaces. Unacceptable extraneous noises generated from mechanical air-handling equipment and the air draft felt at the dining tables were also addressed by mechanical engineers who relocated the HVAC vents to better distribute air throughout the space. Subsequently, a successful solution was achieved, both acoustically and visually, by cladding interior surfaces with high-performing acoustical materials without compromising space, design, or aesthetics.

- The existing library had been discretely located on the second floor of the commons. It no longer met the needs of the resident community; they desired a larger and more accessible space located along the major resident traffic route on the first floor to encourage its utilization and inclusion into the general daily activity of the facility. A newly designed, larger, and more open library is now situated off the main floor where the old cafe / deli and plant room used to be. Bookcases were inserted into the existing walls of the old cafe / deli between 26 and 60 inches, easily accessible to the senior population. The new library has direct access to an outdoor patio, taking advantage of generous views to mature landscaped gardens. As a direct result of these improvements, the library has seen its usage increase by 30 percent.

- The interior design palette of the first floor commons was completely refreshed. This has resulted in both new and existing residents feeling that their community has raised the bar, as it did 20 years prior when Orchard Cove was originally built. The newly revitalized interior environment represents the high level of contemporary design associated with today's CCRCs.

Challenges: What were the greatest design challenges?

Every aspect of this project required the design team to see life through the lens of an aging adult, both of existing residents hesitant to change and those of new residents with different expectations. Building consensus through several design review meetings included the adoption of new program elements, new space concepts, layouts, and locations, as well as the selection of finishes. Favorite spaces in the building were refreshed and upgraded, whereas underutilized spaces were reconfigured and designed to house new amenity concepts maintaining the character and look of Orchard Cove.

Throughout the programming and design phases, careful consideration was given to the residents and staff to help understand their special needs and to expedite the project as they lived through months of phased construction and change. Specifically focused resident committees were formulated by the Orchard Cove administration. The committees included: library, dining, acoustics, fitness / wellness, interior design, and artwork. This process resulted in capitalizing upon the ideas and insights of existing residents and gaining their trust soon after the first phase was completed. By working closely with the various resident committees, the majority of the residents felt that they had been listened to and the final preferred solution was often close to unanimously embraced as a whole.

Innovations: What innovations or unique features were incorporated into the design of the project?

The creation of the new fitness / wellness center has centralized and placed importance on this critical social activity. The new spaces follow an open concept plan which helps maximize natural light and resident interaction. The use of glass walls, some relocated and some built to match the existing, define the different exercise areas, allowing for transparency and natural light making them more pleasant to occupy. This new concept contributed to a 75 percent increase of utilization since put into operation. The space is designed not only for residents to exercise but to foster a lifestyle geared towards wellness.

Rectifying the acoustical reverberation problems at the two major dining venues required research to find materials that would provide highly efficient attenuation, and would not impact the design of the space. The solution consisted of applying a stretched fabric over acoustic fiberglass underlayment at all hard ceiling surfaces. This resolution preserved the shape and look of the cathedral ceilings in the pavilion dining room and allowed the design team to maintain the green-ceilings effect in the garden dining room. Padded window treatments, wooden acoustic panels, and highly absorbent floor coverings also contributed to the renovation of both dining rooms. The resulting design, which also includes new and re-upholstered furniture and new lighting solutions, has won praise from all who work and live in the community.

The updated library space, with its pivotal new location and open configuration, has contributed positively to the life of the Orchard Cove community and has helped tremendously in marketing the community. The open library concept was initially received with a certain level

of skepticism by some residents. However, soon after renovation the new space was embraced by the community. It provided a casual, interactive, comfortable, and beautifully lit library that allowed residents to browse for books, read the daily newspaper, access the internet on provided tablets, or conduct book club meetings. It transformed the library from a secluded and remote space to an interactive space accessible by all, and for all.

Marketing / Occupancy: What issues were encountered regarding marketing and / or achieving full occupancy?

As this was an existing 20-year-old facility, the administration realized that the newer facilities that were attracting residents included up-to-date fitness facilities and libraries that incorporated technological change. The final design solution addressed these issues and has resulted in a significant resurgence of customer interest in Orchard Cove.

Top: Community members and architects discuss floor plan ideas
Photography: DiMella Shaffer

Opposite bottom left: The corridor connecting two wings opens to library materials
Opposite bottom right: The library was converted from a cafe
Photography: Robert Benson Photography

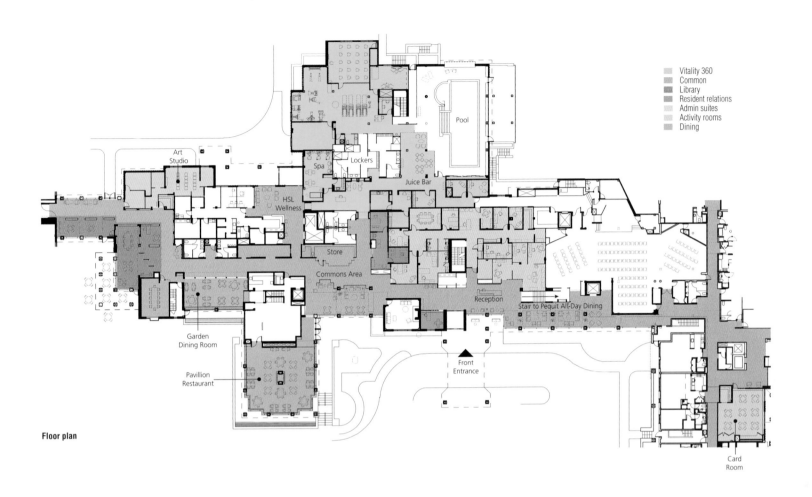

Floor plan

Vitality 360
Common
Library
Resident relations
Admin suites
Activity rooms
Dining

Pool

Art Studio

Lockers

Spa

Juice Bar

HSL Wellness

Store

Commons Area

Reception

Stair to Pequit All-Day Dining

Garden Dining Room

Pavillion Restaurant

Front Entrance

Card Room

Above: Dining area following renovation
Opposite top left: Exhibit space following renovation
Opposite top right: The fitness center repositioned as
  Vitality 360—a wellness program

Photography: Robert Benson Photography

Data / Research: What innovative or unique data collection and / or research was applied during the planning and / or design process?

Surveys and scoping sessions with the existing residents helped to identify what they believed were deficiencies in the facility, or what had become outdated. Numerous meetings and walkthroughs with staff and residents helped direct the design team towards particular spaces and needed amenities. The marketing staff transmitted comments from prospective customers about what the competition was offering. Through this gathering of information, the basis of a master plan program was developed as a wish list of desirable attributes to be included in any renovation to the existing facility.

Collaboration: How did stakeholders, occupants, the design team, and / or others collaborate during the planning and / or design process?

The program data was collected with the full engagement of the residents and staff. The various specialized resident committees worked with the design team reviewing the range of solution options that were developed to encourage the total engagement from the committee members. After the committee members concurred, the design was fully developed, then presented to the entire residential community to allow them to buy into the design as it had already been endorsed by their friends, neighbors, and committee representatives.

Since the design elements were implemented in a phased approach, allowing the community to remain functional, it was crucial that the initial construction projects were well-designed, well-executed, on budget, and completed on time. With careful consideration, an effective structured schedule was implemented to help meet time constraints. The dining room renovations were completed first and were both successes. The result was that subsequent phases were relatively quickly endorsed by the building's population.

Green / Sustainable Features: What green / sustainable features had the greatest impact on the project's design?

Maximized daylighting, conscientious choice of materials, and reuse of existing building structure and / or materials.

What were the primary motivations for including green / sustainable design features in the project?

Support the mission / values of the client / provider and the design team, and stay competitive with other similar / local facilities.

What challenges did the project face when trying to incorporate green / sustainable design features?

Lack of client knowledge about green / sustainability.

Common Spaces: What senior-friendly common spaces are included in the project?

Formal dining, bistro / casual dining; swimming pool / aquatics facilities; dedicated fitness equipment room; dedicated exercise classroom; salon; large multipurpose room; dedicated conference / meeting space; dedicated classroom / learning space; library / information resource center; art studio / craft room; and resident-maintained gardening space.

Stewart & Conners Architects, PLLC

Sharon Towers Dining Renovation

Charlotte, North Carolina // Sharon Towers

Facility type: Independent Living; Assisted Living; Long-term Skilled Nursing; CCRC or part of a CCRC
Target market: Middle / upper middle
Site location: Urban
Project site area (square feet): 1,080,288
Gross square footage of the renovation / modernization involved in the project: 11,507

Purpose of the renovation / modernization: Repositioning
Ratio of parking spaces to residents: 0.96:1
This site is within 1,000 feet of public transportation, and within 1,000 feet of at least 10 basic services with pedestrian access to those services.
Provider type: Faith-based non-profit

Below: Dining foyer
Opposite: Club room

Overall Project Description

Located at the physical and social heart of the community, this CCRC's dining program was not living up to current market expectations. An inefficient and inconvenient design located the main kitchen on the ground floor meaning a slow elevator ride was needed to deliver service to all dining venues, from independent living to nursing. Additionally, the existing plan featured the common and dining areas centrally located between cottages and apartments to both the west and the east. The existing "main street" was unceremoniously diverted at both ends by a large dining room, entirely enclosed, with no transition space to welcome residents to the town center experience. The master plan identified a phased renovation and future expansion to provide new restaurant-style dining, casual dining with a center-stage buffet, a cafe, and club room, all to be supported by an "a la minute" kitchen relocated to the main level.

Project Goals

What were the major goals?

- To upgrade the resident dining experience from single venue, cafeteria-style dining to a more market-driven approach with multiple venues. The project provides restaurant-style dining, casual dining, a cafe, market place and club room, and an "a la minute" kitchen. The casual and restaurant dining were positioned to take full advantage of large north-facing windows with views to a landscaped courtyard, while creating more intimately scaled dining venues.

- To enhance the "main street" experience to build a greater sense of community. The existing CCRC plan featured a common area centrally located between cottages and apartments to both the west and the east. The new plan called for the creation of the cafe and the club room as destination spaces, gracefully terminating primary view axes in both directions, turning the

main commons corridor while also providing a comfortable transition space at either end of the dining program. Both spaces are designed to engage the passersby, similar to a neighborhood sidewalk cafe or pub, with inviting but indirect views through finely detailed art glass and interior windows. The cafe includes sidewalk seating with tables and a banquette seating alcove with a beautifully textured wood accent wall that adds appealing detail along the corridor. The sidewalk seating provides the opportunity for the chance meeting of friends as they pass along the main street corridor with the cafe immediately adjacent. The cafe is sized and arranged to operate at efficient staffing levels, while offering a widely varied menu and a gourmet marketplace. Immediately adjacent is an "a la minute" kitchen that extends the cafe's services even further. The club room features a comfortably appointed wet bar with a double-sided stone fireplace that subtly subdivides the space into well-scaled and varied seating areas to suit any resident's taste. The club room can also operate as a pre-function space for the adjacent casual and restaurant dining, as well as offering its own light dining menu. Both the cafe and club room have been met with resounding approval from the residents as comfortable bookends to their "main street" experience.

Challenges: What were the greatest design challenges?

The existing CCRC (the first phase built in the early 1970s) features Modernist building exteriors, with interiors renovated to suit the current traditional Southern tastes and styles. Anticipating a change in market tastes and desiring a more consistent exterior-to-interior aesthetic, the design team integrated a more open plan that creates greater opportunities for interaction. The transitional design retains the complexities of the Southern aesthetic but transforms the detailing with curved lines, reveals, and textures. The finishes are crisply detailed wood paneling and granite counters with slightly quirky accent lighting that gives the project a comfortable style.

Another major challenge for the design team was to provide an extensive, equipment-intensive program, located in the center (vertically and horizontally) of a functioning community and building, with upscale finishes and within a modest budget, without disrupting services. Where new kitchen equipment requiring vertical runs through the existing nursing was to be installed, the design team planned to shorten horizontal runs and use existing chases or create new chases in unobtrusive areas while avoiding heavy cast-in-place concrete ribs in the existing structure. In keeping with the transitional style of finishes, ceiling planes were expressed with an inexpensive reveal painted black, thus adding detail and visual interest at low cost. Working with the owner and contractor, the architect was able to create a phasing plan that virtually eliminated disruption to the dining services.

Innovations: What innovations or unique features were incorporated into the design of the project?

The project required the addition of multiple, equipment-intensive programs within a limited space while planning for a future expansion. Despite the restrictions, the design team was able to plan a small and efficient service core that delivers behind-the-scenes service without violating resident common spaces, while also planning for future service area expansion without moving major equipment such as hoods and washing equipment. The center-stage buffet cabinet work

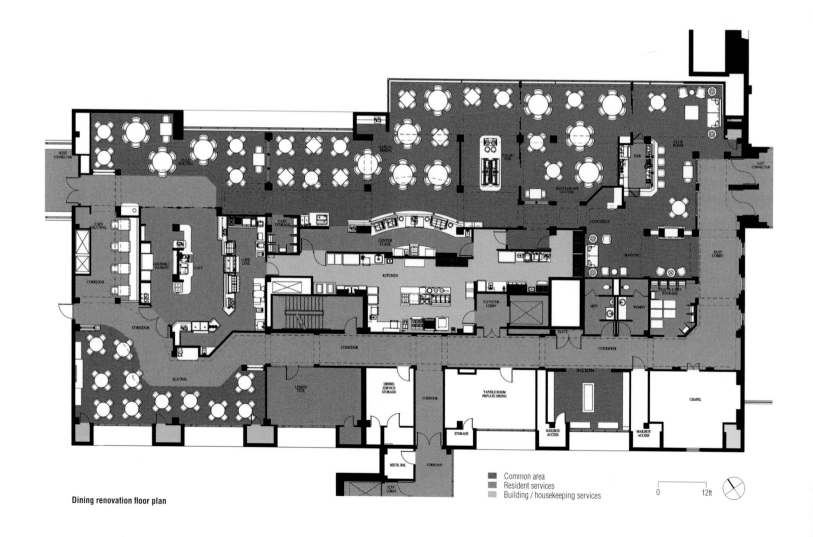

Dining renovation floor plan

■ Common area
■ Resident services
■ Building / housekeeping services

0   12ft

and equipment is planned so that it can be easily relocated with the future expansion without major rework. The multiple resident service and seating venues are defined by interior walls with finely detailed art glass and interior windows, with large sliding doors that allow the space to be expanded and provide greater flexibility.

Collaboration: How did stakeholders, occupants, the design team, and / or others collaborate during the planning and / or design process?

Dining programs are both operationally intensive and unique to every community. The design team was able to provide benchmark data from their extensive database of projects and then tailor the response through team visits to other communities. Multiple design options were created and presented to the stakeholder group.

Common Spaces: What senior-friendly common spaces are included in the project?

Formal dining; bistro / casual dining; coffee shop / grab-and-go; marketplace / convenience store; and club room and lounge.

Top: Casual dining and cafe flex seating
Left: Casual dining and center stage

Photography: Sargent Photography

Lenhardt Rodgers Architecture + Interiors

St. Ignatius Nursing & Rehab Center

Philadelphia, Pennsylvania // Felician Franciscan Sisters

Facility type (date of initial occupancy): Short-term Rehabilitation (September 2012)
Target market: Low income / subsidized
Site location: Urban
Project site area (square feet): 60,000
Gross square footage of the renovation / modernization involved in the project: 6,388
Purpose of the renovation / modernization: Repositioning

Ratio of parking spaces to residents: 0.2:1 on-site; 0.5:1 including off-site
This site is within 1,000 feet of public transportation, and within 1,000 feet of at least 10 basic services with pedestrian access to those services.
Provider type: Faith-based non-profit

Below: Great room view to country kitchen and corridor
Opposite: Great room view to living room

both the residential and common areas, and appropriate medical support in a home-like environment.

- Privacy was provided by the unique redesign of the resident rooms.
- By reducing the bed count in the wing and through careful space planning, it was possible to add a great room, a large open room comprised of a living room, dining, and kitchen.
- Light and bright colors extend a warm and welcoming atmosphere. Materials and details reflect what may be found in homes, such as wood flooring, articulated millwork details, decorative lighting, artwork, accessories, and plants.
- The short-term stay unit is able to provide care for a wide variety of medical needs because of the addition of an oxygen and suction system. This is available at each bed and is concealed in residential-style cabinetry.

Overall Project Description

This community is a faith-based, non-profit, stand-alone long-term-care nursing home in an urban location. It provides assistance to low-income elderly under the ministry of the Felician Franciscan Sisters. Over 90 percent of the residents receive Medicaid. With little to no renovation over the years and a quest to add short-term rehabilitation to their services, the client sought to transform one of their long-term care corridors.

They wanted something drastically different from their existing outdated medical model facility. The physical site, which is only an acre and a half, did not allow room for expansion. The community is comprised of one five-story building with a basement. The first floor (and basement) contain the common and support spaces, including a large dining room and auditorium. Prior to the start of the project, all residents (except those unable to

be transported who received trays) came to the large dining room on the first floor for all of their meals. The second, third, and fourth floors are the residential floors for 176 residents in two wings per floor. The second floor also contains a large chapel where daily services are held. The fifth floor is the convent where the Felician Sisters live. The project scope was limited to one wing on the second floor. The client recognized the need for accommodations that would attract short-term stay residents. Prior to the start of the project, the wing contained 27 residents in side-by-side double rooms. Two double rooms shared one bathroom. The financial model allowed for the reduction in beds from 27 to 22.

Project Goals

What were the major goals?

The goals of the project were to provide privacy for the residents, dining and living room space within the wing, an attractive environment in

Challenges: What were the greatest design challenges?

The limited amount of space in which to achieve the program goals was the greatest design challenge. The financial model did not allow for much reduction in the number of beds and the tight urban site did not allow room for expansion. While all agreed that creating private rooms was ideal, at this site it was not possible. This organization serves a low-income population and it was critical to keep the census high. Due to careful planning, the resulting design only reduced the census by five beds. Suites were created which provide four private rooms and a shared toilet. The support spaces were strategically located to be unobtrusive which allowed for the purposefully designed focal elements to stand forward. While the footprint was small, changing the public spaces from a closed plan to an open plan allowed for the infusion of light, better circulation, and additional common areas.

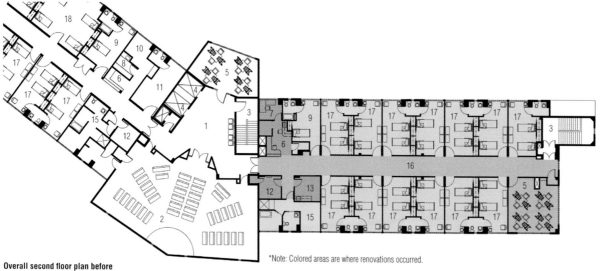

Overall second floor plan before

*Note: Colored areas are where renovations occurred.

1 Lobby
2 Chapel
3 Stair
4 Elevator
5 Dining room
6 Nurse station
7 Office
8 Med room
9 Isolation room
10 Storage
11 Employee area
12 Soiled utility
13 Clean utility
14 Janitors closet
15 Bathing room
16 Corridor
17 Double occupancy resident room
18 Quad occupancy resident room

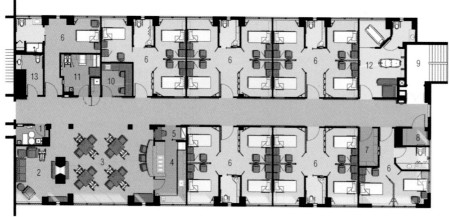

Newly renovated floor plan

1 Soiled utility
2 Living room
3 Activity / dining
4 Pantry
5 Doctors charting
6 Resident suite
7 Linen closet
8 Laundry room
9 Exit stair
10 Nurse / chart / med
11 Storage
12 Spa
13 Toilet

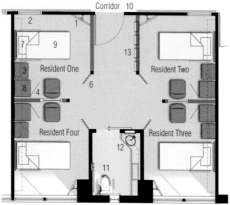

Enlarged newly renovated resident suite

1 Flat screen television with remote control
2 Interior window facing corridor with faux wood blinds for privacy control
3 In wall oxygen / suction inside custom cabinet that coordinates with furniture. A custom nightstand was provided below to match the size of the oxygen suction cabinet.
4 Partial height wall with translucent window for allowing natural light to penetrate corridor-side resident room.
5 Partial height walls to create a sense of personal space. Walls also provide visual privacy from corridor.
6 Curtains for privacy control. Sprinkler heads were located strategically so that mesh was not necessary at the top of the curtain. Curtains were fabricated at longer length to remove the institutional feeling that would normally occur with a shorter curtain.
7 Lighting concealed in a custom shelf provides individually controlled lighting for each resident.
8 Custom wardrobe to fit underneath the lighting shelf.
9 New beds and custom head boards. Footboards were eliminated for a less institutional feeling.
10 Decorative wall sconce connected to the nurse call system
11 Toilets were kept in the existing location to reuse plumbing. Fold down grab bars were added for ease in transfer.
12 Counter space with built-in trash receptacle and cabinets for each residents' personal belongings.
13 In-suite medicine cabinets for each resident.

Innovations: What innovations or unique features were incorporated into the design of the project?

The resident room layout is unique. Space planning was challenging; essential goals were to provide privacy for each resident and update the bathrooms for ADA compliance. Within the existing floor plan, four residents shared a bathroom and two residents shared a room with little to no privacy. In the new plan, suites were created to house four residents. The shared bathroom became enlarged and centrally located. Walls were built to divide the rooms for privacy. Resident rooms are divided with a six-foot-high windowed wall, creating privacy for each resident, while also allowing light to pass through into the adjacent room. The corridor-side resident room has a window that looks onto the corridor which allows these residents a view and creates a sense of spaciousness. The individual rooms are decorated with unique and complementary colors to provide individuality to each space.

Marketing / Occupancy: What issues were encountered regarding marketing and / or achieving full occupancy?

One of the major difficulties this project created for the client was the cost of vacating the wing during the construction. This almost equaled the cost of construction. Once the project was completed, it filled up quickly and has remained full.

Data / Research: What innovative or unique data collection and / or research was applied during the planning and / or design process?

Early in the design process, the client researched the decentralization of dining and providing choice for meal options. A small dining room was set up as a study. After a period of time the staff found that residents' health had dramatically improved with significant weight gain and a number of residents able to be taken off of their feeding tubes. This was the encouragement the facility needed to pursue the project with the ultimate goal of decentralizing dining and offering choice throughout the facility.

Collaboration: How did stakeholders, occupants, the design team, and / or others collaborate during the planning and / or design process?

The Felician Franciscan Sisters, administration, staff, architect, and interior designer participated in focus groups in which collaborative design decisions were made to the ensure the success of this new space. The staff provided valuable insight about the daily care of residents. Through this collaboration the design team was able to provide a state-of-art short-term stay.

Green / Sustainable Features: What green / sustainable features had the greatest impact on the project's design?

Energy efficiency, maximized daylighting, and conscientious choice of materials.

What were the primary motivations for including green / sustainable design features in the project?

Make a better home for the residents.

For a project with a residential component, what was critical to the success of the project?

Improving units / private spaces.

Common Spaces: What senior-friendly common spaces are included in the project?

Great room with living room, dining room, and kitchen.

Top: Spa
Photography: ©2014 Halkin Mason Photography LLC

GGLO

Atria Valley View

Walnut Creek, California // Atria Senior Living Group

Facility type (date of initial occupancy): Assisted Living (April 1976)
Target market: Middle / upper middle
Site location: Urban
Project site area (square feet): 198,198
Gross square footage of the renovation / modernization involved in the project: 98,658

Purpose of the renovation / modernization: Repositioning
Ratio of parking spaces to residents: 0.5 per apartment
This site is within 1,000 feet of public transportation, and within 1,000 feet of at least 10 basic services with pedestrian access to those services.
Provider type: For-profit

Below: Architectural additions at entry and bistro provide connections to resident amenities and activities
Opposite: Remodeled reception area

Overall Project Description

The renovation of Atria Valley View, an assisted living community located in the hills of Walnut Creek, California, is a major building and site renovation of an existing two-story residential care facility with 125 apartments. The renovation work includes the reconfiguration of some existing uses, the expansion and remodeling of the central community areas, and comprehensive updates of the site and landscape features to enhance outdoor living. An overriding goal is to reposition the community to appeal to existing and future residents by providing more amenities with an enhanced quality of design, and with an emphasis on sustainability.

The design concept of this LEED Silver Certified renovation is the redevelopment of the existing site and building so that it is reminiscent of a northern California lodge. One of the primary design ideas is to create strong indoor-outdoor connections. The building concept also incorporates the use

of natural materials and introduces details rich with earth tone colors and textures. Fundamental to the design is the acknowledgement that Atria Valley View is a vibrant community for seniors, their visiting families, and the staff. To this end, the design is welcoming, accessible, and safe.

Project Goals

What were the major goals?

- Reposition to appeal to the market. The welcoming, historic design aesthetic of a northern California lodge inspired the renovation design concept for the existing building and landscape, the greater context of the site in Walnut Creek, California, and the existing resident culture. With an emphasis on design quality, this property renovation incorporates local stone and wood detailing that emphasizes outdoor living, views, and new indoor / outdoor connections at the main dining room and bistro, wi-fi lounge, family lounge, and games room.

The additions of the bistro and bistro terrace, new dining fireplace terrace, massage therapy, spa / salon, fitness center, view overlook deck, and comprehensive landscape renovations bring more amenities and options for daily activities. Enhancements to the main entry, reception, main lounge, theater, library, and lounge terrace work in tandem with the new additions and amenities to complement the design concept and complete the redevelopment of the shared, comfortable, community spaces.

Because existing and future residents are savvy to the benefits of earth-friendly choices, sustainability goals informed the design process. With an emphasis on water conservation, energy efficiency, and construction waste reduction, LEED points were carefully tracked from the design stages through to the end of construction. Tenant education is an ongoing component of the sustainability goals with a comprehensive signage program to educate the occupants and visitors to the benefits of green buildings.

- Provide a hospitality / resort feel. Today's elders are sophisticated and demand more choice and control in meeting their aging-related needs. In response to this, the renovation adapts a newer residential model infused with amenities and services borrowed from hospitality, retail, and resorts. The focus on hospitality is carried throughout the design with amenity-rich spaces such as informal living and lounge areas, a salon with spa services, and a diverse range of dining choices with longer hours of operation and extensive menu choices. This hospitality-oriented residential environment enhances the quality of life for the residents by fostering independence, choice, dignity, and privacy.

- Raise the quality of resident living by offering enhanced choices of extensive amenities. The addition of the bistro and outdoor bistro

Remodeled unit plans level 2

Remodeled unit plans level 1

Studio
Deluxe studio
One bedroom
Corner studio

0   50ft

terrace create dining options; the residents can now choose an informal meal at the bistro or formal dining in the main dining room.

A larger spa / salon created space for more patrons to receive salon services each day. Two new pedicure chairs add to the enhanced spa experience, while the addition of a massage room means residents do not have to leave the campus for this service.

The renovation and additions to the main lounge re-invigorated this community gathering area. This space is akin to the living room of a home, and the new vaulted ceilings, library shelves, grand fireplace, and French doors to the main lounge terrace have all enhanced the comfort and usability of this space.

The remodeled activity room provides a functional and adaptable space for various smaller group activities. The addition of the fitness room, with its connection to the south courtyard and walking paths, gives residents a new single-purpose room designed for exercise, flexibility, and balance.

Challenges: What were the greatest design challenges?

The greatest design challenge was to assure that this total building renovation allowed for a comfortable transition in the existing residents' living environment. To help the residents feel involved in the renovation process, the owner / operator assisted the design team in creating image and materials boards to be posted before

the construction began. These featured design renderings with written descriptions of the new spaces that were being created. The materials included on the boards allowed the tenants to see the selected carpets, tiles, and stone finishes. The design team also focused on creating environments suited to this community's culture of outdoor enthusiasts. The introduction of a view outlook deck brings more options, and allows residents to enjoy the outdoor environment.

Another challenge was integrating a new memory care wing into the renovation design. One of the most difficult aspects of this program is to successfully incorporate security for the

Below: Informal gathering area off main lounge

memory care residents. The Life Guidance wing is a discrete household that provides 11 different private and semi-private rooms. This secure wing has its own kitchen, dining, lounge, library, and medications room. The enclosed outdoor deck and gardens allow the residents access to outdoor spaces while providing safety within tall perimeter fencing. Though the emphasis is on security, the space planning and finish selections create a welcoming environment for the residents and guests.

Innovations: What innovations or unique features were incorporated into the design of the project?

Providing hospitality / resort feel, offering daily choice through extensive amenities, and repositioning to appeal to the market.

Green / Sustainable Features: What green / sustainable features had the greatest impact on the project's design?

Energy efficiency and recycling construction waste and / or diversion from landfills.

What were the primary motivations for including green / sustainable design features in the project?

Support the mission / values of the client / provider and the design team, and make a contribution to the greater community.

What program / organization is being used for green / sustainable certification of this project?

Leadership in Energy and Environmental Design (LEED).

For a project with a residential component, what was critical to the success of the project?

Improving common spaces / amenities.

Common Spaces: What senior-friendly common spaces are included in the project?

Formal dining, bistro / casual dining; salon; large multipurpose room; small-scale cinema / media room; library / information resource center; and family visitation room.

Jury Comments

The transformation from the existing to the new was dramatic and pleasant to the eye. In the jury's opinion the overriding objective of meeting the expectations of today's and tomorrow's seniors was very well achieved. The project's original and outdated 60s look is now completely nonexistent. The exterior renovation transformed the character to one that is now more appropriately reminiscent of a northern California lodge and more in keeping with the region. The ambiance is cheerful and inviting. The entrance was also dramatically transformed—it's more welcoming and upbeat, and the front door has a strong sense of arrival. Finally, the connection between the indoors and outdoors was also enhanced effectively.

Opposite top: Deluxe studio residence featuring open living plan with high-efficiency heating and cooling
Opposite bottom left: New private dining room
Opposite bottom right: New bistro with connection to new outdoor terrace
Top left: New spa salon
Top right: New courtyard terrace with outdoor dining beyond
Photography: © Scott Hargis

Perkins Eastman

Camphill Ghent

Copake, New York // Camphill Village USA, Inc.

Facility type (date of initial occupancy): Independent Living (November 2010); Assisted Living (November 2010); Assisted Living—dementia / memory support (November 2010); CCRC or part of a CCRC
Target market: Middle / upper middle
Site location: Rural; greenfield
Project site area (square feet): 90,860

Gross square footage of the new construction involved in the project: 90,860
Gross square footage of a typical household: 16,500
Number of residents in a typical household: 11
Ratio of parking spaces to residents: 1:1
Provider type: Non-sectarian non-profit

Below: Townhouse and large natural pond
Opposite: Co-house roadside

Overall Project Description

The Camphill Initiative was developed (in Scotland following World War II) to care for children with developmental disabilities. These children have now aged and many of them require the kind of care provided for older adults in assisted living environments. Camphill Ghent is a response that enables this older developmentally disabled population to live in a supportive environment under the community's guiding principles of Anthroposophy, which is dedicated to supporting the potential of all people regardless of physical (or other) disabilities. In the 1970s, the Camphill Initiative established a community in Copake, Dutchess County, New York. Camphill Ghent was conceived as a continuation of the Initiative's mission: allowing their residents to live in an environment that enables them to age with assistance and support.

In keeping with the tradition of these self-sustaining communities, Camphill Ghent Elder Initiative purchased a 114-acre farm capable of supporting several phases of development. The first phase of Camphill Ghent includes two assisted living buildings with a total of 39 licensed assisted living beds, as well as apartments for staff on the second floor.

Approximately 32 apartments (studio, one- and two-bedroom) have been developed for independent seniors who wish to live and work as part of the larger community. Additionally, ten independent living townhouses have been developed (both one- and two-bedroom) for older adults who wish to live in larger residences.

The community has been planned to sit comfortably within the natural features of the site, which climbs over 150 feet from the main entry to the highest point. There are two large natural ponds, around which the co-houses and townhouses are arranged; these serve to handle storm water on the site.

In addition to the co-houses, townhouses, and two assisted living houses, there is a congregate house for developmentally disabled youth, and a replacement barn which contains a health clinic, maintenance and receiving areas, as well as the administrative offices for the community. The master plan includes a community cultural center, manual arts building, and future residential and assisted living buildings on the upper 60 acres of the site.

Project Goals

What were the major goals?

- Enhance the quality of life. Residents live and interact with their caregivers. A caretaker on site 24 / 7 creates a sense of security and well-being for residents.

- Promote wellness. Biodynamic farming, gardening, and pathways encourage residents to be active outdoors and walk from building to building.

- Empower independence. Regardless of physical abilities, residents feel nurtured by an environment that promotes choice and supports their needs. The design, and caretaker and resident involvement create a sense of true community.

- Reinforce personal relationships. Staff and co-workers (independent residents) live among residents in apartments above and attached to the assisted living houses. Co-houses and townhouses with rear patios overlook and surround a large pond; this arrangement promotes chance social experiences.

Challenges: What were the greatest design challenges?

Safety and security were primary challenges for this site, since residents are encouraged to walk and explore the 114 acres of rolling hills. From the entry road to the assisted living houses, the topography changed by 150 feet. Careful site planning allowed for a five percent grade among the co-houses and townhouses, and the barn along the main road. A path between the ponds allowed residents to access the highest point. Minimal re-grading and site changes met LEED certification requirements.

Financial affordability for seniors with a diverse range of incomes was critical. The team worked closely with the client and CM to maintain an economical cost / square foot, which enabled middle-income seniors to live in this supportive community.

Camphill communities traditionally provided housing for developmentally disabled children and adults, and co-worker housing (as part of their wage). This new community—both assisted living and independent living—is the first to develop rental housing for people not part of the Camphill movement. This required a big change in thinking for the client—moving from modest or dormitory-like housing to accessible designs with full kitchens, ample closets, living rooms accommodating diverse furniture, and usable outdoor terraces that appeal to independent seniors.

Innovations: What innovations or unique features were incorporated into the design of the project?

One feature of the project that is unique and noteworthy is the melding of the design and philosophical view of Anthroposophy with state requirements for licensed assisted living residences, and services for frail seniors with development disabilities. The idiosyncratic forms and angled walls, and rooms and building shapes that reflected a belief system challenged the team in creating a building that met state certification. It was an unusual design challenge, and a new example for the Camphill Elder Initiative.

Marketing / Occupancy: What issues were encountered regarding marketing and / or achieving full occupancy?

Camphill Ghent is a unique senior community. It had a constituency that was aging-in-place at another nearby community who were prepared to avail themselves of assisted living services. The independent living apartments, both in the co-houses and above the assisted living care houses, were immediately occupied by staff members from other Camphill communities around the country. Camphill Ghent held open-house events and soon discovered that the independent living apartments filled a need for aging adults in this semi-rural part of New York. As a result, the townhomes and larger apartments filled quickly, and a waiting list was formed before construction was complete. Camphill realized they could have built more apartments and townhomes but were reluctant to increase the first phase cost of the project.

Site plan

0   300ft

House floor plan

Administration
Circulation
Commons
Resident support
Staff
Service
Resident room

Bottom left: House entry
Bottom right: House porch

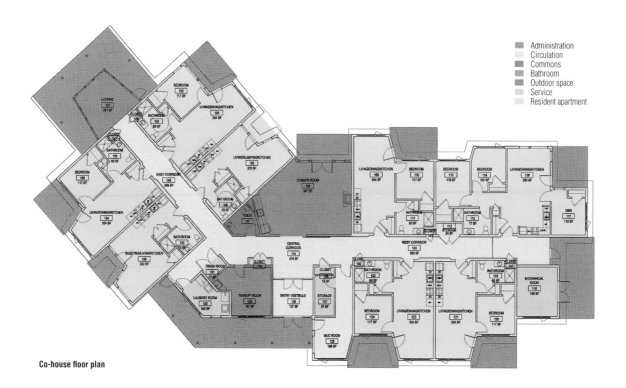

Administration
Circulation
Commons
Bathroom
Outdoor space
Service
Resident apartment

Co-house floor plan

Above: Co-house rear patios overlook the large pond
Opposite bottom: Townhouse quads in natural landscape

Townhouse floor plan

Garage / circulation
Living / dining / kitchen
Bathroom
Outdoor space
Service / storage
Bedroom

Collaboration: How did stakeholders, occupants, the design team, and / or others collaborate during the planning and / or design process?

Community leaders, co-workers, and designers envisioned a nurturing, supportive residence for developmentally disabled seniors. Discussions, brainstorming, and programming meetings pinpointed the key elements of care, as well as philosophical beliefs. Designers then refined the space and functional program, melding their experience in independent living and assisted living housing with the tenets of Anthroposophy and the client's philosophy of community.

Outreach: What off-site outreach services are offered to the greater community?

As a new community, Camphill has not developed any off-site outreach services at this time. They have an active cultural life that includes lectures and concerts, which they advertise locally to encourage the community to attend.

Green / Sustainable Features: What green / sustainable features had the greatest impact on the project's design?

Site design considerations, water efficiency, and recycling construction waste and / or diversion from landfills.

What were the primary motivations for including green / sustainable design features in the project?

Support the mission / values of the client / provider and the design team, and make a contribution to the greater community.

What program / organization is being used for green / sustainable certification of this project?

Leadership in Energy and Environmental Design (LEED).

For a project with a residential component, what was critical to the success of the project?

Improving units / private spaces.

Common Spaces: What senior-friendly common spaces are included in the project?

Formal dining, bistro / casual dining; large multipurpose room; dedicated classroom / learning space; activity room; sitting room; therapeutic room; and community garden / walking path.

Households: What is innovative or unique about the households in the project?

The assisted living households were designed according to the aesthetic principles of Rudolf Steiner while incorporating accessible design elements that would allow residents in a variety of physical states to live comfortably. The Steiner principles affected the overall building geometry, creating many irregular angles in the building form and corridor configuration. Another Steiner principle created single-loaded corridors that limited the number of rooms in series before residents would see a window and orienting

views to the outdoors. Common spaces generally had ceilings that sloped towards the outdoors: a Steiner principle that created a feeling of openness and possibility. Different colors were used as accents which Steiner believed affected a person's mood and tranquility. The inclusion of small nooks inset from corridors, containing a bench and bookcases, encourages residents to rest and read along their daily walks. One of the neighborhoods is attached to an independent living group of apartments, effectively allowing independent residents to participate in the care of the assisted living residents.

Jury Comments

An excellent example of the physical manifestation of organizational philosophy and culture. This project meets the care needs of older adults with developmental disabilities, and applies the principles of "Anthroposophy," which support the potential of all people regardless of physical or other disabilities. The rural campus layout takes advantage of the surroundings with strategic building orientations and a focus on biodynamic farming / gardening, in addition to the wellness initiative with an emphasis on the walking trails. The architecture encourages the relationship focus of the organization by providing staff with living and work areas. The interiors are focused on using ample natural light and providing a variety of textures and colors to engage the senses.

Opposite top: Multipurpose room
Top: Community activity space
Bottom: Dining area

Photography: Sarah Mechling

Perkins Eastman

Moorings Park

Naples, Florida // Moorings Park

Facility type (date of initial occupancy): Independent Living (September 2012); CCRC or part of a CCRC
Target market: Upper
Site location: Suburban; greenfield
Project site area (square feet): 290,000
Gross square footage of the new construction involved in the project: 322,000

Purpose of the renovation / modernization: Repositioning
Ratio of parking spaces to residents: 2:1
This site is within 1,000 feet of public transportation, and within 1,000 feet of at least 10 basic services with pedestrian access to those services.
Provider type: Non-sectarian non-profit

Below: Spacious independent living lifestyle apartments were designed to be completely customized by the owner
Opposite: The event space and outdoor terrace, located next to the independent living residents' building social room

Photography: Chris Cooper

Overall Project Description

Moorings Park wished to enhance its current offerings with a new product, amenities and a lifestyle of wellness that would exceed the expectations of its residents. Beginning with the question: "How can we design a CCRC product for people who don't necessarily feel ready to move to a CCRC?", this community engaged potential future residents in the planning and design process to explore independent living offerings, wellness facilities, outdoor spaces, and dining options.

Moorings Park brings the concept of lifestyle to its reinvigorated campus—from a new concept in independent living to a community center that reflects a philosophy of wellness in concert with the next generation of consumers. Wellness for the whole person—mind, body, and spirit—heavily influenced the design and programming of all new components.

Four new buildings—three residential lifestyle apartment buildings and the Center for Healthy Living—now form a small town square, and include the new upscale restaurant with casual, outdoor, and fine-dining options, as well as beautifully landscaped gardens surrounding social spaces that offer indoor / outdoor connections.

Spacious independent living lifestyle apartments were designed to be completely customized by the owner—essentially blank slates to be configured and finished to suit the resident's lifestyle. Providing abundant outdoor space, communal parks and scenic views, the apartments are situated around a new central lake.

The Center for Healthy Living offers concierge medical services and amenities that include a spa, exercise studios, fitness / weight rooms, and a rehabilitation center. To encourage wellness dimensions beyond the physical, the Center also offers a meditation room, Zen garden, creative arts studios, and lecture space for visiting speakers. Wellness programs are customized to fit each resident's specific desires.

Project Goals

What were the major goals?

- Creating a community for the next generation consumer who does not feel ready to move into a typical CCRC. The design team engaged potential residents in discussions early in the planning and programming, held focus groups, and undertook surveys to determine the most important qualities of next generation lifestyles, and how those factors could be incorporated into the design.

- Designing a product reflecting the community's wellness-based philosophy and offerings, and encouraging personal wellness customization. The architecture supports holistic wellness, from the new lifestyle apartments to the Center for Healthy Living, and to the integrated surrounding landscape. Just as residents may customize their lifestyle apartments, focus groups impacted upon decisions for the new restaurant, from the menus and imagery to food presentation options (eg chef tables, wine pairings).

- Providing a senior wellness environment by applying the principles of an integrative medical model. The interior design supports this goal through blending medical functionality and technology with hospitality-like aesthetics. The plan includes five areas for core wellness activities—a medical clinic, physical therapy, fitness, comprehensive spa, education and social interaction—areas that offer the appropriate transparency between them to reinforce their cohesive whole. Transparency is executed with low partitions, openings instead of doors, and the use of transparent materials, such as glass and 3form, as well as interior landscaped features and planters. The result is supportive functional spaces with definition yet visible to each other, reinforcing their functional integration and role in the wellness continuum.

- Providing opportunities to strengthen mind, body, spirit, and engagement. An abundance of windows and clerestories provide natural daylighting and create an inviting atmosphere. An open floor plan—with interior green spaces, balconies, and rooftop landscaping— promotes a connection to nature. Natural materials and textures, open spaces, and clean lines provide a sense of confidence in the Center's delivery of excellence. Visitors are aware of the facility's scale and have access to all areas; there is a strong sense of arrival. The Center also has the convenience and synergy of connected parts communicating a holistic approach to wellness, as opposed to the one dimensional or singular experience of isolated services / treatments that formerly existed.

- Providing adaptability and flexibility for current and future residents, while addressing changes as the Center grows. Each area has built-in flexibility, including growth in programming, a variety of capacity scenarios, formal and informal spaces, a range of private and open spaces and degrees of energy levels—from the highly charged to the peaceful and meditative. Outdoor living now includes apartments with large exterior terraces, alfresco dining options, and an event terrace located between two of the buildings with an adjacent indoor social room for planned or unplanned use. Enhanced landscaping, with shade structures, canopies, and trees, promotes walking and socializing—a bridge over the lake becomes a spot for fishing with grandchildren; two water features provide added interest. The new town square, bounded by the Center for Healthy Living, a new restaurant, and an existing chapel for larger events, becomes a central gathering spot.

Challenges: What were the greatest design challenges?

Creating three building floor plans (over parking) without any unit plans at the time of going to market—essentially core and shell design allowing maximum customization. Residential floors were designed with no double-loaded corridors; units had co-shared stairs and elevators. All units were thru-units offering apartments with views from both directions, greater natural light, and cross ventilation.

Providing non-obtrusive parking on a site that sits on a high water table. To hide the parking on the first level of the independent living buildings, designers integrated vertical columns into the building design, descending from the second floor down into stilts over the parking area. Landscape design also masks parking, while enhanced roof decks become engaging, habitable social areas.

Creating an inviting, holistic wellness center above two floors of new parking spaces. The only land left on the south end of the property was an over-utilized, on-grade staff parking lot. By pushing the third floor wellness center over a new two-story arcade, the town square appeared as a series of small vertical buildings with a more residential manner, while still including parking.

Expressing the mixed-use quality of the new development, while maintaining privacy for residents living above it. The town square and outdoor spaces, Center for Healthy Living, restaurant, and private residences form a mixed-use quality of development within the campus. This product differentiator addresses new consumer values and desires, but creates a need for separation for people not wanting to live above a restaurant. The building / restaurant entrance feels more like a residential entrance,

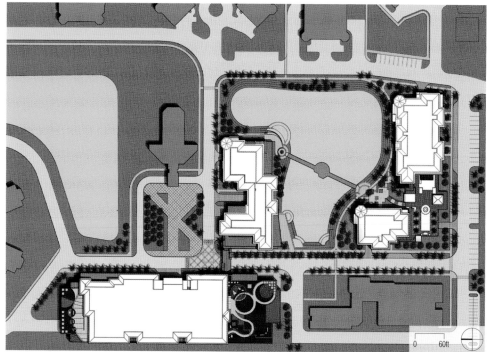

Site plan

since the restaurant opens up to the lake rather than the street, and colored glass canopies identify the restaurant.

Sorting out the final allotment of space in the Center for Healthy Living. Since each area was directed to be its own center of excellence, the development of functional programming kept growing, as did the demand for usable space. Through a series of regular team meetings with designers and operators, all aspects of the space were discussed to arrive at the right balance and commitment of space, to deliver a total experience.

Maintaining a cohesive "place presence" for the entire Center for Healthy Living, while defining each of the wellness activity areas with their own functionality and energy levels. This was accomplished by having a core set of materials—bamboo, brushed stainless steel, linen white, and a palate of blues and greens—that were

applied throughout the space. Each area has the core materials as well as accent colors and materials, such as an orange backdrop to activate the cafe, terrazzo flooring with large leaf inserts to highlight walking paths, translucent glass and natural textures in the spa, and dark accents in the lecture hall.

Innovations: What innovations or unique features were incorporated into the design of the project?

Fully customizable lifestyle residences began with a discussion focused on individual lifestyles: cooking versus not cooking, movie room versus living room, painting studio versus music studio, or even the amount of outdoor living space. These discussions allowed residents to work backwards from their price point, matching lifestyle and entrance fee with square footage and interior design choices.

The athlete plan

The entertainer plan

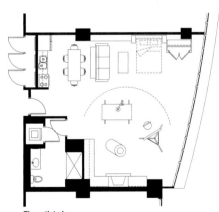

The artist plan

Left: The social room, located next to the outdoor terrace, offers residents a quieter, private space for making connections

Photography: Randall Perry

Marketing / Occupancy: What issues were encountered regarding marketing and / or achieving full occupancy?

Marketing was integrated throughout the design process to address a core issue of the campus repositioning—reinvigorating a traditional campus to attract the next generation of consumers. Potential residents were engaged in design and programming meetings from the very start of the process— participating in focus groups and surveys—to ensure future expectations were being met.

Data / Research: What innovative or unique data collection and / or research was applied during the planning and / or design process?

The design team immersed themselves in the local culture and lifestyle of next generation residents of Moorings Park. The team spent time with potential residents—visiting their current homes and going to their favorite restaurants—to get a hands-on understanding of their personal lifestyles.

Collaboration: How did stakeholders, occupants, the design team, and / or others collaborate during the planning and / or design process?

Engaging current and potential residents was crucial to the success of this project. Resident surveys and management's understanding of their needs were the basis of the entire program. Programming was extensive and done in a team setting where the design team lead the process and held regular meetings to gain input from participants (who were asked to prepare for each meeting), as well as to share understanding as the plans developed, thus allowing the team to operate more seamlessly. Focus groups conducted for restaurant development included tastings, wine pairings, menu development, and design development. Focus groups were conducted with men and women for the spa and salon, touching on desired services, interior design, as well as attitudes about spa treatments relative to wellness; the results helped inform the design and programs.

Detailed design development, functional planning, and coordination happened in smaller meetings where the different wellness areas were discussed in detail. The clinic exam room was mocked up full-scale, and then revised upon with user input from physicians and nurses. National experts were consulted in the initial phases, who provided valuable research and insights to spa services, fitness programs, medical programs, and retail services. A digital virtual tour was created in great detail during the design process (not after) to further vet the design, and to provide the design team, stakeholders, residents and operational management a clear picture of the space qualities.

Outreach: What off-site outreach services are offered to the greater community?

The Center for Healthy Living will be open to the greater community for a monthly membership fee.

Green / Sustainable Features: What green / sustainable features had the greatest impact on the project's design?

Site design considerations; energy efficiency; and reduced solar gain / heat island–effect sunshades, and planting.

Top left: The rehabilitation center is strategically located between the medical clinic and the fitness equipment area
Top right: The waiting area's interiors reflect a cohesive presence by having a core set of materials – bamboo, brushed stainless steel, linen white, and a palate of blues and greens
Opposite: The Center for Healthy Living focuses on promoting wellness for the whole person – mind, body, and spirit

Photography: Randall Perry

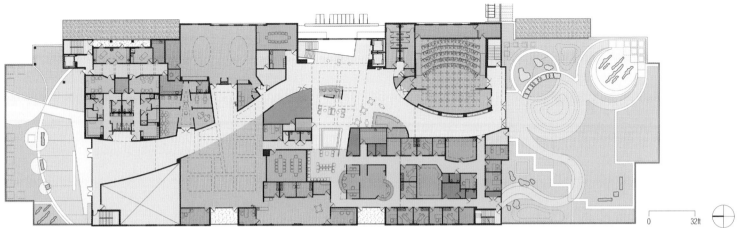

Center for Healthy Living floor plan

0   32ft

What were the primary motivations for including green / sustainable design features in the project?

Support the mission / values of the client / provider, and the design team; retain existing residents; and appeal to what the future residents are demanding.

Top: Trio Restaurant provides residents and visitors with casual, outdoor, and fine dining options
Photography: Chris Cooper

Opposite top: View of the interior dining area of Trio Restaurant
Opposite bottom: Trio Restaurant's lakeside dining terrace faces beautifully landscaped gardens, natural water features and fountains
Photography: Randall Perry

What challenges did the project face when trying to incorporate green / sustainable design features?

Lack of client knowledge about green / sustainability.

What program / organization is being used for green / sustainable certification of this project?

Leadership in Energy and Environmental Design (LEED).

For a project with a residential component, what was critical to the success of the project?

Improving common spaces / amenities.

Common Spaces: What senior-friendly common spaces are included in the project?

Formal dining, coffee shop / grab-and-go; dedicated fitness equipment room; dedicated exercise classroom; dedicated rehabilitation / therapy gym; massage / aromatherapy room; salon; large multipurpose room; small-scale cinema / media room; dedicated conference/ meeting space; dedicated classroom / learning space; library / information resource center; resident-maintained gardening space; geriatric assessment clinic; wellness shop; and outdoor terrace and event space.

Jury Comments

The design goal was to create a product for people who don't necessarily feel ready to move to a retirement community, by exceeding their expectations. Three residential lifestyle apartment buildings, an upscale restaurant, and the Center for Healthy Living now combine with a previously existing chapel to form a small "town square." Spacious independent living lifestyle apartments, situated around a new lake, were "blank slates" which enabled the resident to configure and finish them to suit their individual desires / tastes. The Center for Healthy Living offers concierge medical services and amenities, and wellness programs are customized. A cohesive "place presence" (while also defining functional activity areas) is accomplished by the use of materials. The restaurant offers casual, outdoor and fine-dining options. Contemporary lighting, varied textures, an upbeat color scheme, an open bar, and an exhibition kitchen with a chef's table give this space a "young" vibe.

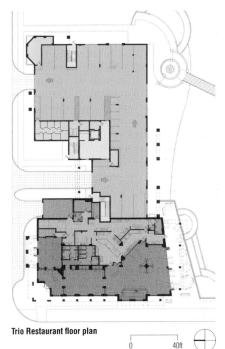

Trio Restaurant floor plan

0   40ft

SFCS Inc.

Rockhill Mennonite Community

Sellersville, Pennsylvania // Rockhill Mennonite Community

Facility type (date of initial occupancy): Assisted Living (March 2012); CCRC or part of a CCRC
Target market: Middle / upper middle
Site location: Suburban
Project site area (square feet): 29,855
Gross square footage of the addition(s) involved in the project: 29,865
Gross square footage of a typical household: 9,955
Number of residents in a typical household: 10

Purpose of the renovation / modernization: Minor renovations in wellness and fitness, including a pool and massage room
Ratio of parking spaces to residents: 1:1
This site is within 1,000 feet of public transportation, and within 1,000 feet of at least 10 basic services with pedestrian access to those services.
Provider type: Faith-based non-profit

Below: An overall view of the personal care building and chapel with the existing health care building to the right.

Photography: Alise O'Brien

Left: The curved facade features multiple balconies and large glass windows with louvered sunscreens. The brick veneer, wood panels, and glass blends with the existing buildings on campus.

Photography: Alan Karchmer

Overall Project Description

The existing CCRC sits on 44 rolling acres in Sellersville, Pennsylvania. A two-phase master plan was produced to expand the community and create a "residential village." This project was the first phase and is the new three-story personal care building for 20 residents, adult day services serving up to 40 residents, and a wellness center.

Personal care offers enhanced person-centered care through a new concept of living and social interaction. It gives an environment to live in that is "home," where the living areas, open kitchens, activity centers, and other spaces allow the same choices for each resident as they had in their previous home or community. Within each home of 10 residents, there are social clusters of four and six residents.

The building's first floor contains newly expanded and renovated wellness rooms, including new massage therapy facilities, and classrooms. The new adult day-services area provides more space for participants, and offers dining, activity, and seating areas, as well as a large enclosed garden area.

The upper two floors are named Gardenview and Skyview given that the design allows dramatic views out into the distant landscape and over the gardens around the building. Arching indirect clerestory windows bring natural light into social spaces without glare or harsh sunlight.

Large expanses of glazing bring natural light in, aided by a light shelf. Each floor contains 10 private studio bedrooms with private bathrooms, surrounded by social spaces in an open floor plan. The brick masonry is curved where it embraces the resident rooms to provide an expanded area for reflection, reading, and personal activities.

The personal care building is LEED-certified, utilizing geo-thermal heat pumps, an energy efficient building envelope, natural light, light shelves, sunshade devices, and other sustainable solutions. Beyond sustainability is the creation of a positive, stimulating environment for each resident; full of natural light, color, and enriched interiors.

Project Goals

What were the major goals?

The existing campus is nondescript, somewhat traditional with a predominately brick veneer and simple in style, in keeping with rural Pennsylvania vernacular. The challenge was to respect the heritage, simplicity, and materiality of the existing campus, but to present a new and bold vision. The design style uses a brick veneer found throughout the campus, blended with glass and Trespa wood panels to provide interest and variety while respecting the organization and surrounding community. Sweeping, curved roofs and exterior facade forms soften the building, and provide gracious living spaces while allowing indirect natural light in from multiple angles. The exterior design followed the intended feel, function, and use of the interior space. The form presents an updated look to the community.

Another goal was the creation of social clusters.

Challenges: What were the greatest design challenges?

The owner and staff wanted to challenge all paradigms of typical assisted living designs while creating a new model that encourages independence and well-being. This challenge was willingly accepted and accomplished through the bold application of the small house or household concept for assisted living. A small house design for 10 residents in each household encourages socialization and family living while promoting independence. The solution creates small households with gracious living units and an emphasis on community and socialization instead of traditional apartment living with services.

While challenging the paradigm of current assisted living models, creating an exciting new vision through design, designers had to support the concepts of sustainable design and energy conservation. Using traditional materials coupled with unique geometry, the design bridges the conservative and tradition of a rural / suburban CCRC with progressive use of material and form inspired by European designers. The geometry used to express the vision enhances the experience of the residents, and supports independence, and wellness.

Innovations: What innovations or unique features were incorporated into the design of the project?

The private room design aided by the curved facade is a unique feature of the community's personal care building. The shape of the room is warm and inviting to the resident. It offers many advantages to the resident, such as room for countless furniture arrangements, personal activities, and visitors. Natural light is abundant in each room with breathtaking views. The design gives the resident a home that they can call their own and empowers them to live independently and comfortably.

Marketing / Occupancy: What issues were encountered regarding marketing and / or achieving full occupancy?

The new household model and contemporary design were a dramatic shift from the traditional personal care facility. Therefore, the marketing program was redirected to attract a new niche

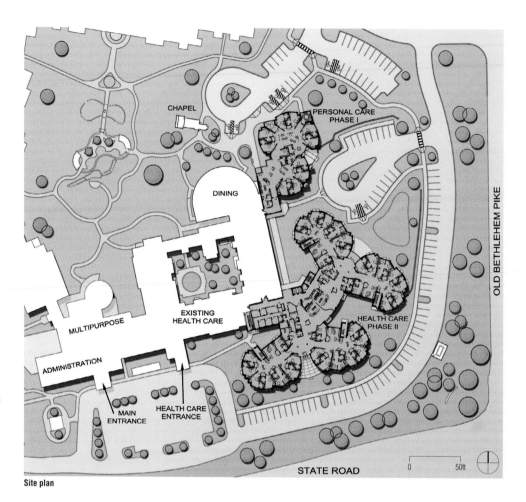

Site plan

in the community. After obtaining the occupancy permit and operating license, the new building filled up within one year, which was expected given the real estate market and economic forces in the local economy at that time.

Data / Research: What innovative or unique data collection and / or research was applied during the planning and / or design process?

There were many programming and design charrettes, as well as mock-up exercises, to determine size and details of all areas. This open planning process was dynamic and provided clear information for both the design team, and the user groups.

Collaboration: How did stakeholders, occupants, the design team, and / or others collaborate during the planning and / or design process?

The owner, administration, and staff had completed substantial research prior to embarking on this design process. They wanted something unique based on the needs of their community and residents.

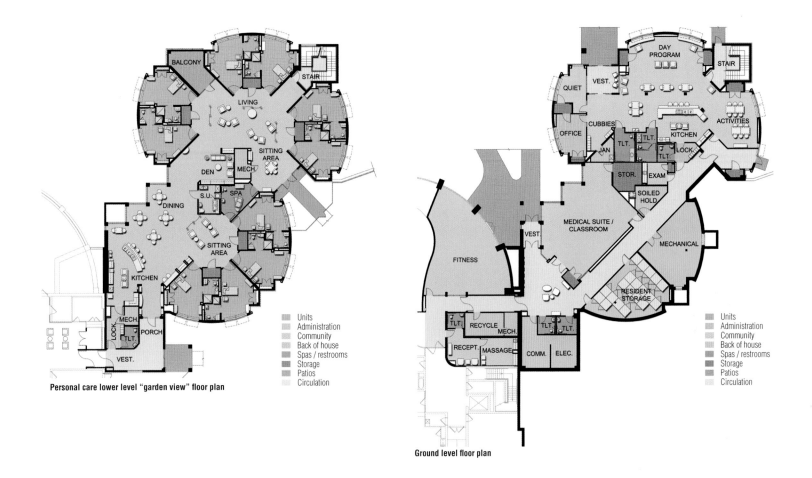

Personal care lower level "garden view" floor plan

Units
Administration
Community
Back of house
Spas / restrooms
Storage
Patios
Circulation

Ground level floor plan

Units
Administration
Community
Back of house
Spas / restrooms
Storage
Patios
Circulation

The design team held a series of charrettes at the community and at retreat locations using the idea of small social clusters within the house as the guiding principle. The design team formed three teams composed of staff, administration, board members, and design team members. After, each team studied a concept unique to that group, the rough sketches were pinned up and debated by the entire group. Each proposed scheme received a nickname. A three-person jury was formed from within the group to make the final concept selection from that first charrette. The jury's goal, if ratified, was to select an idea or series of ideas from each concept and form them into one cohesive, recommended version. This gave the design team a programmatic / physical benchmark.

A month later, staff and board members of the community were once again broken up into three groups. Each group studied a scheme that emerged from the one chosen from the early charrette. They were asked to decide on a scheme. The design team took cues from this final design charrette to propose the scheme that was ultimately constructed and occupied. This was not a new process but the level of involvement from the beginning was noteworthy and significant.

Green / Sustainable Features: What green / sustainable features had the greatest impact on the project's design?

Energy efficiency, maximized daylighting, and conscientious choice of materials.

What were the primary motivations for including green / sustainable design features in the project?

Support the mission / values of the client / provider, make a contribution to the greater community, and lower operational costs.

What challenges did the project face when trying to incorporate green / sustainable design features?

Perceived first-cost premium and lack of client knowledge about green / sustainability.

What program / organization is being used for green / sustainable certification of this project?

Leadership in Energy and Environmental Design (LEED).

For a project with a residential component, what was critical to the success of the project?

Improving units / private spaces.

Households: What is innovative or unique about the households in the project?

Each household of 10 residents is organized into two neighborhoods or social clusters with four to six rooms in each cluster. This allows for close proximity to common areas and the household kitchen / dining area while minimizing walking distances from each room. The reduced walking distance also helps with efficient staffing to provide better and faster care for each group.

All bedrooms and fully accessible bathrooms are private and are adaptable to each resident's needs. Bedroom and living areas allow for personal choice of furniture placement and size to encourage residents to customize their space to not only enjoy life, but to stay independent. Bathrooms are designed to promote independence through the use of barrier-free design, multiple stability devices, and grab-bar locations.

The personal care building gives residents the comfort and privacy of being in their own home. The households are separated from the public circulation to allow privacy. In addition, the breakdown of 20 residents into smaller groups of 10 per floor, and then four to six, promotes a homelike environment and encourages social interaction in a multitude of group sizes.

Top right and top left: Residents can meditate, worship, or take personal spiritual time for themselves in the new chapel.

Opposite: The open dining space provides easy access for families and visitors as well as residents. Arching indirect clerestory windows bring natural light into social spaces without glare or harsh sunlight.

Photography: Alise O'Brien

Abundant natural light and multiple views to the outdoors are enhanced by the open and varied floor plan within each household. Maximum flexibility of use in each space is achieved through geometry, moveable screen walls, and column-free spaces; these allow the residents and staff to customize the use of all common areas.

Common Spaces: What senior-friendly common spaces are included in the project?

Bistro / casual dining; massage / aromatherapy room; dedicated classroom / learning space; religious / spiritual / meditative space; resident-maintained gardening space; adult day-care services suite; and living and reading areas / rooms.

Jury Comments

Natural light entering via the many windows is controlled by light shelves and louvered sunscreens. Sweeping, curved roof lines and exterior facades soften the building exteriors and provide a bold change from existing buildings on the campus.

Open dining spaces are filled with natural light from clerestory windows. The light shelf helps to reduce direct sunlight glare. Resident rooms are nested in clusters of four or six around a semipublic space, providing separation from public space. The bed location in each resident room offers sight lines to window, bath and entrance door.

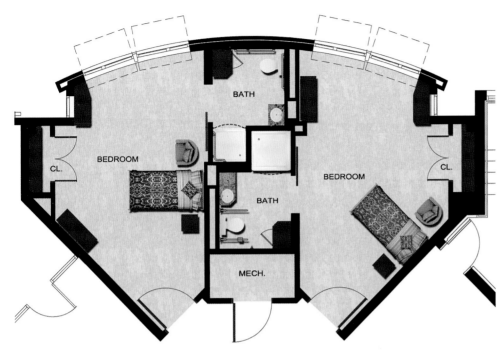

Personal care unit plan

Opposite top: Residential living rooms feature decorative lighting, wood finishes, and an entertainment center
Opposite bottom: The care base is conveniently located to the private resident rooms and activity alcove

Photography: Alise O'Brien

Bottom left & right: Resident rooms include private showers, and the large open space allows for multiple furniture layouts and a private lounging area

Photography: Alan Karchmer

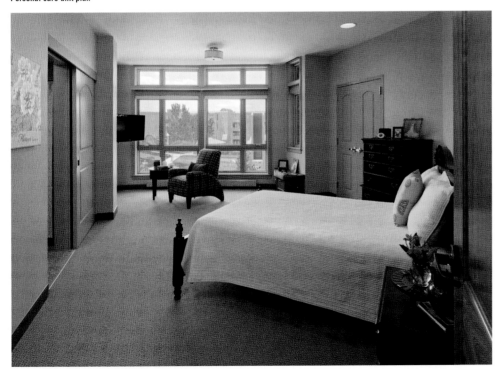

Solomon Cordwell Buenz

The Mather

Evanston, Illinois // Mather LifeWays

Facility type (date of initial occupancy): Independent Living (January 2012); Assisted Living (April 2010); Assisted Living—dementia / memory support (July 2012); Long-term Skilled Nursing (July 2010); CCRC or part of a CCRC
Target market: Middle / upper middle
Site location: Urban
Project site area (square feet): 141,617 (combined site area for both phases)

Gross square footage of the new construction involved in the project: 601,315
Gross square footage of a typical household: 8,800 x 5 distinct households
Number of residents in a typical household: 12
Ratio of parking spaces to residents: 0.65:1; valet parking is provided

This site is within 1,000 feet of public transportation, and within 1,000 feet of at least 10 basic services with pedestrian access to those services.
Provider type: Non-sectarian non-profit

Opposite: View of northeast facade, Mather North
　Photography: Solomon Cordwell Buenz
Left: Rooftop terrace views, Mather North
　Photography: Mather LifeWays

area, group exercise studio, a hair salon, art studio, a cinema / media room, "Possibilities Two" room, and an expansive garden. This phase of the project received LEED Gold Certification in 2012.

Project Goals

What were the major goals?

- The first goal was to create a complete program. Tight urban sites impose limitations on physical area and dictate stacking of program elements. As a result, it was critical to study a variety of planning options that would provide a complete community, replete with dining options, entertainment, health / fitness facilities, access to the outdoors, and housing options, including independent living, assisted living, memory support, and skilled nursing ranging from one bedroom units to two-bedroom plus den units, with ample room for entertaining.

- The second major goal was appropriateness. Sandwiched between the lakefront historic district of single family homes and the edge of the downtown commercial district, the project had to strike a balance by providing the scale and character consistent with a historic area and the street presence to frame the entry to the downtown business area that is occupied by many larger buildings.

- The third major goal was to create open space. A rare commodity in an urban setting is the availability of a welcoming garden or outdoor terrace. A unique feature of The Mather is the availability of outdoor dining terraces, walking paths in an informal multifaceted garden with climbing roses, quiet sitting enclaves, and resident planting beds.

Overall Project Description

The Mather is a CCRC, created in response to its context and location near downtown Evanston. The project replaces two existing seniors residences that had become functionally obsolete. The Mather was born of the need for a modern CCRC that could fulfill the many goals of Mather LifeWays as embodied in their mission of creating "Ways to Age Well."

The 3.2-acre urban infill site encompassed two lots, separated by a street, adjacent to a beautiful residential historic district north of Chicago. From the inception of the phased project, the goal was to capitalize on the advantages of the location—a walkable community on the edge of a vibrant and diverse downtown anchored by Northwestern University, with views of Lake Michigan, and the lakefront historic district, and proximity to mass transit options traversing greater Chicago—and maximize the versatility of the total building program within the limitations of a small urban site.

The first phase of The Mather is an 11-story building completed in 2009. It comprises 141 independent living residences and 57 assisted living, memory support, and long-term care suites. Amenities include six dining venues (including two outdoor dining options), a library with touch-screen computers, a multipurpose "Possibilities Room," a drawing room and living room / performance space, a spiritual / meditative space, and a rooftop terrace. There are unique flex spaces that can be sub-divided using moveable glass partitions (with curtains or large sliding doors) to serve as meeting venues, private dining rooms, or the location of a bridge tournament or a game of Mahjong.

The second phase of The Mather is an 11-story, LEED Gold Certified building providing 99 independent living units, a bistro and rooftop cafe, a wellness / fitness center with massage / aromatherapy rooms, and a rehab-hydro therapy pool, as well as a 20-meter lap pool, sauna, steam showers, cardio and weight training rooms, stretching

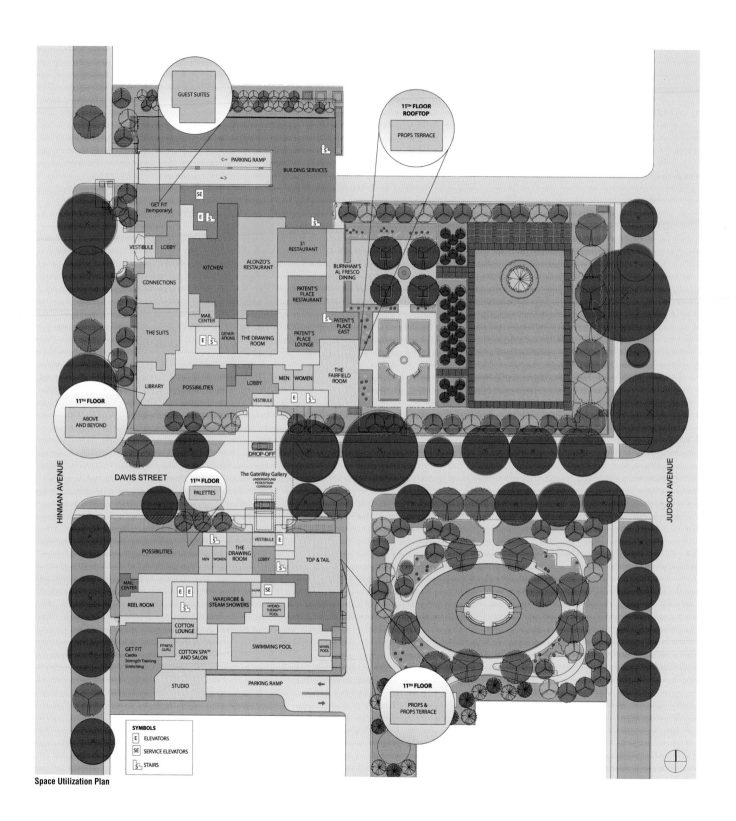

GUEST SUITES

11TH FLOOR
ROOFTOP

PROPS TERRACE

PARKING RAMP

BUILDING SERVICES

GET FIT
(temporary)

SE

E S

S

VESTIBULE LOBBY

31
RESTAURANT

CONNECTIONS

KITCHEN

ALONZO'S
RESTAURANT

BURNHAM'S
AL FRESCO
DINING

PATENT'S
PLACE
RESTAURANT

MAIL
CENTER

THE SUITS

E S GENER-
ATIONS

THE DRAWING
ROOM

PATENT'S
PLACE
LOUNGE

PATENT'S
PLACE
EAST

S

THE
FAIRFIELD
ROOM

LIBRARY

POSSIBILITIES

LOBBY

MEN WOMEN

VESTIBULE

E S

11TH FLOOR

ABOVE
AND BEYOND

DROP-OFF

HINMAN AVENUE

DAVIS STREET

11TH FLOOR

PALETTES

The GateWay Gallery
UNDERGROUND
PEDESTRIAN
CORRIDOR

JUDSON AVENUE

POSSIBILITIES

S

MEN WOMEN

THE
DRAWING
ROOM

VESTIBULE E

LOBBY

S

TOP & TAIL

MAIL
CENTER

REEL ROOM

E E

S

SAUNA

SE

WARDROBE &
STEAM SHOWERS

HYDRO-
THERAPY
POOL

COTTON
LOUNGE

GET FIT
Cardio
Strength Training
Stretching

FITNESS
GURU

COTTON SPA™
AND SALON

SWIMMING POOL

WHIRL
POOL

STUDIO

PARKING RAMP

11TH FLOOR

PROPS &
PROPS TERRACE

SYMBOLS

E ELEVATORS

SE SERVICE ELEVATORS

S STAIRS

Space Utilization Plan

Challenges: What were the greatest design challenges?

The greatest design challenge the team faced was the restriction of square footage. The project faced severe development constraints due to its diminutive site at the edge of a multifamily and single-family district, and the resultant building setback / height restrictions. To fit within the 1.2-acre buildable footprint and to encourage residents to remain active and engaged in the greater community, certain standard CCRC amenities were excluded that are redundant with neighborhood retail offerings, as well as amenities that are often underutilized in many retirement communities.

The compact urban site dictated a vertical community with its footprint in the multifamily district and the 2 acres of open space in the single-family district, and parking below-ground. Parking underground, while expensive, is essential to providing residents and guests with on-site and convenient parking in a busy urban neighborhood. Creative planning was required to accommodate parking below the complex programs of the towers above.

A tunnel, 35 feet below the city street, connects both buildings. This tunnel is fully finished with an elevator service, providing an all-weather connection between the first and second phases of the project. A major feat of engineering was the sequencing of construction: allowing the team to complete the tunnel in two phases, while maintaining significant city infrastructure (sewerage, power lines, water mains). Also, the tunnel and the buildings' deep and significant foundation system required waterproofing. Being so close to Lake Michigan, the tunnel and the building foundations are below the water table.

Innovations: What innovations or unique features were incorporated into the design of the project?

Technological innovations include the computerized wine dispensing system that is located in the ground-floor bistro, which allows residents to purchase individual servings using a pre-paid smart card. Additionally, a formal garden is built over the parking garage, and an underground pedestrian corridor connecting the two phases has been outfitted as a museum and art gallery.

Unique features, such as the maximizing of the rooftop area to provide an expansive outdoor terrace with food service and unobstructed views of Chicago, Lake Michigan, and the mature trees of the historic residential district, provide a valuable amenity for Mather residents.

Marketing / Occupancy: What issues were encountered regarding marketing and / or achieving full occupancy?

The facility achieved full occupancy more quickly than anticipated, despite the economic downturn, with 100 percent of construction financing paid off two years ahead of a schedule that did not anticipate the economic downturn.

Top left: View of southeast facade, Mather South
Photography: Mather LifeWays
Top right: Aerial perspective facing northwest, Mather South building at left, Mather North at right
Photography: Okrent Associates, Inc.

Data / Research: What innovative or unique data collection and / or research was applied during the planning and / or design process?

The entire development of The Mather is a result of market surveys, lifestyle surveys, and discussions with existing residents and future prospects to understand their wants and desires for a new community. The size of homes and finishes were determined by the affordability of the market area and was the outgrowth of a telephone survey. To compete with numerous new empty-nester condo developments, the community homes provide open floor plans and premium finishes (including granite, hardwoods, stainless steel, and gas fireplaces).

The apartment home finish upgrades program features an innovative 90 percent refund program to encourage residents to customize their homes.

With Evanston recognized as the "Dining Capital of the North Shore," expectations run high for the community's dining experience. Movable glass partition walls expand the lobby space, welcoming patrons to experience a Chicago chop house, a bistro featuring an open kitchen, wood-fired brick oven and coffee / wine bar, a Zen-like venue with full-height water wall, an alfresco garden cafe, a rooftop grille, an intimate wine-tasting room, and a Euro-style grocery / cafe.

Evanston residents rank among the most well-educated in the nation. Community spaces encourage intellectual pursuits, with a spacious library / resource center, theatre, and numerous multipurpose spaces for distinct program offerings. There were multiple discussions before and after construction as it related to placement of raised garden beds.

Evanstonians are strong proponents of green strategies and The Mather South is LEED Gold Certified.

Collaboration: How did stakeholders, occupants, the design team, and / or others collaborate during the planning and/or design process?

There was a significant degree of input from everyone on the team that resulted in an evolution of the design based on emerging needs, requests from residents, and the development of the program.

To gain city and neighborhood approval, detailed sets of renderings were invaluable in gaining the trust and buy-in from the community. An initial concern existed not only over the noise and disruption a project such as this would offer, but if the end result would be a welcomed addition to the neighborhood. Detailed renderings went a long way in demonstrating the quality of the proposed development and proved helpful to gain entitlement for the project, as the renderings were incorporated into photographs showing actual trees, building scale, and detail. The team presented a number of views that were of concern to the city and neighbors. More than 25 local architects voiced their support in Evanston for this project, joined by 2,500+ supporters of the proposed community, and a design charrette was held early on in the programming process.

Outreach: What off-site outreach services are offered to the greater community?

Mather LifeWays Community Initiatives are known for Mather's—More Than A Cafe, Cafe Without Walls Programs, Telephone Topics and MoreWays, and reach approximately 3,000 older adults per month. Additionally, more than 150 organizations from 124 cities in 30 states and four countries have attended in-depth workshops and wanted to replicate the Cafe Plus concept.

Green / Sustainable Features: What green / sustainable features had the greatest impact on the project's design?

Site selection, energy efficiency, and maximized daylighting.

What were the primary motivations for including green / sustainable design features in the project?

Support the mission / values of the client / provider, make a contribution to the greater community, and lower operational costs.

What challenges did the project face when trying to incorporate green / sustainable design features?

Actual and perceived first-cost premium.

What program / organization is being used for green / sustainable certification of this project?

Leadership in Energy and Environmental Design (LEED).

For a project with a residential component, what was critical to the success of the project?

Improving common spaces / amenities.

Opposite: Drawing room, Mather South
Top left: Pool and spa facilities, Mather South
Top right: The Georgian Lounge, Mather South
Photography: Mather LifeWays

Households: What is innovative or unique about the households in the project?

New signage was created to show that change had taken place at The Mather in a dynamic and positive way. Employees, residents, and guests now see signs that call administrative offices "The Suits," a multipurpose room is named "Possibilities," physical therapy is "Moving Parts," occupational therapy is "Other Moving Parts," and skilled nursing is the "Life Centre."

Mather LifeWays language surprises people in a good way and engages them in conversation. For example, the word Repriorment™ has a very real meaning for residents of The Mather. Repriorment is the act of rediscovering the joy of long-forgotten pursuits often pushed to the side earlier in life. In similar fashion, administrators are "experience directors," a cook becomes a "manager of culinary delight," public areas are "possibilities spaces" and "experience centers," and the management team is the "possibilities team."

Common Spaces: What senior-friendly common spaces are included in the project?

Bistro / casual dining; coffee shop / grab-and-go; swimming pool / aquatics facilities; dedicated fitness equipment room; dedicated exercise classroom; massage / aromatherapy room; salon; large multipurpose room; small-scale cinema / media room; dedicated conference / meeting space; library / information resource center; art studio / craft room; religious / spiritual / meditative space; resident-maintained gardening space; rooftop terrace cafe; rooftop party room; seven dining venues (total); workshop; guest suites; men's and women's locker rooms in wellness center; whirlpool; steam showers; sauna; computerized wine bar; brain gym; formal living room; mail center; and concierge desk.

Jury Comments

Features include reflective roofing, rainwater harvesting, and a green roof. This repositioning project combines two communities by relocating to a newly constructed building on an urban infill site. The compact urban site dictated a vertical community of 11 stories, parking below-ground, and a rooftop terrace that offers outdoor dining. To compete with empty-nester condo developments, the homes offer open-floor plans, premium finishes, and an upgrade program with a 90 percent refund as an incentive to customize.

Left: View of gardens, The Mather
Right: View across kitchen and dining areas inside a typical two-bedroom plus den unit, Mather North
Opposite: Living area in a typical two-bedroom plus den unit, Mather North

Photography: Mather LifeWays

Brinkley Sargent Architects

The Summit at Central Park

Grand Prairie, Texas // City of Grand Prairie, Parks Department

Facility type (date of initial occupancy): Active adult recreation (May 2010)
Target market: Public facility, age 50+
Site location: Suburban; greenfield

Project site area (square feet): 56,541
Gross square footage of the new construction involved in the project: 56,541
Provider type: Governmental

Below: Lobby
Opposite: Main entry

more athletically inclined adults, with their own secondary entrance. The other side caters to those who prefer their recreation sweat-free, offering craft and game rooms, a pottery center, a teaching kitchen, an 88-seat movie theater, meal program, a cafe, and ballrooms. Members are free to drift outside and between the two sides.

The client's vision also included a sustainability goal to be at least LEED Silver Certified. It achieved LEED Gold.

Data / Research: What innovative or unique data collection and / or research was applied during the planning and / or design process?
Sited on one of the park's lakes, the building features a stunning view and boardwalk access. Outdoor amenities include covered seating and an outdoor grill for special events, gaming courts for bocce, horseshoes and washers, and a greenhouse and garden.

An indoor jogging and walking track overlooks the gymnasium and natatorium. The indoor pool provides lap lanes, a large therapy vortex area, and open areas for both programming and leisure. A large hot tub rounds out this space with views to the lake. Infinity-edge design and ramping provides abundant, yet subtle, accessibility to the pool and hot tub. Cardio-fitness spaces, a group exercise room and locker rooms with wood lockers, towel service, and saunas round out the amenities on the more active side of the building. The "passive" side of the building includes a large dining hall with full-service commercial kitchen, divisible ballrooms with stage and a theatre. Transitional spaces between the main active and passive functions include the lobby and lounge, cafe, games room, arts and crafts room with kiln, classroom, and virtual gaming room.

Overall Project Description

The municipal client sought to create a facility that could cater to traditional public senior center demands, while also being the first municipal "baby boomer center." The project is but one component of a new central park, which was already well underway along a new tollway. The architect served as the prime design professional in charge of master planning the entire development and realizing the first and most significant phase. The site, previously considered unusable due to floodplain issues, was recaptured as viable by re-envisioning flood control as a lake amenity. The first phase included the park infrastructure and roadways, lakes, a 150,000 square foot police station and the active adult center. The entire first phase was conceived and constructed in only 30 months through a fast-track design and construction process to meet client goals. Future pad sites were set aside that will offset park operations costs as they develop.

Additionally, the client envisioned this major endeavor as an opportunity to give the city a new image. Pad sites within the park will be required to be developed aesthetically similar to the city's anchor buildings.

Marketing / Occupancy: What issues were encountered regarding marketing and / or achieving full occupancy?
The project's functional premise is to conceive of a building that is not a senior center, but a community center that caters to those aged 50 and older. It is a multi-generational center that allows both boomers and veterans to equally feel at home.

The answer to the question: "How do you build a facility to wow two dramatically different groups?" turned out to be quite straightforward: split the building in two. The facility is essentially designed to create two distinct, albeit connected, environments. One side houses amenities for

Collaboration: How did stakeholders, occupants, the design team, and / or others collaborate during the planning and / or design process?

Beyond the challenges of arranging the spacial relationships, perhaps the most challenging aspect of the project was the intangible feel of the execution. The client was interested in a contemporary design, but one that was not trendy and that traditional seniors would still embrace. Envisioning the project, words like clean, simple, timeless and warm became the marching orders. It also had to be regionally sensitive. Catering to a mature crowd opened design possibilities with respect to interior materials, though ease of maintenance cannot be overlooked completely in a public facility.

The design response uses a palette of traditional building materials, such as pre-patinated copper, wood and locally sourced stone. Simple building forms with refined detailing provide the underpinning for a richly detailed interior. Steel trellises not only handle the challenging solar orientation necessitated by having lake views, but provide a unifying element for the dominant facades. Furniture was carefully selected to respond effectively to both the needs of the users and the aesthetic of the facility.

From a technical design standpoint, the most challenging space was the natatorium with its wrap-around upper-level jogging track. The track and natatorium cannot share the same air volume,

Master plan

so the desired openness had to be achieved through glazing. Therefore, the modulation of spaces along its path was carefully considered to ensure that the track would not feel like a "hamster tube." Introducing a track above and around the pool deck presented challenges structurally, mechanically, and with respect to lighting, design. Building systems were all exposed in these spaces, becoming part the architecture, and requiring intensive coordination in the studio and in the field.

Green / Sustainable Features: What green / sustainable features had the greatest impact on the project's design?

Reduced solar gain / heat island–effect sunshades, planting, improved indoor air quality, and maximized daylighting.

What were the primary motivations for including green / sustainable design features in the project?

Support the mission / values of the client / provider, make a contribution to the greater community, and lower operational costs.

What challenges did the project face when trying to incorporate green / sustainable design features?

Challenging solar orientation and primary views to the northwest.

What program / organization is being used for green / sustainable certification of this project?

Leadership in Energy and Environmental Design (LEED).

Top left: Control area
Top right: Bar area
Bottom left: Corridor

Common Spaces: What senior-friendly common spaces are included in the project?

Formal dining, bistro / casual dining; coffee shop / grab-and-go; marketplace / convenience store; swimming pool / aquatics facilities; dedicated fitness equipment room; dedicated exercise classroom; large multipurpose room; small-scale cinema / media room; dedicated conference / meeting space; dedicated classroom / learning space; art studio / craft room; member-maintained gardening space; senior craft store; saunas; whirlpool; gymnasium; and indoor jogging / walking track.

Jury Comments

Features include water-conserving landscaping, LED lighting, and maximizing daylight. Contemporary design to attract boomers (aged 50 to 70), but not trendy so traditional seniors, the veterans (aged 70 to 90+), would still embrace it. To accommodate both boomers and veterans the building is split into two areas: active activity side (pool, gym, fitness equipment) and passive activity side (games room, cafe, movie theater) connected by a common area. An indoor pool with generous daylight offers lap lanes, therapy area, and hot tub.

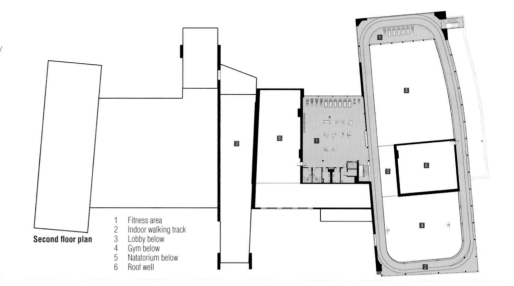

Second floor plan

1	Fitness area
2	Indoor walking track
3	Lobby below
4	Gym below
5	Natatorium below
6	Roof well

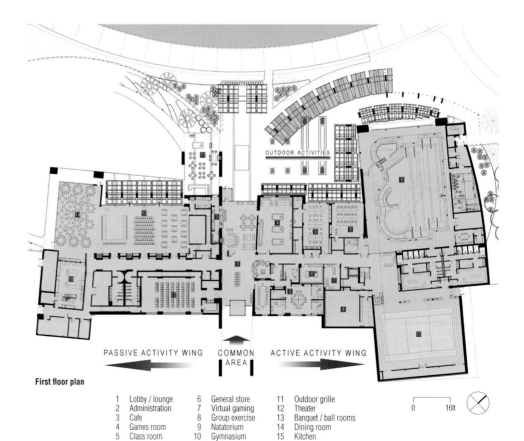

OUTDOOR ACTIVITIES

PASSIVE ACTIVITY WING   COMMON AREA   ACTIVE ACTIVITY WING

First floor plan

1	Lobby / lounge	6	General store	11	Outdoor grille
2	Administration	7	Virtual gaming	12	Theater
3	Cafe	8	Group exercise	13	Banquet / ball rooms
4	Games room	9	Natatorium	14	Dining room
5	Class room	10	Gymnasium	15	Kitchen

0   16ft

Left: Pool
Below: Outdoor area
Middle left: Dining hall
Bottom left: Games room
Bottom right: Theater

Photography: Charles Davis Smith, AIA

RLPS Architects

The Townhomes on Hendricks Place

Lititz, Pennsylvania // Moravian Manor

Facility type (date of initial occupancy): Independent Living (June 2012); CCRC or part of a CCRC
Target market: Middle / upper middle
Site location: Urban
Project site area (square feet): 152,460
Gross square footage of the new construction involved in the project: 42,584

Ratio of parking spaces to residents: 2.5:1 (including garages)
This site is within 1,000 feet of at least 10 basic services with pedestrian access to those services.
Provider type: Faith-based non-profit

Below: Vehicle access to the townhomes
Opposite: Exterior sidewalk connections

Overall Project Description

The townhomes provide a new independent living option for residents of a CCRC located in Lititz, Pennsylvania. The neighborhood of 12 attached, two-story cottage-style townhomes offers residents the opportunity to live, work and play within blocks of their new homes. These upscale, two-story townhomes, configured around a central green, are designed for one-floor living, with all necessary amenities on the first floor and bonus space for additional bedrooms, hobby areas or office space on the second floor.

They are built to accommodate active adults who prefer to maintain a house-sized residence, but enjoy the perks of maintenance-free living within a retirement community. Three different models, ranging from 2,609 up to 2,833 square feet, all include two bedrooms plus a den and rear-loaded two-car garage. Other features include nine-foot ceilings, walk-in closets, an eat-in kitchen, covered porch, gas fireplace, laundry room and an optional sunroom with patio.

Located on 3.5 acres, the townhomes are designed to architecturally emulate the character of their surroundings in downtown Lititz. An interconnecting sidewalk network provides residents with direct pedestrian access to the Center Green and to Lititz Borough's sidewalk and trail network. The townhomes are in close proximity to the Main Street shops and restaurants, Lititz Springs Park, farmers' markets, and other amenities, including physicians and dental offices—each located less than a block away. In addition to access to all of the retirement community's amenities, townhome residents also receive annual membership to the neighboring Lititz Recreation Center. Located across the street from the existing CCRC, the townhomes continue the community's practice of seamlessly blending into the town, rather than trying to recreate the small town feel on a separate campus.

Project Goals

What were the major goals?

- Taking advantage of existing amenities / infrastructure in the surrounding neighborhood. This infill site in downtown Lititz is located across from the CCRC's main campus and within easy walking distance to a wide range of services and amenities ranging from physicians and dental offices to the Lititz Recreation Center, and an English-style pub. Targeting active adults, the new townhomes overlooking a common green are interconnected via a sidewalk system that leads to the adjacent retirement campus, and the town's sidewalk network. Townhome residents will not only have easy access to the CCRC's services and amenities, but also are just steps away from a thriving small town environment with a vibrant network of shops and unique events. About half a mile from the townhomes, Lititz Springs Park hosts a wide range of art shows, cultural events and holiday celebrations throughout the year.

- Aging in place. The team was challenged to design marketable units that provide desirable living amenities and flexibility to allow for aging in place. The two-story townhomes were carefully planned so that residents could live very comfortably on the first floor, with the second floor functioning as a bonus area for a guest bedroom, games room, office or hobby area. All homes were designed with an elevator shaft to provide the option of a residential elevator to access the second-floor loft. Other more discreetly supportive features for accessibility, ranging from wider door clearances through higher countertops to lower shower thresholds, are designed into all of the townhomes as well.

- Responding to local conditions. A design priority was creating a traditional neighborhood development which complements the historical context of the surrounding downtown. The character of the townhomes was developed with reference to the Lititz / Warwick joint strategic comprehensive plan, designed to preserve and enhance the predominant characteristics of the region. To reinforce the residential scale, the building facades take on the appearance of attached buildings along the town's streetscape. The varied color palette and building materials reflect the local vernacular to blend in with the existing community.

Challenges: What were the greatest design challenges?

Implementing the necessary stormwater quantity and quality control measures without compromising the design concept of interconnected townhomes arranged around a common green challenged the design team to explore a non-traditional approach. A combination of rain gardens to define the boundaries between the private and public green spaces, and underground stormwater storage (below the center green), allowed for the desired building configuration within the constraints of a tight infill site.

Another challenge for the design team was obtaining variances from traditional zoning and planning regulations to allow a unique, higher density design solution on the site that was zoned for residential use. Lititz borough officials are sensitive to the aesthetics for this type of infill project. A series of meetings, utilizing concept images and a street-view rendering to illustrate the primary concept of clustering traditional townhomes around a center green, helped to secure the necessary allowances to proceed with the project.

The target market for the townhomes is active adults who wish to live in a spacious home within a pedestrian-friendly town. While one of the primary design goals was to accommodate aging in place, those accommodations could not be at the expense of the residential aesthetic. Prospective residents were clear that they did not wish to live in a home where accessibility features were apparent. Therefore, wider doorways and similar measures, such as extra blocking in showers, allow for future accommodations when needed by the residents living in the home.

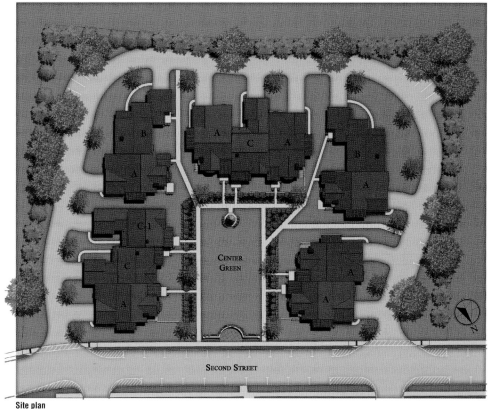

Site plan

Innovations: What innovations or unique features were incorporated into the design of the project?

The facades for the townhomes were designed to provide dual front doors. The alley side provides vehicle access and views, while the courtyard side facing the common green provides sidewalk access and views from Second Street, which runs in front of the townhomes. Although the design tucks the garages behind the street facade, covered, connected parking that is typical to a traditional residence was a priority for prospective residents. The dual front door design solution blends the townhomes into the streetscape while responding to the expectations of the target market.

The owner wished to utilize the available in-fill site to provide a new independent living housing option on its campus for active seniors who are not necessarily interested in downsizing. The most important feature for the townhomes was creating spacious, open floor plan residences that allow for first-floor living, but provide ample space for amenities found in traditional residences. This includes the second-floor bonus space, which can be accessed via a residential elevator. A secondary feature was providing ample outdoor connections through covered porches and optional sunrooms. Each townhome has a covered porch leading to the sidewalk network connecting the homes around the center green.

Marketing / Occupancy: What issues were encountered regarding marketing and / or achieving full occupancy?

This relatively modest 12-home independent living expansion was the first in almost a decade for this community. Based on the upscale design concept and larger size of the townhomes, combined with an uncertain housing market, the design allowed for the townhomes to be constructed in a multiphased approach as units were sold. Initially there were concerns due to a slow market response; however, once the first phase of homes was constructed, ongoing marketing results improved to the point that construction could continue uninterrupted. Full occupancy was achieved ahead of schedule, and there

Opposite top: Exterior views toward street
Below: Exterior views from street

is now a waiting list for the homes. Based on feedback from prospective residents, the owner believes the townhomes met the needs and expectations of active adults who otherwise would not have been ready to move to a retirement community.

Data / Research: What innovative or unique data collection and / or research was applied during the planning and / or design process?

The owner held a series of focus groups to verify market demand for this type of upscale product. The focus groups, in addition to education sessions provided by the architect, helped to identify current trends and consumer expectations related to housing for active adults.

Collaboration: How did stakeholders, occupants, the design team, and / or others collaborate during the planning and / or design process?

The design team, including the owner, architect, and civil engineer met extensively with local officials to discuss how the proposed townhomes on the residentially zoned site would support the goals of the Lititz-Warwick joint strategic comprehensive plan, including the borough's objectives to maintain the historical integrity of the town. Presentations, incorporating concept images and a street-view rendering, conveyed the design objective to seamlessly expand independent living within the community. The goal of strengthening connections to the town rather than creating the more typical inward-focused campus resulted in a number of measures to blend the townhomes into the existing context. This included minimizing signage and connecting to the existing sidewalk network. These measures were a major selling

point in the borough's acceptance of several zoning variances, including allowances for a higher density residential model. The introduction of a landscaped median strip in front of the townhomes eliminated the possibility of street parking in front of the courtyard, to maintain the desired aesthetic.

Green / Sustainable Features: What green / sustainable features had the greatest impact on the project's design?

Site design considerations, maximized daylighting, and relocating an existing home on the site rather than demolishing it.

What were the primary motivations for including green / sustainable design features in the project?

Support the mission / values of the client / provider, make a contribution to the greater community, and stay competitive against other similar / local facilities.

What challenges did the project face when trying to incorporate green / sustainable design features?

Implementing stormwater quantity and quality control measures without compromising the design concept of interconnected townhomes on a tight urban infill site.

Right: View of the two-story great room

Unit A Townhome Second Floor

Unit B Townhome Second Floor

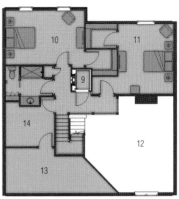

Unit C Townhome Second Floor

Unit A Townhome

1	Great room	8	Optional elevator
2	Library nook	9	Den
3	Kitchen	10	Optional sunroom
4	Dining	11	Bedroom
5	Garage	12	Open to great room
6	Mechanical area	13	Bonus room
7	Master bedroom	14	Storage

Unit B Townhome

1	Great room	8	Den / bedroom
2	Kitchen	9	Optional elevator
3	Dining	10	Bedroom
4	Mechanical area	11	Bonus room
5	Garage	12	Open to great room
6	Optional sunroom	13	Attic
7	Master bedroom	14	Storage

0 ___ 8ft

Unit C Townhome

1	Great room	8	Optional sunroom
2	Kitchen	9	Optional elevator
3	Dining	10	Bedroom
4	Garage	11	Bonus room
5	Mechanical area	12	Open to great room
6	Master bedroom	13	Attic
7	Den / bedroom	14	Storage

For a project with a residential component, what was critical to the success of the project?

Improving units / private spaces.

Common Spaces: What senior-friendly common spaces are included in the project?

Courtyard and gazebo.

Jury Comments

Infill project added 12 attached two-story cottage-style townhomes, creating a pocket neighborhood. Homes are located around a semipublic center green, providing separation from the public street, giving more privacy to occupants of the townhomes. The interconnecting sidewalk network offers direct pedestrian access from townhome porch to center green then to Lititz Borough sidewalks and trails. Rain gardens provide a boundary and some separation between private townhome and semipublic center green. Vehicle access and garages are located off the loop road that runs behind the townhomes, placing garage doors out of sight from street. Dual front doors provide an entrance from the green for those who walk and an entrance garage-side for those who arrive by car. The second-story bonus space provides for an additional bedroom or hobby area or office space.

Top: Sunroom looking out to center green
Bottom: First-floor master suite
Opposite: Eat-in kitchen

Photography: Larry Lefever Photography

EGA PC

White Oak Cottages at Fox Hill Village

Westwood, Massachusetts // White Oak Cottages

Facility type (date of initial occupancy): Assisted Living—dementia / memory support (May 2012); CCRC or part of a CCRC
Target market: Middle / upper middle
Site location: Suburban; greenfield
Project site area (square feet): 3,663,660 (campus); 238,450 (impacted)

Gross square footage of the new construction involved in the project: 19,050
Gross square footage of a typical household: 8,526
Number of residents in a typical household: 12
Ratio of parking spaces to residents: 1:1
This site is within 1,000 feet of public transportation.
Provider type: For-profit

Below: Typical exterior with varied roofline and architectural treatment, including cupola / light monitor
Opposite: View of private garden and house beyond with a skylight

Overall Project Description

The project is the first of its kind as a Green House® assisted living facility in the state. It consists of two houses for the care of residents with dementia (and other memory-related issues), and a third structure for marketing and administration. Each house has private bedrooms and baths for 12 residents and includes a kitchen, dining room, living room, and den.

The houses are designed to maximize the amount of natural light available in all public spaces and resident rooms. Each house is arranged around a secure garden, allowing free access for the residents when weather permits.

The project was undertaken to fill a need in the offerings of a large CCRC on the same campus that was previously offering memory care in a nursing setting only, and in a space far removed from the currently advocated best practices for residents with dementia.

The scope included all site work and building construction for the two houses and marketing building, and no scope related to the existing CCRC on the campus.

Project Goals

What were the major goals?

- Finding a location on a site, which was significantly constrained by existing buildings and wetlands, for two houses, a separate administration building, and significant landscaped areas, while maintaining the elegant character of the entrance to the existing CCRC. A small area was found that was large enough for the proposed development. It required significant ledge removal and zoning modifications to be usable, as well as the addition of some retaining walls and other grade revisions to allow the houses to sit at close to the same level (for accessibility). All attempts were made to retain the character of the existing entrance drive through the siting of

the new buildings and the development of the landscaping. This project occupies a prominent location on the existing campus, and effort was made to reduce the prominence of these houses within the limitations imposed by the site.

- Maximizing natural light. Natural light is always important in any residential project, but takes on a higher level of importance for those with dementia and Alzheimer's, and maximizing natural light is often a struggle on projects employing the Green House® and small house models—because of the relatively high ratio of resident rooms to commons. In this project the building was articulated in such a way as to allow large exposures into the main common spaces, and skylights were added to those other public or semi-public spaces that otherwise lack access to more conventional sources of natural light.

- Connecting those homes to secure gardens. From the beginning of the design process the gardens were thought of as rooms in the project, and as such received high priority during the master planning phase of the development. This put greater strain on the already limited site, but resulted in a carefully rendered and safe outdoor space, accommodating the needs of residents of varying mobility, and providing a diversity of activities in what is otherwise a relatively small area.

Challenges: What were the greatest design challenges?

The greatest challenges to the project were related to site constraints, local regulatory officials, and the difficulties inherent in providing adequate natural light to a house with 12 bedrooms.

The site severely restricted the ability to locate the houses because much of the area not previously developed as part of the CCRC that shares the campus is either filled with exposed ledge or is impacted by wetlands.

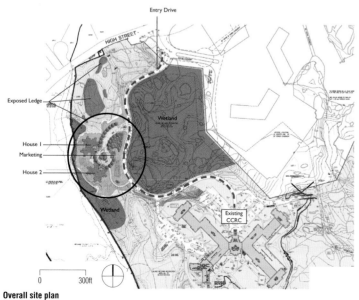

Overall site plan

Entry Drive

HIGH STREET

Exposed Ledge

Wetland

House 1

Marketing

House 2

Wetland

Existing CCRC

0   300ft

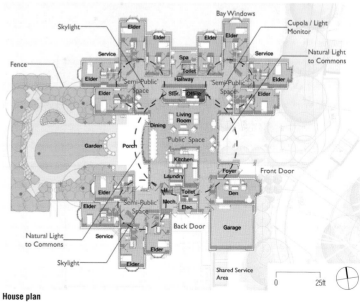

House plan

Skylight

Bay Windows

Cupola / Light Monitor

Service

Elder

Elder

Elder

Elder

Spa

Service

Natural Light to Commons

Fence

Elder

'Semi-Public' Space

Toilet

Hallway

'Semi-Public' Space

Elder

Elder

Stor.

Office

Elder

Living Room

Garden

Dining

'Public' Space

Elder

Porch

Kitchen

Foyer

Front Door

Laundry

Den

Elder

Natural Light to Commons

Elder

Toilet

Mech.

'Semi-Public' Space

Elec.

Service

Garage

Skylight

Back Door

Elder

Elder

Shared Service Area

0   25ft

The local regulatory officials in the town were risk-averse, despite the long and high-quality track record of the existing CCRC. They required the project to meet standards for long-term care that otherwise are not required in assisted living, and were initially resistant to the food service concept presented to them. It took waivers from the local health advisory board to achieve the results.

Residential model projects, including the Green House® and its variants, face one major difficulty when it comes to the architecture. The large number of bedrooms—compared with the relatively small amount of commons space—often means projects suffer from having too little natural light in the common spaces. A more highly articulated building envelope, one that fractures the building enough to allow more opportunities for windows in the common spaces, is one solution. A side benefit of that fracturing is that it makes the exterior appearance of the building more interesting and smaller scaled, despite the more than 8,000 square feet in the house.

Innovations: What innovations or unique features were incorporated into the design of the project?

The houses are organized so that there is a hierarchy of spaces from public to private. The resident rooms are all organized around lounges that provide a buffer between the bedrooms and the main commons spaces. This is similar to the arrangement of a typical house, where bedrooms rarely are accessed directly off of the main living spaces.

The resident rooms all have bay windows. This has two main benefits: otherwise small, otherwise ordinary rooms are made more interesting; and these rooms get the benefit of natural light from three directions, greatly increasing the amount of natural light in the rooms. Most rooms also have a small window located over the bed to provide additional natural light, and which adds interest.

Each of the houses has an attached two-car garage, much like in a typical single-family house. This was originally conceived as a place for overnight staff to park, but also provides a means for separating deliveries and other service related access from the front door of each house. It also provides another area for additional storage in each house, both in the short term for deliveries of larger items, and for long-term storage of general-use items.

Marketing / Occupancy: What issues were encountered regarding marketing and / or achieving full occupancy?

There were no challenges as it relates to marketing. The project is small and was generally very well received by the market from the start. The greater challenge was in staffing up in a way that allowed the owner to feel confident that they were providing the highest possible quality product. As a result, initial occupancy took longer than expected as the staff and their related processes took longer than expected to be refined.

Collaboration: How did stakeholders, occupants, the design team, and / or others collaborate during the planning and / or design process?

This project was done for a for-profit entity, something relatively rare among those adopting the Green House® and small house models of care. As such, there was particular attention paid to cost / benefit across the entirety of the design and construction process.

It was also achieved through a design-build collaboration between architect and general contractor.

Outreach: What off-site outreach services are offered to the greater community?

The administration building on the site includes a space for meetings that, in addition to the staff and families associated with this project, is used by residents of the larger campus (though not with any significant regularity).

Green / Sustainable Features: What green / sustainable features had the greatest impact on the project's design?

Energy efficiency, water efficiency, and maximized daylighting.

What were the primary motivations for including green / sustainable design features in the project?

Support the mission / values of the client / provider, make a contribution to the greater community, and lower operational costs.

Opposite: Dining room with views of living room

What challenges did the project face when trying to incorporate green / sustainable design features?

Actual and perceived first-cost premium.

For a project with a residential component, what was critical to the success of the project?

Improving common spaces / amenities.

Households: What is innovative or unique about the households in the project?

The principal innovation of the project is employing the Green House® principals for assisted living, of which there are few precedents. The Green House® model was conceived as a long-term care model with no particular emphasis on dementia or memory care. Adopting the original principals of de-institutionalization, while shifting the emphasis to those requiring less medical care (but all with levels of dementia), required adjustments mostly related to the specific issues associated with dementia and Alzheimer's. Issues of daylight, artificial lighting level, queuing, appropriate finishes, and colors all played a large role in the design of the project.

A strong emphasis was also made on providing a hierarchy of space within each house, from public to private, with a transition space between the resident bedrooms and the main commons spaces; similar to a typical home, but often not found in other projects of this type.

Common Spaces: What senior-friendly common spaces are included in the project?

Formal dining, and bistro / casual dining; salon; small-scale cinema / media room; dedicated conference / meeting space; and resident-maintained gardening space.

Jury Comments

The project is a Green House® design for assisted living, specifically for dementia and memory care. Two residentially scaled structures, each serving 12 residents, plus a third building for administration are sited to maintain the entrance drive and complement the elegant character of the existing CCRC. There is a strong emphasis on the hierarchy of space within each house. Three pockets of four recessed resident rooms are organized around lounges that provide a buffer between bedrooms and common spaces, similar to a typical home. The building is articulated to allow large exposures of natural light in the common areas. Light is further maximized through the use of skylights. Resident rooms have natural light from three directions, including bay windows. Each house has an attached two-car garage, which provides a means for separating deliveries and other service-related access from the front door, as well as accommodating additional storage.

Opposite top: Living room with fireplace, and resident rooms beyond and skylights
Opposite bottom: Typical resident bedroom with windowseat and window over bed
Above: Living room with kitchen and dining areas beyond

Photography: Jarred Sadowski

SFCS Inc.

Armed Forces Retirement Home

Gulfport, Mississippi // Armed Forces Retirement Home

Facility type (date of initial occupancy): Independent Living (October 2010); Assisted Living (November 2010); Long-term Skilled Nursing (November 2010); Skilled Nursing—dementia / memory support (March 2012); CCRC or part of a CCRC
Target market: Military veterans
Site location: Urban
Project site area (square feet): 4,791,600

Gross square footage of the new construction involved in the project: 842,514
Gross square footage of a typical household: 25,790
Number of residents in a typical household: 12
Ratio of parking spaces to residents: 1:1
This site is within 1,000 feet of public transportation, and within 1,000 feet of at least 10 basic services with pedestrian access to those services.
Provider type: Governmental

Below: Entrance to the Hall of Honors, a formal display space for treasured artifacts of veterans' military service
Opposite: Outdoor spaces featuring reflecting pool, dining terrace, swimming pool, and walking paths
Photography: Alan Karchmer

Overall Project Description

A veterans' facility in Gulfport, Mississippi, was severely damaged by Hurricane Katrina in 2005, and the building could not be salvaged. Most of the 600-plus residents were relocated after the hurricane, but they are now home again to a larger and more bountiful environment.

The project is now a vibrant 842,514-square-foot LEED Gold Certified building, situated on 46 acres on the coast of the Gulf of Mexico. It rises majestically above palm trees on the Mississippi Gulf Coast like a grand hotel in the spirit of the art deco architecture of Miami Beach. The building is composed of three, eight-story residential pavilions, which are designed to withstand a category 5 hurricane and remain self-sustaining for weeks thereafter.

The Commons or Main Street level was raised 15 feet above the existing grade to survive extreme storm surge conditions like those

experienced during Hurricane Katrina. The main entrance has a covered porte-cochere and reflecting pool directly outside the glass enclosed lobby. These elements provide a formal, yet symbolic feeling of entry from either pedestrian arrival or vehicular arrival.

Upon entering the ground level lobby, there is access to the main level via a monumental staircase or elevator. A skylit rotunda greets visitors and residents coming up from below. The lobby provides access to commons level spaces, which include the formal reception area, pre-function space, dining, Main Street, and the Hall of Honors. The commons level contains the main kitchen, chapel, clinic, bank, arts and crafts studios, post office, fitness center, recreation, administration, and other activities / services. Themed graphics, materials, and color support wayfinding for residents. This 160,000-square-foot area represents the residents' downtown or Main Street.

Elevators provide access to each of the three residential towers, which house independent living and assisted living, and a fourth elevator tower to a dedicated memory support suite and long-term care suite. The green roof over the commons level provides a verdant garden for residents on the second floor.

A typical floor has 24 apartments; 12 on each side with a larger room for couples in the center, an elevator, resident laundry, and a family / day room. Each apartment, approximately 450 square feet, allows multiple furniture layouts. There is a view of the ocean from every apartment and a spacious balcony canted toward the ocean and accommodates outdoor dining and socializing opportunities.

Project Goals

What were the major goals?

- The first goal was protecting the building from extreme weather conditions, such as hurricanes, by raising the main level 15 feet above-grade. It is a self-contained town where even neighbors can visit and experience the amenities.

- Another goal was creating more room / space and amenities for residents. Each resident in the old structure had 98 square feet of living area. Most residents had a swivel seat on rollers and would wheel around from bed to bathroom to refrigerator. Now they have full apartments over four times the original size and significant social gathering spaces both inside and out. Each resident is much more aware of their environment and their neighbors. There is also a view of the ocean from every apartment and a balcony that is canted toward the ocean. The balcony is large enough to have a couple of chairs and a small table for eating or socializing. This premise was fundamental to the design, so each resident would be have a view of the gulf from their living unit.

Challenges: What were the greatest design challenges?

From the programmatic constraint indicated by the Gulf Coast site and the tragic experience of Hurricane Katrina, the team developed a solution that raised the lowest occupied floor 15 feet above-grade. The commons level, safely elevated above potential storm surge, contains a full array of resident services and amenities that are carefully organized into a single floor. If necessary, residents can remain in the building after a major storm event for two weeks completely independent of outside electricity, water, and sewer services. The design solution fulfills the challenging engineering requirements for survivability and sustainability.

It was also quite a challenge to create an environment for 600+ retired military persons. Efficient circulation is key to resolving a complex program. One of the features that makes this design a success is the compactness of the plan and the efficiency by which it is served by horizontal and vertical circulation. The grouping of multiple, relatively short residential towers atop a plinth containing all support activities, results in multiple vertical circulation cores accessing a relatively square compact plinth level (first floor). The advantage of this arrangement is that the travel distance is reduced between any vertical circulation core to any particular destination on the plinth level.

The design / build team was authorized to proceed with design in October 2007, and residents started to move back in July 2010. This was an extremely aggressive, compressed schedule for a large-scale, complex project. The design portion of the team worked very closely with the construction group so that building foundation work could start in

Top and bottom: Large apartment bedrooms and spacious balconies with sun-shading canted for ocean views
Photography: Alan Karchmer

January 2009 when the overall design was less than 35 percent complete. This fast-track approach was a tremendous coordination challenge, requiring design decisions to be made very early and with finality. The team was successful in assimilating user program, engineering, code, and budget requirements on a continuously updated basis, allowing construction to proceed even as the design was being finalized.

Innovations: What innovations or unique features were incorporated into the design of the project?

The commons floor is located above the category-5 hurricane storm surge elevation, and the area functions as a small town supporting the residential towers above. The first floor is bisected east–west by a main street, where residents can access major activities, such as dining, theater, banking, and shopping. The cross "streets" lead to the clinic, library, fitness center, and administration offices. Each destination along Main Street is identified by varied architectural detailing. The PX (market)

fronts Main Street with floor to ceiling glass as on a shopping street. In this way, the design is truly unique in providing a "town" for its residents.

Residents have convenient access to multiple dining venues, social, recreational and therapeutic activities—including an outdoor swimming pool (lap swimming and water aerobics); a professionally equipped fitness center and physical fitness programs; individual work areas for arts and crafts, woodworking, painting, and other hobbies; a bike shop; and an on-campus pharmacy, as well as clinical, and dental services. Other areas of interest include a full service bar and lounge with large-screen televisions; coffee shop; a bank; barber and beauty salon; bowling center; movie theater; multipurpose area for live entertainment and dances; computer room, and library. The complex also features spacious landscaped grounds with walking paths; bicycle trail; a nine-hole golf course; basketball court; an area for games of horseshoes; beach access via a private walkway; and bus tours to area attractions.

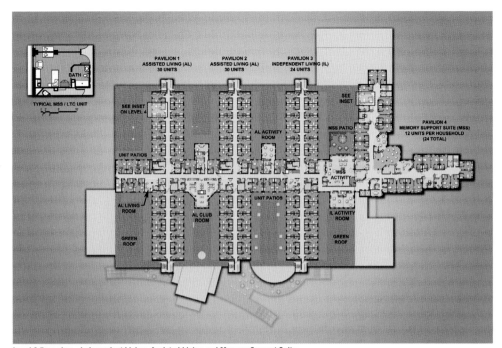

Level 2 floor plan – Independent Living, Assisted Living and Memory Support Suite

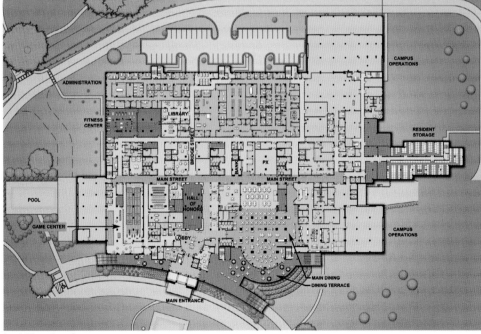

Level 1 floor plan – Commons

Data / Research: What innovative or unique data collection and / or research was applied during the planning and / or design process?

There were many programming charrettes and mock-up exercises to determine size and details of all areas. This open planning process was dynamic and provided clear information for both the design team and the user groups.

Collaboration: How did stakeholders, occupants, the design team, and / or others collaborate during the planning and / or design process?

The design / build team met with the owner / staff in October 2007 for three days to conduct a design charrette. The goal of the charrette was to discover architectural design ideas, discuss critical design features and explore full-size mock-ups. The charettes later incorporated the owners' comments so that the design team could provide the ultimate design for approval and development into Construction Documents. The design team worked to incorporate revisions, additions, and other information discussed at the charrette into the floor plans and submitted revised plans for approval. In development of the architectural floor plans the design / build team worked to resolve several critical issues.

The residents were also an integral part of the process and their insights invaluable. Their input seemed as if they were rebuilding their own home.

- Administration
- Campus operations
- Clinic
- Main street
- Main entrance / lobby
- Circulation
- Community / activity
- Dining
- Fitness center
- Hall of honors
- Restrooms / spa
- Storage
- Units
- Patios / porches
- Roof / skylight
- Green roof

0   64ft

They were involved from beginning to end; from looking at the plans to going through mock-ups of their rooms, to walk-throughs during construction.

Green / Sustainable Features: What green / sustainable features had the greatest impact on the project's design?

Site design considerations, improved indoor air quality, and conscientious choice of materials.

What were the primary motivations for including green / sustainable design features in the project?

Support the mission / values of the client / provider, make a contribution to the greater community, and lower operational costs.

What challenges did the project face when trying to incorporate green / sustainable design features?

Perceived first-cost premium and lack of client knowledge about green / sustainability.

What program / organization is being used for green / sustainable certification of this project?

Leadership in Energy and Environmental Design (LEED).

Top left: Private bedrooms include multiple light sources and types, a custom-built headboard, armoire, television and stand
Top right: Bowling tournament facilities, situated within the building
Above: Residential living room with comfortable furnishings and an abundance of natural light

Photography: Alise O'Brien

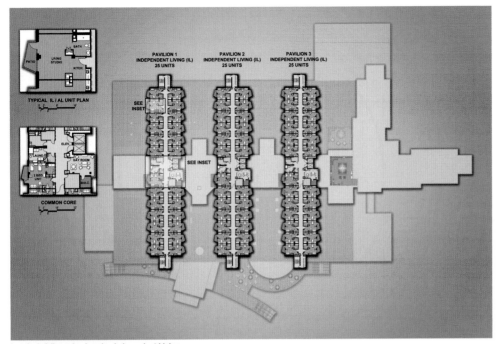

Levels 4–8 floor plan housing Independent Living

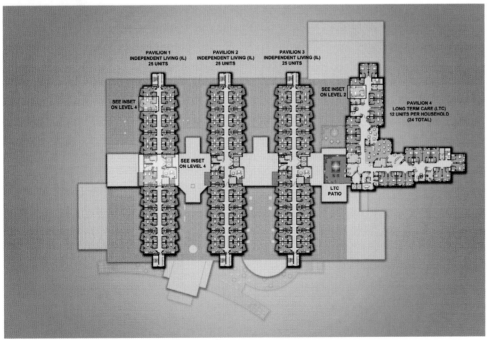

Level 3 floor plan housing Independent Living and Long-term Care

Households: What is innovative or unique about the households in the project?

The owner operates on a core philosophy of person-centered care, and understands the need to listen and respond to its residents accordingly.

The residential living spaces are inviting and reinforce the sense of community and openness within the household. Comfortable furnishings promote social interaction, and an abundance of natural light provides a visual connection throughout. Finishes are warm, inviting, and, durable yet not institutional.

Residents' personal rooms include a full bathroom with showers, and can accommodate multiple furniture arrangements. The bedroom includes a custom headboard providing storage, and multiple lighting sources. Significant attention was given to ensure comfort, including occupant controllability of both thermal and lighting controls.

Large, secure outdoor spaces are provided in each household for both long-term care and memory support suite residents. This suite features a gazebo and other shade devices, as well as activity zones and landscaping.

Common Spaces: What senior-friendly common spaces are included in the project?

Formal dining and bistro / casual dining; coffee shop / grab-and-go; marketplace / convenience store; swimming pool / aquatics facilities; dedicated fitness equipment room; dedicated exercise classroom; dedicated rehabilitation / therapy gym; salon; large multipurpose room; small-scale cinema / media room; dedicated conference / meeting space; dedicated classroom / learning space; library / information resource center; art studio / craft room; religious / spiritual / meditative space; and resident-maintained gardening space.

THW Design

Cohen Rosen House

Rockville, Maryland // Hebrew Home of Greater Washington

Facility type (date of initial occupancy): Assisted Living—dementia / memory support (October 2012); CCRC or part of a CCRC
Target market: Middle / upper middle
Site location: Urban
Project site area (square feet): 83,370
Gross square footage of the new construction involved in the project: 16,361

Gross square footage of a typical household: 308
Number of residents in a typical household: 1
Ratio of parking spaces to residents: 1:0.33
This site is within 1,000 feet of public transportation.
Provider type: Faith-based non-profit

Below: Main entry exterior
Opposite: Resident courtyard

(green roofs) and thoughtful follow-through during construction (recycling of materials) are as integral as the staff's cleaning and maintenance methods (low VOC products). These key aspects demonstrate a commitment to sustainability.

Challenges: What were the greatest design challenges?

To honor the individual residents and to comfort them, the house features many parts that they might have enjoyed in their previous homes. Each room meets the needs of the community and the individual resident. Colors, materials, and textures span not only from room to room, but also from the indoor to the outdoor spaces. Just inside the front door and welcoming foyer, the gallery showcases pictures and memorabilia of residents' families. At the center of the home is the social core, an open living room with large spans of windows for natural daylighting, and views into the courtyard. The living room setting, with high-performing acoustic treatment, is anchored with a fireplace, an aquarium, and placement of a piano nearby. The adjacent dining space with an open family kitchen provides the familiar sounds and aromas of daily cooking. An extension to this space is the four-seasons porch for enjoying views into the courtyard. The two resident wings each feature one central bath and nine private resident rooms, each overlooking outdoor gardens. Personal spaces are clearly separated from public zones, while back-of-house services are hidden in corridors that connect the kitchen to the adjacent assisted living areas.

Innovations: What innovations or unique features were incorporated into the design of the project?

For this project, wellness begins with the dignity of the resident as reflected through the use of a non-institutional design approach and space relationships that encourage interaction and connectivity with others, and with nature. Specific features include the therapeutic nature of the exterior courtyard

Overall Project Description

This project is a new 18-bed, assisted living / memory care house in the midst of a larger CCRC that includes independent living, assisted living, and rehab and recovery. Completing the continuum of care, this project is an assisted living residence that stands as a home in physical form (and in meaning) for their residents requiring memory support. The concept behind the house is the connection between the timeless elements of home and thousands of years of Judaic tradition, all within a connected community of 1,000 residents. The eighteen individuals calling this house their home benefit from an open design centered around them, their families, and their life stories.

Project Goals

What were the major goals?

- Creating an environment suitable for memory care that still represents the qualities of home. Finishes, furnishings and scale all are indicative of a home environment. Clerestory windows allow daylight into the public and private areas to aid the circadian rhythms of residents, thereby reducing sundowning.

- Maintaining the connection to the overall campus. The house is constructed on an underutilized outdoor space for the adjacent assisted living residents; however, careful siting of the building allowed for pedestrian access to the greater campus.

- Providing a safe outdoor space for residents of all abilities that does not look institutionalized. A fenced and gated courtyard features pondless water features, sculptures, and nontoxic plantings, with ample shade and seating for residents, families, and caregivers.

- Achieving LEED Silver certification. To achieve LEED Silver certification, many aspects of the home, from concept to construction to operation, come together. Innovations in design

with water features, gardening tables, and paths and amenities to encourage outdoor activities. Artwork is installed throughout, and the large art room promotes both physical and mental activities. Activities in the dining area kitchen and the adjacent library / parlor are intended to also help residents as part of their daily routines. LEED certification is being pursued so the residents will also enjoy the healthy benefits of sustainable design.

Marketing / Occupancy: What issues were encountered regarding marketing and / or achieving full occupancy?

The facility filled in two months, ahead of schedule, based on the strength of the programming and the positive physical environment. There is a waiting list.

Top: Arrival perspective

Data / Research: What innovative or unique data collection and / or research was applied during the planning and / or design process?

As part of the design process, research was conducted on the sun angles of the project location and the clerestory windows were designed accordingly. Large expanses of windows also warm the spaces with sunlight. As a result, interior lighting is rarely used during daylight hours. Multiple sources tout the benefits of natural light and its healing qualities, especially in the treatment of residents suffering from sundowning. Traditional residential detailing is used on the exterior to camouflage the size and use of the facility. Through the use of residential-scaled materials, finishes and details, artwork, exterior spaces, and integrated furnishings and accessories, the house has the character and feel of a home in the interior common areas, not an institutional facility. The result is a residence where memory impaired residents can live with dignity and experience healthy opportunities for activities and relationships as they age in place.

Collaboration: How did stakeholders, occupants, the design team, and / or others collaborate during the planning and / or design process?

Early on in the design process, the client engaged the design team to develop a plan to work within an existing framework of zoning and environmental constraints. Previous developments of the overall campus had resulted in a small building pad surrounded by a tree conservation area on two sides, with parking and existing buildings on the others. Strict state stormwater regulations and a goal of LEED certification further added complexity to the project. To successfully work within these limits, the client employed a diverse team that included staff, residents, legal counsel, and design consultants. Further, a contractor was brought in to provide pre-construction services. In addition to presentations to the surrounding community, the design team met regularly to ensure an interactive planning / design process and to make sure each stakeholder's concerns were considered through to construction.

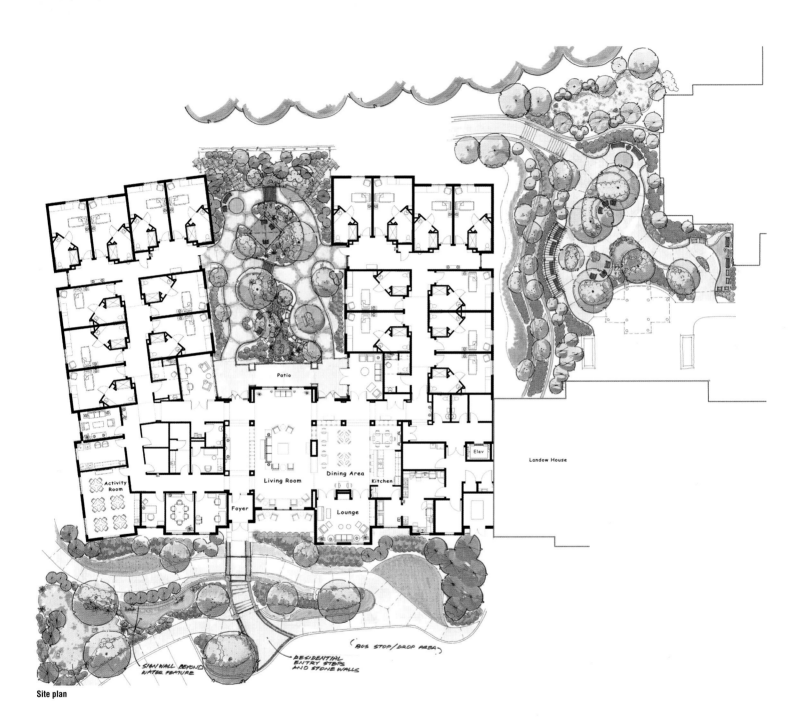

Patio

Activity Room

Living Room

Dining Area

Kitchen

Elev

Foyer

Lounge

Landow House

SIGN WALL BEYOND
WATER FEATURE

RESIDENTIAL
ENTRY STEPS
AND STONE WALLS

(BUS STOP/DROP AREA)

Site plan

Outreach: What off-site outreach services are offered to the greater community?

This community as a whole offers various outpatient services, home care services, and an outpatient medical practice serving approximately 100 per day.

Green / Sustainable Features: What green / sustainable features had the greatest impact on the project's design?

Site design considerations, energy efficiency, and reduced solar gain / heat island–effect sunshades, and planting.

What were the primary motivations for including green / sustainable design features in the project?

Support the mission / values of the client / provider and design team, and make a contribution to the greater community.

Top left: Memory curio space outside each resident's room
Top right: View of corridor
Opposite: Living room with views to dining room
Photography: Alain Jaramillo

What program / organization is being used for green / sustainable certification of this project?

Leadership in Energy and Environmental Design (LEED).

For a project with a residential component, what was critical to the success of the project?

Improving common spaces / amenities.

Households: What is innovative or unique about the households in the project?

Each resident has an individual room and large memory curio that can reflect their unique personality. Just like their previous homes, residents are free to wander and visit with other residents, or enjoy the view from the four-season porch, the quiet room, or the library / parlor. Outdoors, a secure and accessible courtyard gives residents a safe place to enjoy nature. Complete with walking paths, seating areas for individuals or groups, sculptures for wayfinding, and bird baths and feeders to attract wildlife, the courtyard is surrounded by the household wings, and blurs the line between indoor and outdoor space. Raised vegetable planters give residents opportunities to socialize in a meaningful activity and individually contribute to their own meals. At the heart of the courtyard is a dry streambed feature. At its origin, a self-contained stone waterfall disappears underneath a bridge feature. With a natural stone edge and colored tumbled glass to represent the flow of water, the feature continues through the courtyard and ends with flowing statuaries just outside the floor-to-ceiling windows in the living room. These windows give an uninterrupted view back into the courtyard where a sukkah sits beside the dry streambed, offering space for gatherings. Non-toxic and native landscaping not only fills the courtyard and adds to the natural feel of the outdoor room, but also screens the ornamental fence gates, giving the residents and staff the security they need.

Common Spaces: What senior-friendly common spaces are included in the project?

Bistro / casual dining; massage / aromatherapy room; library / information resource center; art studio / craft room; and exterior memory courtyard / garden.

SmithGroupJJR

Good Shepherd Cottage, Santa Teresita, Inc.

Duarte, California // Carmelite Sisters

Facility type (date of initial occupancy): Assisted Living (December 2012)
Target market: Middle / upper middle
Site location: Suburban; greyfield
Project site area (square feet): 60,000
Gross square footage of the new construction involved in the project: 19,704
Gross square footage of a typical household: 9,500

Number of residents in a typical household: 11
Ratio of parking spaces to residents: .9:1 (20 total spaces for 22 residents)
This site is within 1,000 feet of public transportation, and within 1,000 feet of at least 10 basic services with pedestrian access to those services.
Provider type: Faith-based non-profit

Below: Building main entrance.
Opposite: Mountain range views connect the Good Shepherd Cottage to the surroundings.

Overall Project Description

Santa Teresita's project is a response to the vital need for new and better models of care for a growing elderly population. The "Rose Gardens at Santa Teresita" shifts from a medical model to resident centered care by creating "home" in a custom-designed cottage meant to be flexible for assisted living, memory care or skilled nursing. Founded by the Carmelite Sisters of the Most Sacred Heart of Los Angeles, Santa Teresita provides care for the aging community and is motivated by a profound compassion and supported by a commitment to professional excellence.

Good Shepherd Cottage is the first of nine such cottages to be built into the Neighborhood of Care, along with a wellness center, town center for social amenities, and engaging outdoor spaces, such as meandering walkways through a variety of gardens, putting green, and performance stage. The building is designed to

promote the uniqueness of each individual, in the context of community. The cottage concept was developed to embrace the notion of household design; it is meant to be comfortable, supportive and distinctive, creating both a physical and spiritual space reflective of the mission of the Carmelite Sisters. The vision for the cottage as part of the developing Neighborhood of Care is to create interrelationships between indoor and outdoor spaces, as well as other buildings, that facilitate interactions among residents, their families, and staff.

Designed to house 22 residents, the two-story cottage balances community living and kitchen areas with private rooms to create a social and dynamic environment. Each floor accommodates 11 or 12 residents and features an open kitchen, dining area, living room, den, outside patio, and private, personalized bedrooms with storage, and private bathrooms. All of the common spaces, while clearly defined by functionality,

flow together with visibility throughout. Resident rooms are located at the perimeter allowing for scenic views to the outside, as well as direct connection to the social spaces.

Familiar elements and detailing present deliberate reflections of home, and create a sense of comfort for residents. Natural light abounds. Sustainable design strategies that achieved LEED Silver certification included such things as operable windows, low VOC materials, and access to the outdoors to reinforce a healthy living environment.

Project Goals

What were the major goals?

- Make the cottage design interchangeable in order to serve all levels and types of care. In order to allow for future flexibility as the master plan is built out, the original design intent of the cottage is that it can be used as memory care, skilled nursing, or assisted living.

- Provide quality of life. The main goals for the project were to profoundly respect the dignity of each person at every stage of the human experience and to provide comprehensive quality service to all. The architecture helped achieve this by creating a high-quality, attractive setting where residents want to live. The creation of engaging space addresses the common challenge of isolation for the elderly. The building provides a vibrant and engaging lifestyle by focusing on direct access to social areas that have abundant natural light and multiple connections to the outdoors. The floor plan, with a central communal living room, provides options for both group and private activities. The patios and outdoor gardens on the first floor become places for residents to interact. The second floor has accessible common decks with views of the San Gabriel Mountains.

- Increase independence. The individual resident rooms allow for privacy and are designed to promote independence. Each room faces away from the main front door and includes a private bathroom and kitchenette to allow residents the option of entertaining family and friends. The bathrooms have roll-in showers with built-in benches, and toilets have fold-down grab bars. Accessibility is blended into the cottage and campus design, including adjacencies and ease of movement between functional spaces, which allow residents to navigate as independently as possible. Care stations are integrated into the casework at the library with a writing desk so it maintains an unobtrusive and residential appearance. These universal design details function to assist residents as they age. Residents also have access to meals and snacks from the open kitchen and have the opportunity to participate in the preparation. A large residential laundry room is designed to support and ensure that residents can maintain their independence.

- Invite and integrate the surrounding community. A natural flow between indoor and outdoor space, and open relationships with the surrounding campus buildings create a sense of interconnectivity to life as it is happening all around. The abundance of natural light, window / door transparencies, entry way sequencing, and adjacencies create an inviting atmosphere. The naturally lit living room, dining room, and kitchen are all at the center of the house, with two sides in direct access of the garden patios.

Challenges: What were the greatest design challenges?

Working to a strict and tight budget was a challenge for this project. Together with the owner, project manager, and general contractor, cost effective materials and fixtures were sourced. Finish selections were cost efficient: all walls are painted

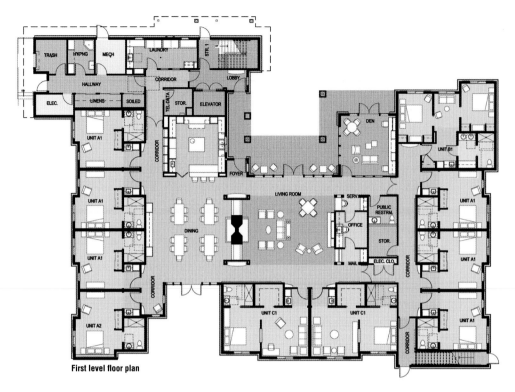

First level floor plan

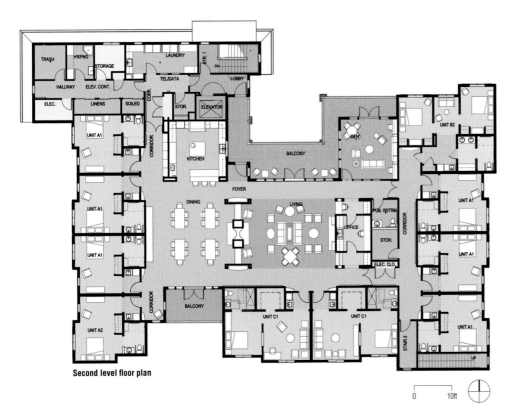

Second level floor plan

0   10ft

and the palette was limited to three colors; exposed wood received a clear finish rather than a stain; and, the casework design is similar throughout, allowing for efficiency of construction. When possible, furnishings were selected from local sources, minimizing shipping costs.

A key challenge was to create an open floor plan that allowed the light-filled common areas (to encourage resident gathering and socializing) to include direct access to eleven resident rooms. Code approval of the open area was a challenge: it was viewed by the regulatory agency as a traditional assembly space, however, the design team was able to convince them that these were living rooms and family rooms, just like in one's home. The number of public bathrooms and multiple-use categories were reduced to eliminate the separation between these spaces and hallways. The project was permitted as completely residential use and occupancy.

Innovations: What innovations or unique features were incorporated into the design of the project?

Resident room spaces are designed with as much attention to detail as the rest of the household. Molding, small storage nooks, and casework give the resident room a character and identity that match the building and the community's high level of care.

Common indoor spaces were designed to flow directly into active outdoor spaces. The living and dining rooms have natural light from two sides.

The entry cues set the tone of the home and promote a sense of respect. The entry foyer serves as an introduction space. It is comfortable and allows visitors to orient themselves, take their coat off, and proceed naturally to the living room.

Opposite: The dining room flows into the kitchen around a central hearth, creating home-like spaces.
Left: The communal living room with a hearth and open patio provides space for social interaction.

The residential kitchen is open and inviting, an integral part of the core of the household. The kitchen, dining room, and outdoor dining patio all serve as functional workspaces and social hubs. There is ample walker storage in an area adjacent to the dining room, so residents have access to all areas of the house and enjoy meals with one another. Common spaces are designed to be inviting and engaging for all members of the family, who are encouraged to be involved in the daily living of the residents.

Marketing / Occupancy: What issues were encountered regarding marketing and / or achieving full occupancy?

The building's occupancy levels filled according to plan.

Data / Research: What innovative or unique data collection and / or research was applied during the planning and / or design process?

The Sisters engaged in a rigorous educational process prior to engaging the design team. They did research, went on field visits to other household model communities and observed operational models across the western United States. Their research informed their own operational model and helped to shape their vision for how the building would support their

residents. They followed up their visits with focus groups with potential residents, resident families, caregivers, and staff. The Sisters then kept stakeholders involved throughout the entire design and construction process, allowing them to view progress drawings, ask questions, and give input.

Collaboration: How did stakeholders, occupants, the design team, and / or others collaborate during the planning and / or design process?

The role of the contractor was unique to this project. The contractor has a close relationship with the Sisters and was involved and integral to all aspects of the design process, advising and guiding the group.

Green / Sustainable Features: What green / sustainable features had the greatest impact on the project's design?

Site selection, energy efficiency, and water efficiency.

What were the primary motivations for including green / sustainable design features in the project?

Support the mission / values of the client / provider, stay competitive against other similar / local facilities, and lower operational costs.

What challenges did the project face when trying to incorporate green / sustainable design features?

Actual and perceived first-cost premium.

What program / organization is being used for green / sustainable certification of this project?

Leadership in Energy and Environmental Design (LEED).

For a project with a residential component, what was critical to the success of the project?

Improving common spaces / amenities.

Households: What is innovative or unique about the households in the project?

Generous balconies were designed to give residents second-floor access to quality outdoor garden spaces. Each balcony provides distinct views and feelings—one with serene views to the San Gabriel Mountains, the other with more active views to the community and first-floor garden below.

Common Spaces: What senior-friendly common spaces are included in the project?

Resident-maintained gardening space; small-scale family-style dining space, outdoor dining, and activity kitchen; small-scale gathering space; outdoor, flat, paved areas for exercise classes and community gatherings.

Wheeler Kearns Architects

Mather More Than a Cafe

Chicago, Illinois // Mather LifeWays

Facility type (date of initial occupancy): Mather Cafe, I, Galewood (June 1999); Mather Cafe, II, Norwood Park (June 2000); Mather Cafe, III, Portage Park (June 2002); Mather Cafe, IV, Chatham (June 2004)
Target market: Middle / low income
Site location: Urban; greyfield
Project site area (square feet): 18,600 aggregate
Gross square footage of the renovation / modernization involved in the project: 18,600 aggregate

Purpose of the renovation / modernization: Upgrade the environment
This site is within 1,000 feet of public transportation, and within 1,000 feet of at least 10 basic services with pedestrian access to those services.
Provider type: Non-sectarian non-profit

Below: Acoustic clouds limit background noise to allow easy conversation in the dining area
Opposite: Different seating arrangements allow members to vary their social involvement

Overall Project Description

The project comprises four neighborhood senior cafes completed in Chicago neighborhoods. The first cafe, located in a 6,000-square-foot storefront in the Galewood neighborhood, served as the prototype for subsequent cafes in Norwood Park, Portage Park, and Chatham.

The cafes serve as neighborhood-based administrative outposts, as well as senior services centers. Along with the social component of the cafe, the senior services provided include computer classes, medical assistance, financial counseling, and exercise classes.

All of the cafes comprised completely new interior tenant buildouts. The architectural details and palette developed in the prototype facility continued through to the other cafes—cherry shadowbox cafe tables (filled with objects provided by members), tectum floating ceiling panels, naturally colored MDF, and brightly colored volumes.

Project Goals

What were the major goals?

The primary goal was to offer Chicago residents an alternative to the large regional governmental senior centers that were cavernous and impersonal. As evidenced by feedback collected from early surveys intended to inform the design process, patrons desired spaces that avoided the clichéd palettes of senior centers, which were dominated by dark wood and burgundy hues.

Each patron is greeted warmly upon entry in the intimate context of a cafe. Beyond the inital greeter's desk, the main dining spaces are broadsided by an open kitchen, allowing staff to converse with the first arrivals in the morning. The bright chromas and hues of the palette set a tone that suffuses the atmosphere with vitality.

Challenges: What were the greatest design challenges?

The greatest design challenge was avoiding the anonymity that usually characterizes local senior centers. By keeping the facilities neighborhood-scaled, encouraging conversation upon entry, and allowing the incorporation of personal effects, the cafes have an intimate ambiance.

Innovations: What innovations or unique features were incorporated into the design of the project?

In order to allow patrons to "put their marks" on the facilities, each cafe was outfitted with glass-topped shadowbox tables where memorabilia could be shared with a group.

In addition to the large group tables, a variety of seating options were included on the periphery for those preferring to talk with staff at the lunch counters or observe from a distance.

In each cafe, the acoustic environment was improved to eliminate the echos and background noise that dominates the larger regional centers.

Marketing / Occupancy: What issues were encountered regarding marketing and / or achieving full occupancy?

Critical grassroots outreach was accomplished during the earliest planning stages for each cafe to make certain that a critical mass of patrons were likely to enroll as members upon opening. By treating patrons as members from the outset, a sense of community was immediately established.

Data / Research: What innovative or unique data collection and / or research was applied during the planning and / or design process?

Most data was collected through grassroots polling in faith-based and community organizations. Although the research was conducted in a traditional manner, the results were notably not expected: Seniors wanted an environment that differed from those of the homes they had or environments they previously occupied; they wanted something that was forward looking, innovative, and which embraced the future.

Collaboration: How did stakeholders, occupants, the design team, and / or others collaborate during the planning and / or design process?

An initial design team, which had a large senior-focused practice, was dismissed in the early stages of the prototype's design because it had a difficult time reinventing a senior facility.

Outreach: What off-site outreach services are offered to the greater community?

The cafes have led to the development of the Cafe Plus concept, which has been emulated in numerous locations. For organizations that have applied the Cafe Plus concept: 65 percent increased community outreach and engagement; 57 percent offer different types of classes and programs; 57 percent increased customer engagement and involvement; 46 percent re-trained staff on customer service techniques; 38 percent enhanced culinary services; and, 38 percent are utilizing new marketing techniques.

Green / Sustainable Features: What green / sustainable features had the greatest impact on the project's design?

Maximized daylighting, reuse of the existing building structure and / or materials, and low background noise levels.

What were the primary motivations for including green / sustainable design features in the project?

Support the mission / values of the client / provider and design team, and make a contribution to the greater community.

Common Spaces: What senior-friendly common spaces are included in the project?

Bistro / casual dining; coffee shop / grab-and-go; dedicated fitness equipment room; dedicated exercise classroom; large multipurpose room; dedicated conference / meeting space; dedicated classroom / learning space; and library / information resource center.

Opposite: Glass-topped shadowbox tables, designed for sharing memorabilia, allow patrons to quickly put their "fingerprints" on the cafe
Left: The central greeting area and computer lab at Portage Park

Photography: Steve Hall

Lizard Rock Designs, LLC

Tohono O'odham Elder Home

Sells, Arizona // Tohono O'odham Nursing Care Authority

Facility type (date of initial occupancy): Assisted Living (February 2013)
Target market: Low income / subsidized
Site location: Rural; greenfield
Project site area (square feet): 18,300

Gross square footage of the new construction involved in the project: 8,000
Gross square footage of a typical household: 8,000
Number of residents in a typical household: 12
Provider type: For-profit

Below: Elder home for Native American residents. Adapts Green House® model to Native American culture.
Opposite: Patios allow access to the outdoors. The outdoor fireplace preserves traditional cooking methods over a mesquite fire. The use of natural materials (wood and stone) reflects the residents' input into building materials.

Overall Project Description

This project is the first of four 12-bedroom, assisted living, Elder Homes located adjacent to the Archie Hendricks Skilled Nursing Facility on the Tohono O'odham Indian Reservation. The Elder Home contains 12 private bedrooms with bathrooms, as well as common kitchen, dining, living, and social areas. The home is based on the Green House® model of care, although the model has been adapted to work within the culture of the Tohono O'odham people. The Tohono O'odham people place great value on respect for nature, and many of the residents have lived most of their lives outdoors. The design reflects this by opening the common areas and surrounding patios completely to the exterior, and orienting them to focus on important natural landmarks and views (sacred mountains east and west). The design also includes spaces between resident rooms and public areas to acknowledge that most residents are used to more privacy, having lived in dispersed rural conditions for most of their

lives. The house opens to outdoor patios, cooking areas, and walkways and seating areas surround the homes.

The Elder Home is a place where elders can receive assistance with activities of daily living, without the assistance becoming the focus of their existence. Each resident enjoys a private room with access to all areas of the house, including the kitchen, living, and outdoor patios. The elders are free from a rigid institutional schedule and engage in activities as they choose. Staff prepares meals in the open kitchen and serves them at a large dining table. The living space is focused on the hearth, with high levels of natural light, views, and several easily accessible patios.

Project Goals

What were the major goals?

- After an extensive survey of senior care needs by the firm American Indian Health Management & Policy, the Tohono O'odham

Nation determined that there was a significant need for assisted living services on the reservation. These homes are an effort to meet that need. Seniors are often faced with a choice between extended stays in the existing nursing home or returning to home environments that are unsafe. However, traditional assisted living models do not work in dispersed rural environments. This project attempts to provide assisted living in small clusters that could be spread throughout the reservation.

- The owner's second goal was to rethink the Green House® model of elder care to adapt it to the Tohono O'odham culture. Many focus groups were held with residents, family members, staff, and the board of the Archie Hendricks Skilled Nursing Facility to shape the design of the homes. Two key priorities emerged: maximize outdoor views, access, and living space, and provide layers of privacy between individual suites and common areas. The floor plan reflects both priorities—providing multiple ways to live and be connected to nature, and locating den space outside resident rooms to separate them from the main common room.

- The owner's third goal was to create a project that could be replicated in each of the 15 districts on the reservation. Long travel distances and a dispersed population present unusual challenges, and traditional methods of providing home care, assistance with meals, and assisted living may be adapted to work in this environment. The Tohono O'odham Nursing Care Authority hopes to create a network of Elder Homes to anchor other services, such as home care, wound care for seniors with diabetes, and assistance with meals. This is the first Elder Home to be built for the Tohono O'odham people.

Challenges: What were the greatest design challenges?

The first challenge for the project was to find a model for assisted living that would be both affordable to operate and appropriate to the Tohono O'odham culture. The owner chose to adapt a model of care in the style of the Green House®, but faced the challenge of convincing residents that they would be comfortable in a group-living situation. This was achieved by adapting the model to provide den spaces outside each cluster of resident rooms to offer an additional layer of privacy between the most public areas and the rooms.

The second challenge was to create a cluster of homes that fit the operational model sought by the owner (that is, a series of independently staffed homes that are supported by the infrastructure of the adjacent nursing facility).

The final challenge was to relate the new homes to the existing skilled nursing facility in such a way that they feel residential and take advantage of important views and connections with nature. Both views and access to nature were listed as the residents' top priorities, and there was concen that too close an association with the nursing home facility could compromise the residential character of the Elder Home.

Innovations: What innovations or unique features were incorporated into the design of the project?

The project is innovative because it adapts the Green House® model to a different culture. The Tohono O'odham people place great value on respect for nature, and many of the residents that were interviewed stated that they have lived most of their lives outside. The design reflects this by opening the common areas and surrounding patios completely to the exterior, and orienting them to focus on important landmarks (a sacred mountain and a mine that many residents worked in). In addition, spaces between resident rooms and the main common room reflect the fact that most residents are used to more privacy, having lived dispersed from their neighbors across the reservation.

The site design is innovative because homes can stand alone or be grouped in twos or fours. This was done to support a model where the nursing care authority seeks to provide assisted living services across a widely dispersed area (15 separate districts).

The project provides both indoor and outdoor cooking areas as requested by residents. Many residents spent most of their adult lives cooking outside over mesquite fires, and the residents requested the ability to do the same in the Elder Homes.

Green / Sustainable Features: What green / sustainable features had the greatest impact on the project's design?

Site design considerations, reduced solar gain / heat island–effect sunshades, planting, and maximized daylighting.

What were the primary motivations for including green / sustainable design features in the project?

Support the mission / values of the client / provider and the design team, and lower operational costs.

What challenges did the project face when trying to incorporate green / sustainable design features?

Perceived first-cost premium and lack of board or leadership support.

For a project with a residential component, what was critical to the success of the project?

Improving common spaces / amenities.

Households: What is innovative or unique about the households in the project?

Land and nature are sacred to the Tohono O'odham people, and important natural monuments play a significant role in their culture. The Green House®

residential model of care accommodates the Tohono O'odham people's way of life, as privacy, connection with the outdoors and preservation of the traditional hearth are emphasized.

Common Spaces: What senior-friendly common spaces are included in the project?

Large multipurpose room, and dedicated conference / meeting space.

Opposite top left: Open kitchen allows staff to prepare meals, as well as residents and their visiting family members.
Opposite top right: Location of dens outside the residents' rooms offers an additional layer of privacy between public and private areas.
Opposite bottom: Living and dining spaces focus on the hearth, which is central to the culture of this Native American tribe. Wood ceiling and exposed framing recall traditional structures on the reservation.
Top: Each room has multiple windows, and most have corner windows, allowing for a strong connection with the outdoors.

Photography: Liam Frederick Architecture & Photography

AG Architecture

Haven Hospice Custead Care Center

Orange Park, Florida // Haven Hospice

Facility type (date of initial occupancy): Hospice (September 2012)
Site location: Suburban; greenfield
Project site area (square feet): 271,330
Gross square footage of the new construction involved in the project: 29,276

Gross square footage of a typical household: 7,000
Number of residents in a typical household: 9 (patients)
Ratio of parking spaces to residents: 5.3 stalls per unit
This site is within 1,000 feet of public transportation.
Provider type: Non-sectarian non-profit

Below: Porte-cochere
   Photography: Eric Harrmann / AG Architecture
Opposite: Reception
   Photography: John Bateman Photography

Overall Project Description

Historically, hospice care center environments have been largely modeled after a typical skilled nursing facility with some additional lounge space provided for family use. The provider knew that there had to be an alternative to meet the needs of the patient and their family as they participate in the ultimate resident-centered care experience. Having been inspired by trends in the long-term care marketplace, the provider modeled their new care center after household designs more commonly used in memory care and resident / family-centered solutions.

Carefully sited within a collection of mature live oaks, the new structure is a stark contrast to this provider's previously constructed buildings. The new care center is divided into four distinct zones. An entry pavilion contains administrative areas, counseling rooms, a chapel, and a strong visual connection to a landscaped courtyard. The main care center itself is divided into two distinct nine-bed neighborhoods organized around residential-scaled living rooms for family use, again with a strong outdoor orientation. Finally, a service wing encloses the various back-of-house components.

Special features such as larger resident rooms to accommodate families, private family bathrooms, which support dignified extended stays, and a conscious effort to create a residential-scaled, household-type environment make this hospice a compelling, carefully crafted and peaceful alternative to the more institutional industry norm.

Project Goals

What were the major goals?

- Creating a resident / family-centered environment. For those choosing to receive hospice care in this 18-bed care center, the provider insisted on creating an atmosphere and environment that is filled with the kinds of spaces that in use, scale, and detail are patterned after a single-family home. When

first entering the households, one is greeted by a residential-style kitchen and a small children's play area. Each household features residential-scaled parlors separated by a fireplace and each with a front window that looks out into a landscaped courtyard. Patient rooms frame and surround these parlors, but to insure privacy, walls are strategically placed to screen patient room doorways from the public areas. The patient rooms themselves are large by typical skilled nursing facility standards in order to allow opportunities for personalization, gathering multiple family members, and foldout chairs that allow loved ones to sleep overnight. The exterior and interior design palette was carefully chosen to enhance and emulate a particular residential style that is familiar to those living in this location. Care stations, medicine preparation areas, and other support areas are discreetly hidden, yet significant thought was given to their respective locations in order to facilitate staffing efficiencies.

- Connecting to nature. The provider's directive to the design team was to "bring the outdoors in and the indoors out." Promoting a positive connection to nature is a critically important aspect of hospice care for patient and family alike. Efforts were made in a number of ways starting with the patient rooms themselves. Enlarged windows are used throughout and special consideration was given to the location of the bed to insure easy views outdoors. The living areas for each household have large windows and nearby doors to encourage both patients and family members to use a landscaped exterior courtyard. Several screened porches allow another option for patients to enjoy the outdoors. The family dining area has a thoughtful exterior view and an outdoor veranda for use when weather allows. The L-shaped configuration of the care center itself was consciously used in combination with the adjacent administrative office component to enclose a large exterior space, which is used as both an exterior destination and a large-scale exterior gathering area for annual memorial services.

- Promoting a sense of community. Multiple family members often participate in the hospice experience together. They are joined together during this difficult time and find themselves sharing a similar experience with other patient's families at the same time. The building was designed with this phenomenon in mind. Four distinct, yet centrally located, living rooms create casual settings where families (related, and unrelated) can sit, chat or help console each other. A community dining area allows social interaction between family members and staff. All can share the family kitchen and children's play area. The outdoor spaces, whether enclosed porches or landscaped courtyards, are common destinations that can be shared as well. The adjacent community space in the adjoining administrative pavilion is a community-wide resource that can be used by many to raise the awareness and support of hospice care.

Challenges: What were the greatest design challenges?

Condensing and separating the residential components from the administrative and service components was a design challenge. Two strategies were used. The first strategy was to create four distinct zones. One zone is an entry pavilion that has lighter administrative space and a small chapel. The second is a service pavilion that encloses the back-of-house components. The third and fourth zones are the residential households themselves. The second strategy was to use a center raceway component as a method to both tie the household together, but also to discreetly and centrally locate important support areas like medicine preparation, linen functions, and equipment storage in the center of the plan, to maximize staff efficiencies.

Siting the building to preserve the largest number of existing live oak trees proved to be an interesting challenge. After exploring many options, it became clear that the fact that the administrative pavilion was not directly connected to the care center allowed the design team the flexibility to move and manipulate the site's shape to find the optimum placement of the buildings to both preserve trees and to frame a significant exterior courtyard. The

finished floor elevation and footings were raised to build on top of live oak roots so as not to disturb existing trees. Parking areas were also manipulated to save specimen trees.

Designing to withstand hurricane forces. Poured concrete in insulated concrete forms was used for the exterior wall construction to provide exceptional thermal and sound attenuating performance, as well as strength. The provider required that the large community room also serve as a special needs storm shelter that is capable of sheltering patients, staff, and their families. As a result, all structural and exterior components were upgraded to withstand 130 mph winds. Mechanical and electrical systems were added to a backup generator, and redundant communication systems were added.

The mechanical system—the unsung hero of the project. The provider challenged the team to find an alternative to the typical thru-wall PTAC unit but to retain individual controls in each patient room. The solution ultimately accepted was a variable refrigerant flow system with simultaneous heating and cooling. This type of mechanical system is efficient, quiet, and has a low lifecycle cost. It offers individual controls as one patient

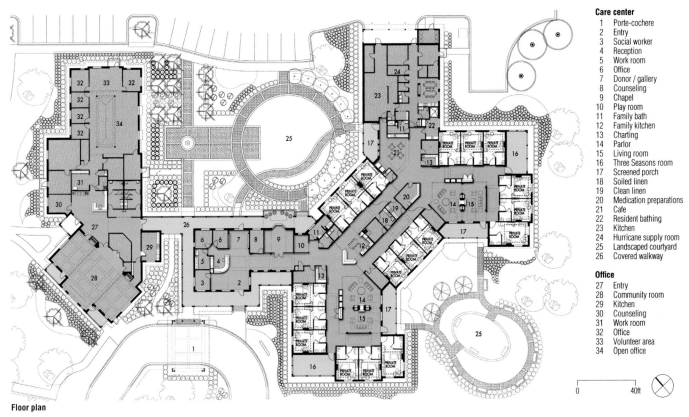

Floor plan

Care center

1	Porte-cochere
2	Entry
3	Social worker
4	Reception
5	Work room
6	Office
7	Donor / gallery
8	Counseling
9	Chapel
10	Play room
11	Family bath
12	Family kitchen
13	Charting
14	Parlor
15	Living room
16	Three Seasons room
17	Screened porch
18	Soiled linen
19	Clean linen
20	Medication preparations
21	Cafe
22	Resident bathing
23	Kitchen
24	Hurricane supply room
25	Landscaped courtyard
26	Covered walkway

Office

27	Entry
28	Community room
29	Kitchen
30	Counseling
31	Work room
32	Office
33	Volunteer area
34	Open office

Opposite left and right: Comfortable spaces throughout the care center reinforce personal relationships and promote a sense of community.

Top: The Florida Cracker—style residential typology allows for breezeways, deep verandas and other residential details and embellishments that enhance the appearance of a large rambling house rather than that of a traditional-looking skilled nursing home.

Photography: John Bateman Photography

room may be cooling while another is heating. The lack of an exterior wall mechanical unit or a furnace room meant that the windows could be larger and the patient rooms more spacious, both were critical to the success of this project.

Innovations: What innovations or unique features were incorporated into the design of the project?

The Florida Cracker–style residential typology allows for breezeways, deep verandas, and other residential details and embellishments that enhance the appearance of a large rambling house, rather than that of a traditional-looking skilled nursing home. This residential architectural style, carefully placed within a collection of mature live oaks, provides a therapeutic setting, which demonstrates a sincere respect for this intense moment in the human experience.

The interiors combine the Florida Cracker–style with a clean and contemporary approach. This was achieved with the use of white beadboard wainscot applied throughout much of the commons area, as well as the resident rooms. These clean white materials are combined with cool blue tones, seafoam greens and sand brown tones on the walls and floors for a refreshing yet cool and calm interior. Hospitality design details were incorporated into the patient rooms to lessen the medical feel of the space. A hospitality-inspired, built-in wall unit was designed to house the desk, wall-mount flatscreen TV, built-in charting, and wardrobe space. Warm wood tones (such as the headboard, footboard, and nightstand) complement the white beadboard and pastel walls, while providing a contemporary hospitality styling. Functional sofa beds and pull-out sleeper chairs allow family members to be comfortable while they remain close to their loved one.

The Florida Cracker–style and hospitality design details are key elements that support the expression of resident-centered care.

Marketing / Occupancy: What issues were encountered regarding marketing and / or achieving full occupancy?

The facility filled up faster than expected largely due to the lack of a suitable alternative in the market.

Data / Research: What innovative or unique data collection and / or research was applied during the planning and / or design process?

The provider's years of experience in hospice care, and lessons learned at four prior care centers, served as the foundation for the planning and design process as the team developed a new model—an alternative model that meets the needs of the patient and their family as they participate in the patient-centered care experience.

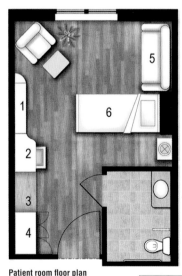

Patient room floor plan

1 Media center
2 Built-in patient workstation
3 Custom bench with built-in storage
4 Custom built-in wardrobe with separate caregiver workstation
5 Furniture for visitors
6 Patient bed on headwall with concealed equipment

0   4ft

Collaboration: How did stakeholders, occupants, the design team, and / or others collaborate during the planning and / or design process?

An intense series of meetings were held by the entire development team to fully tap the resources of the provider's caregivers. As the newest structure in a five-building hospice system, the provider was determined to break from the past to create a more family-oriented design solution. The provider's years of experience, and the existing facilities, served as the data that pushed the team to create a new innovative model for hospice care.

Outreach: What off-site outreach services are offered to the greater community?

The care center itself does not offer off-site outreach services; the organization does.

Green / Sustainable Features: What green / sustainable features had the greatest impact on the project's design?

Site selection, site design considerations, and maximized daylighting.

What were the primary motivations for including green / sustainable design features in the project?

Support the mission / values of the client / provider and the design team, and lower operational costs.

What challenges did the project face when trying to incorporate green / sustainable design features?

Developing a building while minimizing disruption to existing mature live oaks and other specimen trees, and maximizing outdoor views for public spaces.

Households: What is innovative or unique about the households in the project?

While addressing the medical needs of the patient is a priority, it is the comfort in which these services are delivered that sets this hospice apart. The intent of the design was to create the sense of peace and comfort one has in their own home. As such, the household design plays a key role in creating a calm environment for the patient. Larger rooms were designed to accommodate families, allowing them to remain close to their loved one receiving hospice care. Private family bathrooms were included to support

privacy and dignity throughout their extended stays. Each room was carefully situated directly adjacent to shared amenity spaces to create a residential-scaled, household-type environment. The necessary medical equipment, monitors and devices were cleverly disguised behind panels or located in nurse nooks or closets to help maintain the residential appeal of the environment.

Common Spaces: What senior-friendly common spaces are included in the project?

Bistro / casual dining; large multipurpose room; dedicated conference / meeting space; dedicated classroom / learning space; religious / spiritual / meditative space; and resident-maintained gardening space.

Opposite: Special features, such as larger resident rooms to accommodate families, concealed equipment, private bathrooms and a connection to nature, provide a carefully crafted and peaceful alternative to the more institutional industry norm.
Top left: Chapel
Top right: Maintaining positive connections to nature
Photography: John Bateman Photography

Perkins Eastman

Laclede Groves

Webster Groves, Missouri // Lutheran Senior Services

Facility type (date of initial occupancy): Independent Living (May 2013); Long-term Skilled Nursing (December 2012); Short-term Rehabilitation (December 2012); CCRC or part of a CCRC
Target market: Middle / upper middle
Site location: Suburban
Project site area (square feet): 2,745,587
Gross square footage of the new construction involved in the project: 197,750

Gross square footage of the addition(s) involved in the project: 59,350
Gross square footage of the renovation / modernization involved in the project: 87,200
Gross square footage of a typical household: 6,780
Number of residents in a typical household: 14
Purpose of the renovation / modernization: Repositioning
Ratio of parking spaces to residents: 1:1
Provider type: Faith-based non-profit

Below: Town Center entrance
Photography: Sarah Mechling, Perkins Eastman
Opposite: Town Center lobby
Photography: Chris Cooper Photography

Overall Project Description

Lutheran Senior Services engaged in a journey of exploration and discovery in search of a campus heart for Laclede Groves. The existing campus evolved over decades from a Catholic convent to new buildings and programs, each with a complement of social and activity spaces. During planning workshops, everyone spoke of the importance of community, and breaking down the barriers between levels of care and service. The location of community spaces was scattered, circulation was confused, and the physical environment thwarted community at every turn.

This search for community began a process of change that resulted in a new town center (campus heart) with enhanced amenity space, wellness programs, and dining venues; residential (independent) living apartments; upgrades to the quality and capacity of skilled care; and, improved campus circulation.

The new town center provides a focal point for the campus and features a vehicular plaza and covered drop-off, lobby / reception, fine dining / bistro, and pool link. A new 80-unit, four-story residential living apartment building connects to the town center, providing new, larger marketable units. Renovations to the first and second floors resulted in enhanced fitness / wellness, therapy pool / lockers, media room, spa / beauty salon, meeting rooms, offices, and a physical and occupational therapy clinic.

The organization's journey toward culture change faced roadblocks related to the physical environment; organization leadership recognized that this roadblock would not allow them to implement their goals without a physical change to the building. New end-wing clusters were attached to the existing skilled nursing building, which opened up the opportunity to create 10- to 14-bed houses with private rooms; three houses connect to a central kitchen, dining, and living room for greater efficiency and community. Renovated skilled nursing areas increased for a high percentage of private rooms.

Project Goals

What were the major goals?

- Create community with a new town center—"campus heart"—and enhanced amenity spaces. To achieve this goal, skilled Medicare beds and administrative offices were relocated from the historic Lutheran Convalescent Home to the new additions. The lower two floors of the skilled care building were then converted into amenity spaces, which featured dining and therapy pool additions, along with fitness / wellness, spa / salon, clinic, physical and occupational therapy areas, classroom, meeting, arts and crafts, media room, library, and activities.

- Create a total integration of the culture change model into all levels of skilled nursing. To accommodate this change, it was critical to expand short-term rehabilitation, and offer more private rooms using the household model of care (both renovations and new additions); eliminate three-person rooms and facilitate hospice services within rooms; redo the entry lobby and add administrative offices, and create an in-patient / out-patient physical and occupational therapy clinic with an improved entry, and parking.

- Add revenue through new marketable residential living (independent) product. Eighty new residential living apartments with connections to the town center and underground parking increase the offerings of this campus. Marketing and administrative offices are located near the town center connector for potential residents' ease of access.

- Address circulation, public entrances and parking that enhances community. Establishing a new public "campus heart" entry at the front door of the re-purposed town center (old convent) and rededicating the south building entry as the skilled care entrance were critical to a greater sense of community. The new residential living underground parking garage offers public / visitor parking spaces, and integrating the parking bays along the redeveloped roadways with landscaping, lighting, and signage upgrades improves wayfinding and ease of access.

Challenges: What were the greatest design challenges?

Management of existing spatial, structural, and mechanical / plumbing / electrical conditions in the building, while trying to incorporate the new town center program. On the upper first floor, the new interior gallery walkway was shifted to the front wall to help facilitate larger space needs in a single-loaded fashion and to take advantage of the exterior windows for natural lighting. Mechanical systems were re-evaluated to make better use of available equipment locations and limited ceiling plenums.

The significantly sloped, wooded central area of the site was also the opportune location for the new residential living apartment building, and it provided difficult challenges related to the building footprint, building massing, parking-garage configuration / entry points, and blending of surrounding mixed vernaculars. The residential living apartment building's three wings were designed with a canted pattern that frames the two primary site circulation paths—main entry and skilled entry—into well-proportioned visual sequences; and the canting allowed the bifurcation of the double-loaded corridor to appear to visually shorten travel distances. The exterior facade design carefully blends and integrates with multiple existing vernaculars on campus in a sensitive way.

The plan to relocate the existing skilled care program and residents from the lower two floors of the building (new Town Center) to the skilled care upgrades at the south building renovation and additions offered challenges for how to manage bed count and staff needs in the new household plan arrangement, and for the integration of the short-term rehab program. Much thought went into determining the right mix of semi-private vs private rooms, short-term rehab vs long-term care, and how to distribute clinical support spaces throughout.

Opposite: Town Center formal dining room
Photography: Chris Cooper Photography

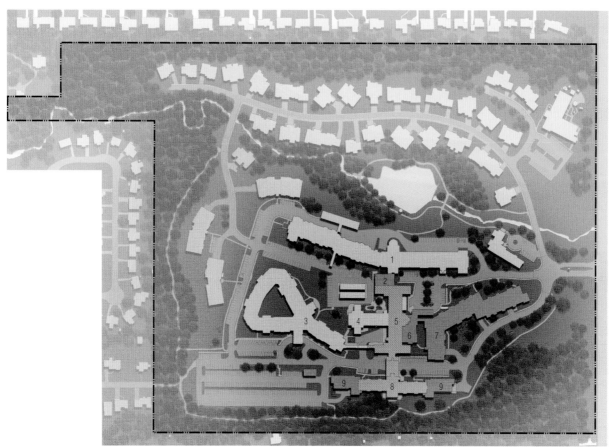

1 Laclede Oaks Manor – existing apartment building
2 Therapy pool addition
3 Existing assisted living building
4 Existing chapel
5 Existing Lutheran Convalescent Home: lower two floors renovated to Town Center; upper two floors renovated skilled nursing resident rooms
6 Fine dining, bistro, entry lobby addition
7 New 80-unit apartment building
8 Existing South Building – skilled care (renovated)
9 East/West South Building additions – skilled care households

0   200ft

Site plan

Innovations: What innovations or unique features were incorporated into the design of the project?

A dramatic change of campus culture emerged with the conversion of the lower two floors of the historic skilled care building into the central Town Center and new "campus heart;" this conversion also required the creative use of very challenging physical constraints. The existing first floor was used for service and office space, but it was in a poorly located, strategically central campus location. These spaces were moved out to create new resident amenity spaces.

The new residential living apartment building comprises three wings in a canted pattern that frames the two primary site circulation paths—main entry and skilled entry—into well-proportioned visual sequences; and it offers a terraced underground parking garage that facilitates parking needs on a significantly sloped and wooded area of the site. The exterior facade design carefully blends and integrates with multiple existing vernaculars on campus in a sensitive way.

In addition to the new skilled nursing wings, a traditional 24-bed long-term care building was converted into six houses by carefully adding new private rooms and shared living space.

The pool addition creatively utilizes adjunct outdoor space between the buildings where fire rating and egress code requirements were challenging. A portion of the historic skilled nursing building exterior wall has been purposely left exposed at the west wall of the pool compartment to provide residents with a meaningful visual legacy.

Data / Research: What innovative or unique data collection and / or research was applied during the planning and / or design process?

Designers offered the client a view of the existing CCRC's potential as a reinvented campus, and the client was teamed early-on with a market feasibility consultant to support this potential with first-hand research. The team held focus group interviews with existing residents and future residents to understand their current and future desires. Informational / hands-on meetings were held with multiple departments to gather detailed design needs of various aspects, such as staff / resident relations, adjacencies, casework, storage, lighting, communications, finishes, etc. This led to the integration of the results from the focus group findings with the results of a group visioning process to determine the best plan and model for the entire campus, as well as for each specific product.

Collaboration: How did stakeholders, occupants, the design team, and / or others collaborate during the planning and / or design process?

The project commenced with an initial strategic planning workshop that was structured to help the client determine strategic ways to develop new opportunities and to create, reposition, and reinvent existing services and environments for seniors. Meetings engaged executive teams, board members, and key staff in a process that integrated forward-thinking design, thoughtful economic analysis and thorough market assessment to create sustainable strategies for this community.

The workshops focused on identifying needs and challenges, creating a vision based on new consumer trends, developing concepts, and financial testing, and then finalizing the plan based on key stakeholder input, discussion, and consensus. During the process, the client group defined and presented their vision of a successful campus, which led to a consensus opinion that the campus lacked a "heart" and then recognition that one of the campus' original buildings—the old Catholic convent building—was the best location for creating a new Town Center. A series of Webex presentations between the owner and the architect allowed for a collaborative, creative planning process to result in a final repositioning plan.

Outreach: What off-site outreach services are offered to the greater community?

Laclede Groves does not provide services outside the community. Lutheran Senior Services (LSS) has a division called In-Home Services that brings services to wherever older adults call home. Some of these services are provided to residents who live at Laclede Groves, others live in the surrounding community. Under In-Home Services, LSS provides skilled home care, hospice care, private duty non-skilled home care, living safe technologies, and three United Way Programs—Good Neighbor, Volunteer Money Management, and Outreach Social Services, all of which provide geriatric care management.

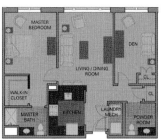

Independent Living Unit A plan

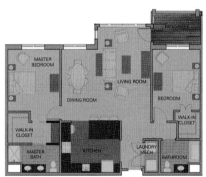

Independent Living Unit B plan

Independent Living Unit C plan

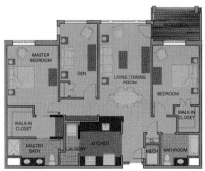

Independent Living Unit D plan

0   8ft

Top: Open, spacious, and light-filled independent living apartments

Photography: Chris Cooper Photography

Bottom: Skilled nursing household living room

Photography: Sarah Mechling, Perkins Eastman

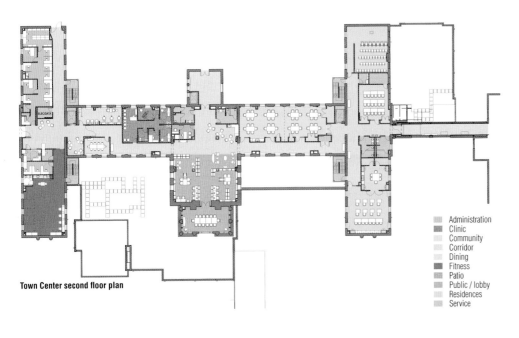

Town Center second floor plan

Administration
Clinic
Community
Corridor
Dining
Fitness
Patio
Public / lobby
Residences
Service

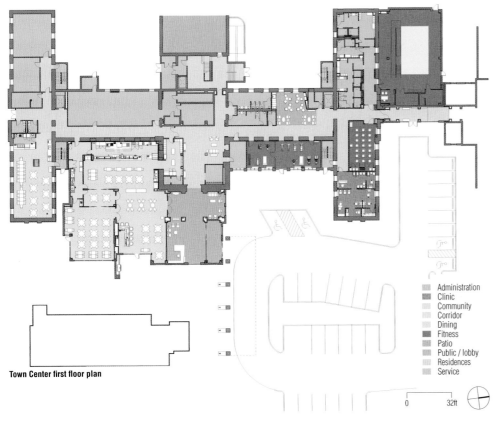

Town Center first floor plan

Administration
Clinic
Community
Corridor
Dining
Fitness
Patio
Public / lobby
Residences
Service

0   32ft

Green / Sustainable Features: What green / sustainable features had the greatest impact on the project's design?

Maximized daylighting, and recycling construction waste and / or diversion from landfills.

What were the primary motivations for including green / sustainable design features in the project?

Support the mission / values of the design team, make a contribution to the greater community, and promote good public relations.

What challenges did the project face when trying to incorporate green / sustainable design features?

Actual and perceived first-cost premium, lack of board or leadership support, and lack of resident support.

For a project with a residential component, what was critical to the success of the project?

Improving units / private spaces.

Households: What is innovative or unique about the households in the project?

The new household model of skilled nursing care is a complete culture change for this community. The renovated portion of the building now offers private rooms with finishes upgrades, while the winged addition offers all new private rooms with a household kitchen, dining, living, staff and support spaces.

Common Spaces: What senior-friendly common spaces are included in the project?

Formal dining, bistro / casual dining; coffee shop / grab-and-go; marketplace / convenience store; swimming pool / aquatics facilities; dedicated fitness equipment room; dedicated exercise classroom; dedicated rehabilitation / therapy gym; salon; large multipurpose room; small-scale cinema / media room; dedicated conference / meeting space; dedicated classroom / learning space; library / information resource center; and art studio / craft room.

HKIT Architects

Mary Helen Rogers Senior Community

San Francisco, California // Chinatown Community Development Center & UrbanCore

Facility type (date of initial occupancy): Independent Living (January 2013)
Target market: Low income / subsidized
Site location: Urban; brownfield
Project site area (square feet): 16,500
Gross square footage of the new construction involved in the project: 95,000

Ratio of parking spaces to residents: 0.27:1
This site is within 1,000 feet of public transportation, and within 1,000 feet of at least 10 basic services with pedestrian access to those services.
Provider type: Non-sectarian non-profit

Bottom left: The design of this affordable senior community has a contemporary look that embodies the urban feel of the neighborhood
Bottom right: A south-facing active and secure courtyard is available to residents
Opposite: Community meeting space with access to a private south-facing courtyard

Overall Project Description

This residential community was the winning entry in a design competition sponsored by the former San Francisco Redevelopment Agency (SFRA), and was made possible by the SFRA's acquisition of seven of the 22 parcels left by the demolition of the Central Freeway following the 1989 Loma Prieta earthquake. The development of these former freeway off-ramps provided an opportunity to further the city's affordable housing goals while also meeting the changing needs of the Western Addition neighborhood.

One of San Francisco's newest affordable housing developments, this senior community includes 100 apartments for low- and very-low income seniors, including 20 units set aside for formerly homeless seniors under the Department of Public Health's Direct Access to Housing program. This development offers preference to SFRA certificate–holders—this certificate was issued to households that were displaced from the community during the redevelopment era of the 1960s, allowing those displaced to relocate to the community affordably. The facilities include administrative and service provider offices, a community room, a commercial / retail area with provisions for a commercial kitchen, as well as a large, ground-floor courtyard and several elevated terraces. MHRSC was designed to complement an adjacent redeveloped freeway site, Parkview Terraces, to form a "senior campus" with shared programs, which include physical activities and computer courses for seniors.

The project was named to honor the memory of Mary Helen Rogers, co-founder of the Western Addition Community Organization in 1966 and a long-time community activist. Mary Helen Rogers, a mother of 12, had a long track record of community activism and organizing. She worked tirelessly to tear down the barriers that prevented fair and equitable treatment to African American families, school-aged children, welfare recipients, minority businesses, and community churches.

Project Goals

What were the major goals?

- Provide smaller apartments with ample natural light, full kitchens and acoustic controls on a site that is located at a busy urban intersection. The apartments provide large window areas to allow as much natural light and air as possible. The windows are highly rated for acoustic controls. The apartments facing the busy streets include a "Z" duct in each apartment so that natural ventilation can be provided without compromising acoustic control.

- Connect to the surrounding neighborhood. Named for a prominent community leader, MHRSC was planned in conjunction with another building a block away to create a "senior campus," with shared programs, including physical activities and computer courses. There is a strong and prominent entry to the main lobby that is welcoming, but also provides security through an intercom system and reception desk. Large, high windows add a connection to the streets from the lobby, offices, and community room. Retail space that is located on the ground floor will include a cafe for both resident and community use.

- Provide amenities and convenient proximity to outdoor spaces. There is a protected, large, south-facing, and secure courtyard that is comfortable for residents to access for both passive and active recreation. There are also auxiliary courtyard spaces with plantings and seating areas on the 6th floor that take advantage of quiet areas and feature spectacular views. Additional amenities include south-facing, private balconies that are larger than usual, and which provide more usable space than typical apartment balconies.

- Use of durable / cost effective materials that are visually appealing, stimulating, and home-like for seniors. The apartments have hard-surface

Sixth level floor plan

1   Studio
2   One bedroom
3   Laundry
4   Janitor
5   Trash
6   West roof terrace
7   South roof terrace

▓ Residential
▓ Residential support
▓ Circulation building support

Second level floor plan (typical)

1   Studio
2   One bedroom
3   Laundry
4   Janitor
5   Trash

▓ Residential
▓ Residential support
▓ Circulation building support

Entry level floor plan

1   Main entry
2   Reception
3   Office
4   Conference room
5   Common room
6   Storage / maintenance
7   Cafe / retail entry
8   Cafe / retail
9   Cafe kitchen
10   Courtyard
11   Garage entry
12   Redwood alley

▓ Residential lobby
▓ Residential support
▓ Circulation building support
▓ Cafe

0   20ft

wood flooring and cabinets made from sustainable products. The use of cork, linoleum, and bright, warm colors creates an interesting, engaging environment. The products used are easily cleaned and were selected because of their high durability.

- Balance the SFRA's desire for modernist architecture with a suitable environment for seniors who may be used to a more traditional San Francisco aesthetic. The modernist approach to the design includes contemporary-style bay windows and a facade that is broken up by stepped planes and color blocks to create the illusion of smaller scaled buildings and relate the design to the texture of the surrounding neighborhood.

Challenges: What were the greatest design challenges?

This brownfield site is a former highway off-ramp, and considerable cost went into the removal of existing below-grade foundation elements. This added cost was balanced with the overall construction budget.

Height and bulk requirements set by City Planning / SFRA posed a challenge to get the desired number of units on the small site and maximize the building envelope. The design response was to step the building mass at both ends of the "L" shape, creating outdoor areas that take advantage of the available views and provide more open space for the residents.

Structural shear walls were positioned to allow as much open area for windows as possible. The structural system had to be carefully designed and placed to provide as much building flexibility as possible. The units are long and deep, so the window area was important to allow for as much natural light into the units as possible. The bay windows have a wrap-around glazing feature, which helps to maximize the daylight.

The ground floor includes the main entrance and lobby for private residents, as well as the cafe that is open to the public and which required its own identity and a separate entrance. The south-facing courtyard is shared by both the cafe and the residents and provides a protected landscaped area with seating and activity space, yet retains secure access to and from the apartment lobby for the residents.

Innovations: What innovations or unique features were incorporated into the design of the project?

For an affordable senior building that is an area of high-end condominiums and market rate developments, it was important that this affordable senior community blended with the surrounding neighborhood and not stand out as a stigmatized low-income project. As such, it was designed with a very contemporary flair that embodies the urban feel of the neighborhood, and uses color and materials (e.g., the stone for the ground floor) that enrich the look and sophistication of the building—all within a limited budget.

Marketing / Occupancy: What issues were encountered regarding marketing and / or achieving full occupancy?

There were over 3,000 viable applications for 100 apartments. Accommodations were made for SFRA certificate–holders, who received first preference to return if they desired.

Data / Research: What innovative or unique data collection and / or research was applied during the planning and / or design process?

This was a collaborative effort between all stakeholders, including the SFRA, neighborhood, and potential future residents, and meetings were held for input and information gathering. This is a prominent site with great access and exceptional views to the surrounding urban landscape, so all of those factors were taken into account. The location of outdoor spaces, entry points, and visual presence on the street were examined through 3D computer models, as well as with physical models which were used as presentation materials to communicate with the stakeholders.

Collaboration: How did stakeholders, occupants, the design team, and / or others collaborate during the planning and / or design process?

This was a unique process in that the development went through three separate developers / owners during the design and documentation phases— each time the design was handed over it entailed incorporating new thinking on the part of the developer. The challenge was to provide both a program space and include retail area use for the community's benefit that all stayed within the basic envelope of the building. The entry points for specific uses were evaluated and also a straightforward approach was taken regarding security issues for public vs private areas.

Outreach: What off-site outreach services are offered to the greater community?

This building works in conjunction with another new senior community (also developed by the SFRA) a block away. They share services for health care, wellness, and social services. Each building has specific programs that can be shared and are also accessed by the greater senior community. These programs collectively provide services for 200 apartments, plus a very large senior community that exists on adjacent blocks.

Green / Sustainable Features: What green / sustainable features had the greatest impact on the project's design?

Site design considerations, energy efficiency, and maximized daylighting.

What were the primary motivations for including green / sustainable design features in the project?

Support the mission / values of the design team, make a contribution to the greater community, and lower operational costs.

What challenges did the project face when trying to incorporate green / sustainable design features?

Perceived first-cost premium.

For a project with a residential component, what was critical to the success of the project?

Improving common spaces / amenities.

Common Spaces: What senior-friendly common spaces are included in the project?

Large multipurpose room, and dedicated conference / meeting space.

Left: Residential lobby with contemporary furnishings
Photography: David Wakely Photography

Leddy Maytum Stacy Architects

Merritt Crossing

Oakland, California // Satellite Affordable Housing Associates

Facility type (date of initial occupancy): Independent Living (June 2012)
Target market: Low income / subsidized
Site location: Urban; brownfield
Project site area (square feet): 15,000
Gross square footage of the new construction involved in the project: 62,000

Ratio of parking spaces to residents: 1:5
This site is within 1,000 feet of public transportation, and within 1,000 feet of at least 10 basic services with pedestrian access to those services.
Provider type: Non-sectarian non-profit

Below: Southwest facade with screen wall facing adjacent freeway
Opposite top left: Southwest façade with living screen wall
Opposite top right: Main entry flanked by management office (left) and community room (right)

Overall Project Description

Located at the edge of Oakland's Chinatown, this affordable senior housing development transforms an abandoned brownfield site near a busy freeway into a community asset for disadvantaged and formerly homeless seniors, while setting a high standard for sustainable and universal design. The LEED Platinum, 70-unit building includes on-site supportive services, management offices, a community room, community kitchen, and a landscaped courtyard and garden.

Merritt Crossing is a product of the social mission of Satellite Affordable Housing Associates (SAHA) to provide affordable, service enriched housing that promotes healthy and dignified living for people with limited options. Based on the organization's strong commitment to sustainable design in affordable housing, SAHA set a goal of maximizing sustainable strategies that benefit their residents the most.

To track the development of goals, SAHA decided to simultaneously test a variety of sustainable ratings systems:

- LEED for Homes Mid-Rise Pilot Program (Platinum Level)
- Build-It-Green GreenPoints (206 Points)
- EnergyStar Rated Building (Certified as first in California)
- Bay Friendly Landscaping (104 Points)

Project Goals

What were the major goals?

Based on the organization's strong commitment to sustainable design in affordable housing, SAHA set a goal of maximizing sustainable strategies to benefit their residents. The three important goals identified:

- Enhancing a sense of community. An array of outdoor spaces was provided, including a lawn for tai chi and other activities, an orchard and community garden, and patio seating areas

with a soothing water feature. These provisions resulted from a minimization of the parking footprint so that the indoor and outdoor community spaces could reinforce each other.

- Healthy living. This goal resulted in special attention being paid to indoor air quality, daylight, and views. In addition, the community room and other amenities were placed on the ground floor so that residents will be exposed to activities and exercise before going up to their units.

- Energy efficiency. The energy efficiency goal focused on a highly effective building envelope, energy efficient systems, and renewable energy. The efficiency has resulted in lower operating costs for the non-profit developer and lower energy bills for the low-income residents.

Challenges: What were the greatest design challenges?

The biggest challenge was the freeway being immediately adjacent to the project site. To address that, a variance was obtained to place the backyard on the longer side of the building not facing the freeway, to shelter it from noise and wind. To address air quality, a central air intake system takes air from the roof of the building through a HEPA filter providing constant air movement throughout the building. Another challenge was the project's scale and fitting the required number of units on the small site. This was addressed by providing design enhancements, such as recessed facade layering with balconies that visually break up the massing, and the smaller parking footprint to better accommodate the common areas.

Innovations: What innovations or unique features were incorporated into the design of the project?

A living screen wall on the side that faces the freeway not only provides privacy but it is also a distinctive design feature, and it enhances sustainable design by providing shading and plants. In order to keep amenities such as the community room on the ground floor, further linking it to the neighborhood, the size of the garage was reduced by providing parking in a lift system. On upper floors full glazing at both ends of the corridor allow daylighting and views.

Marketing / Occupancy: What issues were encountered regarding marketing and / or achieving full occupancy?

The residential community was built for low-income seniors and roughly half of the residents are formerly homeless; full occupancy was achieved quickly.

Collaboration: How did stakeholders, occupants, the design team, and / or others collaborate during the planning and / or design process?

The developer brought the contractor on board early to collaborate with the design team, which offered benefits, such as constructability input and estimates at concept design, schematic design, design development, 50 percent construction documents, and 100 percent construction documents, ensuring the project remained on budget. The contractor was also able to provide testing and mocking-up of products, which helped provide nicer finishes and other tenant upgrades.

Top: Centrally located community room visually connected to street, entrance and social services
Bottom: Corner apartment with enhanced ventilation, daylight and outdoor views

Photography: Tim Griffith

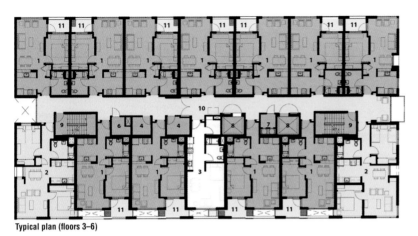

Typical plan (floors 3–6)

1	One-bedroom unit	5	Lounge	9	Stairs
2	Two-bedroom unit	6	Electricals / phone	10	Hallway
3	Studio unit	7	Trash	11	Balcony
4	Storage	8	Elevator		

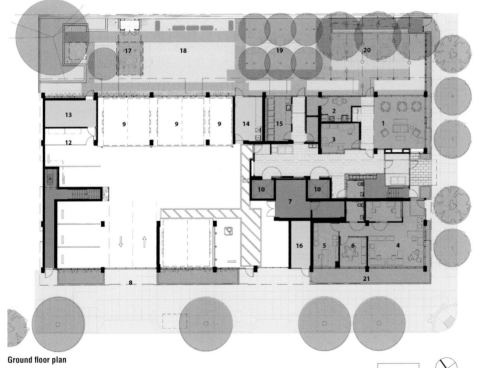

Ground floor plan

1	Community room	7	Trash room	13	Electrical room	19	Orchard
2	Kitchen	8	Garage entry	14	Maintenance shop	20	Courtyard
3	Service office	9	Parking lift	15	Laundry	21	Stormwater planter
4	Management office	10	Elevator	16	Pumps		
5	Manager's private office	11	Stairs	17	Trellis seating		
6	Conference room	12	Bicycle storage	18	Community garden		

0 15ft

Green / Sustainable Features: What green / sustainable features had the greatest impact on the project's design?

Energy efficiency, improved indoor air quality, and the project addressed multiple sustainable features to meet guidelines for Platinum certification in LEED for Homes rating system, 206 GreenPoints and EnergyStar rating.

What were the primary motivations for including green / sustainable design features in the project?

Support the mission / values of the client / provider, make a contribution to the greater community, and lower operational costs.

What challenges did the project face when trying to incorporate green / sustainable design features?

Fulfilling client goals within budget.

What program / organization is being used for green / sustainable certification of this project?

Leadership in Energy and Environmental Design (LEED).

Common Spaces: What senior-friendly common spaces are included in the project?

Large multi-purpose room; resident-maintained gardening space; outdoor patio; orchard, and seating area with water feature; social services office; and community kitchen.

Stewart & Conners Architects, PLLC

Rydal Park Repositioning

Rydal, Pennsylvania // Presby's Inspired Life

Facility type (date of initial occupancy): Independent Living (July 2013); Assisted Living (September 2012); Assisted Living—dementia / memory support (September 2012); Long-term Skilled Nursing (October 2011); Skilled Nursing—dementia / memory support (October 2011); Short-term Rehabilitation (October 2011); CCRC or part of a CCRC
Target market: Middle / upper middle
Site location: Urban

Project site area (square feet): 952,657
Gross square footage of the new construction involved in the project: 142,862 (medical center addition)
Gross square footage of the addition(s) involved in the project: 2,443 (commons and club room addition)
Gross square footage of the renovation / modernization involved in the project: 102,061 (total area of renovation)

Gross square footage of a typical household: 7,800
Number of residents in a typical household: 12 or 13
Purpose of the renovation / modernization: Repositioning
Ratio of parking spaces to residents: 0.63:1
This site is within 1,000 feet of public transportation, and within 1,000 feet of at least 10 basic services with pedestrian access to those services.
Provider type: Faith-based non-profit

Opposite: Front entry facade renovation
Left: Medical center addition – west elevation

Photography: Steve Wolfe Photography

Overall Project Description

The project is in a northern suburb of Philadelphia, in an existing, successful and well established, 22-acre, CCRC campus that proactively sought to reposition its community to meet future market expectations. Utilizing an interactive team process involving administration, the architect, development consultant, staff, and selected residents, the repositioning project included the following:

- Campus entry and site upgrades, including new site lighting, a renovated porte-cochere and new entry pavilion;

- Renovated formal and casual dining, cafe, and club room addition;

- Commons renovation and expansion;

- Renovated therapy and wellness facilities, and salon;

- Renovated independent living apartments in the Hillside Building;

- New nursing, patio / outdoor terrace, chapel and salon, and nursing administration;

- New memory support; and

- Renovated assisted living areas.

The repositioning project did not include any work on existing independent living apartments in portions of the Hillside Building and in Woodside and Parkside.

Project Goals

What were the major goals?

- Create community through designing internal and external connections. The repositioned community plan has created connected nodes of activity at all levels of service that are easily accessible, comfortable and inviting, encouraging greater social engagement. External connections, such as a pedestrian entry pavilion, covering a required accessible ramp, expand choice and community without operational cost.

- Enhance quality of life by creating greater choice and personal autonomy. The level of choice has been expanded, including amenities and social spaces for the enjoyment of the residents.

- Improve efficiency of process—reposition without compromising on-going operations. The phased project delivery resulted in no revenue-producing units ever being out of service for an extended period of time. The integrated development team delivered the complex project on time and on budget.

- Reposition the lifestyle amenities to enhance community engagement and customer satisfaction. There is now better access and increased utilization of amenities, an example is the dining area, which has seen an increase in average stay.

- Reposition the medical center to help enhance a sense of community, feeling at home. Welcoming residential-style accommodations have received positive reviews from residents, their families, and guests. There is increased utilization of guest rooms—people want to stay. The unobtrusive delivery of services means no carts in halls, no call bells and alarms, and a quiet, peaceful and comfortable experience.

- Connect to extended community and off-site amenities—urbanism. An enhanced connector with gateway pavilion and covered access ramp has made a physical and figurative connection to the local community and which has been greatly used by residents. On-site improvements have spurred new up-grades in the adjacent shopping center.

- Enhance the dining experience. To accomplish this goal a little-used interior courtyard (adjacent to the front lobby and the corridor outside dining area) was enclosed to become a signature club room, welcoming residents and visitors and inviting both to linger for conversation, drinks and appetizers prior to proceeding to dining. Also, extending the dining experience is a coffee kiosk with adjacent seating for those visiting with a friend, who might happen along the main lobby corridor. Directly off the main lobby and separated by gently curving partial height walls with art glass, is a bustling cafe that has become the center of resident activity. Adjacent to the café, and divided by multiple large pocket doors to allow for flexibility, is the new center stage casual dining and an intimate waitstaffed restaurant dining area with a water wall feature. All of these features have enhanced the dining experience, which is reflected in the fact that average stays in the dining areas have increased by 25 minutes.

Challenges: What were the greatest design challenges?

Initial master planning for the repositioning of this CCRC campus concluded that the only available land for a desperately needed nursing replacement of 114 private rooms was at the front entrance of the site, in a floodplain; and, the new plan must fit within a previously approved NPDES permit that included an outdated building footprint based upon 60 semi-private rooms. To add to the challenge, the new addition is located on 50 existing parking spaces, which needed to be retained in that location with 50 additional parking spaces, and not violate strict zoning height limitations.

Working closely with local planning and zoning officials, as well as officials from the Pennsylvania Department of Environmental Protection, the design team was able to create a plan that included two levels of under-building parking (50 spaces each), with building engineering and maintenance services, two levels with 45 private beds each, distributed into 22- and 23-bed neighborhoods, and one level with a memory support neighborhood for 24 private beds, with adjacent resident services and administrative spaces. Despite the site falling away on the low side, making it difficult to align with existing floors for operational efficiency and resident comfort, and still remain within the height limitations, the team was able to formulate a successful design that dealt with the floodplain, and height limitations, while satisfying programmatic requirements.

The delivery of services from the existing program spaces, particularly dining, laundry, recycling, and trash to resident areas, had to operate without using resident corridors. Utilizing a portion of the first-floor parking level, the design team created parallel service and resident corridors—the resident corridor with lots of windows and views to the entry courtyard, and the parallel service corridor with high windows to borrow natural light. The service corridor leads to a service core with double-loaded service elevator,

trash, recycling, and laundry chutes that open to a back-of-house area on resident floors, with direct access to trash rooms and a service pantry.

Innovations: What innovations or unique features were incorporated into the design of the project?

The existing CCRC and medical center (located at the front of the site) presented a bulky, institutional facade, and the JC Scott Medical Center addition needed to redefine the campus and blend in with the existing buildings.

The addition utilizes indigenous stone and stucco to not only ground the building to the region and site, but also to add texture, detail, and scale. The scale is further modulated with soaring expanses of glass that are topped by graceful sheltering, standing seam metal roofed arches, and sunscreens that both control the light entering the building, as well as add pleasing detail and color to the exterior. The addition's materials and details were then

judiciously projected across the front of the existing building on a corridor that is connected to the independent living commons; a finely detailed entry pavilion repeats the arched forms and is also firmly connected back to the earth by stone columns, spreads into the landscape as a retaining wall.

Collaboration: How did stakeholders, occupants, the design team, and / or others collaborate during the planning and / or design process?

From pre-design to project completion, the design progressed through an interactive team process involving all stakeholders, including administration, architect, development consultant, staff, selected residents, resident committees, and zoning and code officials. Initial high-level master planning involved administration, architect, development consultant, and select staff analyzing broad programmatic requirements, site constraints, and budget. As direction and scope became clear, the stakeholder team

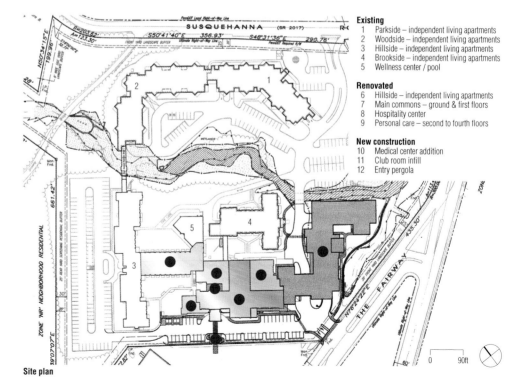

Existing
1   Parkside – independent living apartments
2   Woodside – independent living apartments
3   Hillside – independent living apartments
4   Brookside – independent living apartments
5   Wellness center / pool

Renovated
6   Hillside – independent living apartments
7   Main commons – ground & first floors
8   Hospitality center
9   Personal care – second to fourth floors

New construction
10   Medical center addition
11   Club room infill
12   Entry pergola

Site plan

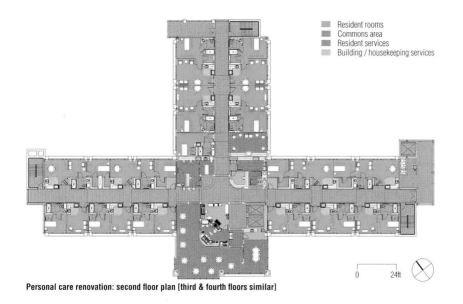

Resident rooms
Commons area
Resident services
Building / housekeeping services

0   24ft

Personal care renovation: second floor plan [third & fourth floors similar]

Above: Personal care renovation – main dining room

Photography: Steve Wolfe Photography

Medical center addition: second floor plan – Nursing [third floor similar]

Resident rooms
Commons area
Resident services
Building / housekeeping services

0   24ft

Medical center addition: fourth floor plan – Nursing memory care

expanded to include engineers, interior designers, and select residents to develop a detailed program and conceptual plans through multiple design charettes. With a viable schematic design in hand, a contractor was added to the team to investigate technical issues, check scope, budget, and schedule. At all milestones, input was sought from facility departments and resident committees, and plans were presented to all of the residents for comment.

Green / Sustainable Features: What green / sustainable features had the greatest impact on the project's design?

Site design considerations, maximized daylighting, and reuse of existing building structure and / or materials.

What were the primary motivations for including green / sustainable design features in the project?

Support the mission / values of the client / provider, make a contribution to the greater community, and stay competitive against other similar / local facilities.

For a project with a residential component, what was critical to the success of the project?

Improving common spaces / amenities.

Households: What is innovative or unique about the households in the project?

Each household is designed with bedrooms that are clustered around individual family rooms, which are the primary living spaces for the residents. Each neighborhood dines at an intimate dining room with treetop views, and the levels of finish and service are equal to that of residents who are in independent living.

The design accommodates wandering patterns that avoid any deadend corridors, thereby discouraging elopement, without frustrating residents. Additionally, care areas are incorporated into the plan for maximum operational efficiency, and avoid any institutional overtones, which strengthens the desired homelike atmosphere.

This project enhances the quality of life of its residents by incorporating design principles that influence a sense of wellbeing. Similar to a well-designed home, there is a public-to-private gradient, which consists of an entry threshold that is adjacent to more public areas (such as kitchen, dining and living rooms), which proceeds to private bedroom areas that are in turn are clustered around individual family rooms (the

primary living spaces for the residents). Within each graciously sized bedroom, there is a seating area with lots of light and treetop views, a private bathroom with accessible shower, and opportunities for self-expression at the front door niche / memory box and writing desk (with shelves).

Common Spaces: What senior-friendly common spaces are included in the project?

Formal dining, bistro / casual dining; coffee shop / grab-and-go; marketplace / convenience store; dedicated rehabilitation / therapy gym; massage / aromatherapy room; salon; dedicated conference / meeting space; dedicated classroom / learning space; library / information resource center; art studio / craft room; and religious / spiritual / meditative space.

Top left: Medical center addition – living room (memory support)
Top right: Medical center addition – resident room (nursing memory care)
Opposite: Main commons renovation – club (left); center stage (top right); hospitality center (bottom right)

Photography: Sargent Photography

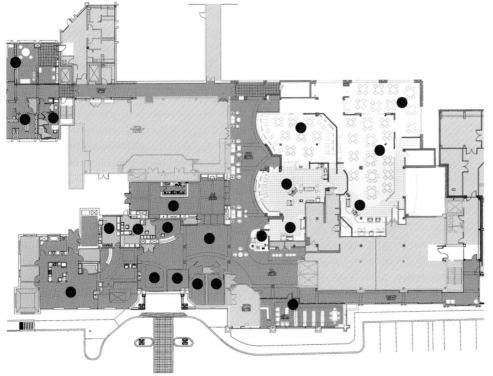

Commons renovations: first floor plan

1   Vestibule
2   Lobby
3   Reception / concierge
4   Lounge
5   Hospitality / center
6   Security
7   Work room
8   Toilet room
9   Library
10 Club room addition
11 Coffee kiosk
12 Marketplace
13 Cafe
14 Casual dining
15 Center stage
16 Formal dining
17 Bank
18 Mail room
19 Patio / outdoor terrace

▨ Resident rooms
▨ Commons area
▨ Resident services
▨ Building / housekeeping services

0   24ft

SFCS Inc.

The Deupree House and Nursing Cottages

Cincinnati, Ohio // Episcopal Retirement Homes Inc. (ERH)

Facility type (date of initial occupancy): Independent Living (February 2007); Long-term Skilled Nursing (June 2009); CCRC or part of a CCRC
Target market: Middle / upper middle
Site location: Urban; brownfield
Project site area (square feet): 104,544 (Nursing Cottages); 483,952 (new Independent Living / Community Center)

Gross square footage of the new construction involved in the project: 173,200
Gross square footage of the addition(s) involved in the project: 16,300
Gross square footage of the renovation / modernization involved in the project: 4,500
Gross square footage of a typical household: 11,080

Number of residents in a typical household: 12
Purpose of the renovation / modernization: Upgrade the environment
Ratio of parking spaces to residents: 2:1
This site is within 1,000 feet of public transportation.
Provider type: Faith-based non-profit

Project Goals

What were the major goals?

A dated retirement community in the upscale Hyde Park area of Cincinnati was losing appeal as a place that seniors felt comfortable calling home. Common areas and amenities were undersized for the population and very limited. Dining was undersized and in need of a program update. Physical and spiritual wellness programs lacked dedicated spaces. Administration offices were cramped and there were no large multipurpose spaces for resident programs, art and cultural programs, or group meetings.

In addition to physical challenges, residents who needed skilled nursing care or assisted living were transferred to a sister community on an adjacent campus, which lead to marketing challenges and caused frustration for families.

Goals of the project included the following:

- Provide updated amenities for state-of-the-art programs;
- Create nursing care in a resident-directed model;
- Develop a model that would enhance and sustain the business outcomes of the campus; and,
- Maintain good relations with neighbors and community while being good stewards of the environment.

Each of the goals was accomplished. New amenities include a wellness center with pool, lockers, and exercise room. A new chapel, multipurpose room, office suite, completely renovated dining, and enhancements to the library / club room more than doubled the dedicated spaces for residents. Exterior gardens encourage active and passive connection to the outdoors.

Overall Project Description

This retirement community in Cincinnati, Ohio, underwent a comprehensive planning effort to reposition the existing campus. The original community offered independent living accommodations with limited amenities, and lacked nursing care. Critical to this project was a cost-effective solution that provided a new revenue stream, to allow for the expanded services and amenity upgrades. By creating a new five-story, 60 unit, one- and two-bedroom luxury apartment building (with under-building parking), revenue was produced to support the campus upgrades and resort-style amenities. These amenities included renovated and expanded dining venues, a new events center, and a state-of-the-art wellness center, complete with a heated indoor pool and spa, exercise facilities, administration areas, and chapel.

The new pedestrian bridge connects the existing building to the new amenities and provides social connectivity between the two apartment buildings. The repositioning also involved the creation of two distinctive, skilled nursing cottages that look, feel, and operate like a home.

Each cottage has twelve private residential rooms with showers, and two suites that allow for separate living and sleeping areas. A shared courtyard and walking paths encourage resident interaction and enjoyment of the outdoors. The innovative "small cottage" concept offers 24-hour supportive nursing care. Thoughtful design sensitivities were incorporated throughout the small cottage households. The Deupree House went from a standalone independent living apartment building with modest amenities to a state-of-the-art campus offering contemporary amenities, services, and nursing care. A new culture, rooted in resident choice and resident involvement in directing their care and daily lives has evolved, and it guides all aspects of the community.

The cottages support 24 private residents divided into two households (of 12 residents each) that look, function, and are home to the residents. Each household is self-directed by staff and residents and are an example of the implementation of the philosophy of resident-directed care at all levels.

The addition of 60 new independent living apartments diversifies offerings on the campus and brings in new revenue, which is necessary for overall campus upgrades. The resident mix is now more in balance and the community has a new vibrancy.

Through methodical discussions with neighbors during the planning and re-zoning process, the owner was able to gain support and continues to have a good relationship with neighbors, the City of Cincinnati, utility companies, and all stakeholders. Existing trees on the adjacent property were surveyed and protected during construction. Proffers on building height, materials, screening of mechanical equipment, and enhanced landscaping are among many agreements that were a part of the good neighbor approach.

Some features of the environmental stewardship that was a guiding principle for the entire team:

- Redevelopment of a former light industrial site;
- Improvement to the quality of stormwater run-off to Duck Creek;
- Mitigation of minor wetlands;
- Preservation of trees on adjacent hillside;
- Upgrades to the existing combined sanitary / stormwater system;
- Nature gardens and preservation of vegetation along Duck Creek; and,
- Energy-efficient mechanical systems and low-e glazing.

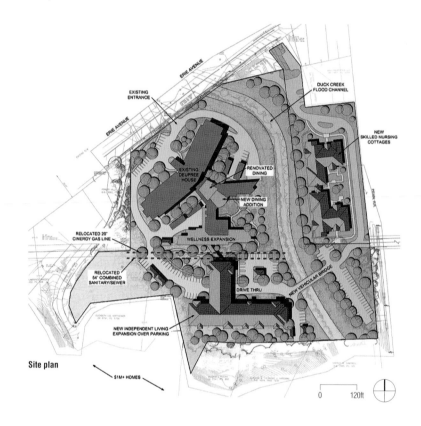

Site plan

0   120ft

Independent living apartment unit plan – Observatory

Independent living apartment unit plan – Victoria

Independent living apartment unit plan – Grandin

0   8ft

Opposite left: The new independent living apartments provide spacious accommodations to meet the needs of today's seniors
Opposite right: Independent living apartment – kitchen / dining
Photography: Michael Houghton

Challenges: What were the greatest design challenges?

The team worked closely with the city planning commission throughout the design process to solve several major design and development challenges for the independent living apartments, wellness center, and the cottage additions.

The steep site topography on the south side along with the Duck Creek channel (a stormwater channel) and the utility easements required the independent living building design to have a drive-thru at the lowest level to enable complete site access to the entire campus. Also, due to utility easement requirements, the team relocated the 54-inch sanitary sewer / storm line to sit adjacent to the 20-inch high-pressure gas line (which supplies the upper northeast quadrant of Cincinnati) to allow an adequate clearance to the existing building. By not relocating the gas line and working around it, this provided a cost-effective solution for the project. The gas line also had a vertical clearance requirement for future maintenance, which lead to a second-floor pedestrian bridge design solution. The bridge connector allows residents in the original and new independent living communities equal access to the new wellness center, new amenities, and the dining venues.

The small house cottages site originally located on a brownfield (zoned for industrial / commercial use and occupied by a warehouse storage facility) covered about half of the site. A zoning change was necessary to allow for this new nursing home use. The team also had to relocate the main entrance to meet new city traffic regulations. In addition, the location for the small house cottages site was separated by the Duck Creek channel. The team solved this issue by designing a vehicular bridge that would connect the two properties, allowing the nursing home a more private location, while keeping the entire campus accessible.

Lastly, the team faced neighborhood opposition to the proposed independent living apartment building. The residents of an exclusive neighborhood overlooking the site were concerned about the effect that the removal

of trees would have on their views. To minimize concern, the team developed a three-dimensional model to provide multiple views from each of their patios and adjusted the independent living building geometry, scale, height, and material palette to accommodate the design goal of unaltered views from the neighbors' homes.

Innovations: What innovations or unique features were incorporated into the design of the project?

Innovative features are incorporated throughout the campus. Perhaps the most noteworthy innovations are not merely design features, but the overall campus plan that reacts to the market and the person-centered care philosophy; the campus has been reinvented despite the multitude of complex site constraints, roadblocks and challenges.

Site constraints, restrictions, and challenges included, but were not limited to:

- Concerns from the exclusive neighborhood bordering the site adjacent to the proposed expansion;
- Steeply sloping neighboring site with a wet creek and specimen trees that needed to be protected;
- An 8-inch, high-pressure gas mains that traversed and bisected the site;
- An existing 52-inch combined sanitary / stormwater line that traversed and bisected the site;
- City of Cincinnati "paper street" that needed to be closed;
- Duck Creek channel and 100-year floodway bisected the property—Corp of Engineers approval required;
- Light industrial site required clean-up and re-zoning;
- Light-rail crossing and acoustic control required for the nursing cottages;
- Access across the property was limited and required a bridge to allow access across Duck Creek;
- Bridge across Duck Creek for access to the nursing cottage site; and,
- Re-zoning requirements.

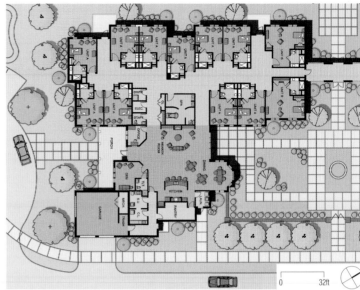

Nursing cottages floor plan

Each of these challenges were successfully solved by innovative design and site planning, careful and methodical negotiations with multiple utility providers, the Corp of Engineers, City of Cincinnati, neighborhood associations, railway officials, and other regulatory agencies and stakeholders.

Innovative features, such as bridges (three in total on this site), leak detection for the gas mains crossing, acoustic berm / barrier adjacent to the railway, and creative site layout and planning all came together to allow the project to proceed and succeed. The nursing cottages are in themselves innovative.

Marketing / Occupancy: What issues were encountered regarding marketing and / or achieving full occupancy?

For the cottages, there was a delay in full occupancy. While right-sized at 24 accommodations to serve primarily the independent living residents, there were not 24 residents who needed to move at the time of licensure. In the effort to be fiscally responsible the first outreach was to residents at the sister property who wished to move and then to the community at large for admissions.

Data / Research: What innovative or unique data collection and / or research was applied during the planning and / or design process?

The project team had the added benefit of a culture change planner, who directed the provider to visit communities where culture change models had been incorporated into the campus. The provider was then able to see how the Green House®, small house, and household models for nursing all function together, and achieve an environment for residents, staff and families that supports the philosophy that all residents have choice and freedom in their lives. The architect's own experience in designing similar projects and post-occupancy evaluations of these projects provided research-based data that contributed to this design. In addition, planning charettes brought together residents, staff, and management to discuss important aspects of the small cottage design to achieve the residential character of "home."

Staffing ratios, meal services, development costs, resident profiles and the influence of design details and features were researched and benchmarked against similar developments.

Collaboration: How did stakeholders, occupants, the design team, and / or others collaborate during the planning and / or design process?

A series of planning charettes brought together residents, staff, and management to discuss important aspects of the nursing cottage design to achieve the residential character of "home." Resident committees were formed, and they participated in visual listening exercises to help them explain to the design team what "home" meant to them and how to create a community that is meaningful to their generation. Residents participated by using inspirational photos from magazines to communicate and interpret elements such as color and texture. The design team applied the exercise to create an end product that matched the residents' opinions of a home.

Top left: The cottage's Craftsman-style living room provides a warm and inviting atmosphere with a fireplace, and comfortable furnishings for relaxed entertainment
Photography: Alise O'Brien

Outreach: What off-site outreach services are offered to the greater community?

The owner models good stewardship toward the surrounding local community by providing a variety of outreach programs. Through a variety of programs, the average is over 16,000 staff outreach and volunteer hours. Parish Health Ministry extends the mission and ministry outside the walls of the retirement communities and into the surrounding communities of southern Ohio. Through Meals on Wheels, the owner provides older adults with warm, nutritious meals delivered to their homes on the east side of Cincinnati. Up to 350 meals are delivered per day. The Council for Life Long Engagement (CLLE) is an action-learning project that creates positive interactions between grade-school students and elders over a period of time, furthering the education of young people. There are more than 100 residents involved in CLLE that annually touch the lives of 500-plus students.

Green / Sustainable Features: What green / sustainable features had the greatest impact on the project's design?

Site selection, site design considerations, and energy efficiency.

What were the primary motivations for including green / sustainable design features in the project?

Support the mission / values of the client / provider, make a contribution to the greater community, and attain appropriate-use approvals, while protecting the existing environment and minimizing impact to neighbors.

What challenges did the project face when trying to incorporate green / sustainable design features?

Actual and perceived first-cost premium, and neighbor resistance to expansion and added density.

What program / organization is being used for green / sustainable certification of this project?

Leadership in Energy and Environmental Design (LEED).

For a project with a residential component, what was critical to the success of the project?

Improving common spaces / amenities.

Households: What is innovative or unique about the households in the project?

The cottages' detached, single-story buildings represent a new approach, utilizing unique design features to support the residents' needs in creating "home."

Each cottage houses 12 nursing care residents in private bedrooms suites. The bedrooms have been designed to include full bathrooms complete with showers, and are designed to accommodate lifts and multiple-person transfers.

The cottages are designed with the private areas—such as the bedrooms and spa—separated from the more public spaces of hearthroom, dining, and kitchen areas. Public spaces are accessed from the covered front porch and door of each cottage. Upon entry, visual access is created across the cottage through the hearthroom and dining room directly to the outdoors. The open plan of the hearthroom and living areas allows residents to see all the activities and to participate in daily life in the home.

Activities such as television, cards, or special meetings take place in a separate den just off the front entry. The den is designed as a guest room, using a fold-down bed, for use by families who find that they need to stay close to a relative during illness or at end of life.

A garage allows for materials and supplies to the cottages to be delivered from the main campus without the trucks parked at the front door. Delivery vehicles pull into the garage out of the elements and out of sight. Residents can board transportation for outings fully protected from the weather.

Just off of the garage entry are the back-of-house functions of the cottage. The garage entry provides easy access to all utility rooms, as well as the preparation kitchen.

Each of the cottages takes on its own architectural style, one being a Craftsman style while the other is a traditional Colonial style. The cottages are connected through a glass corridor, which compliments both architectural styles and serves as an enclosed walk between the cottages; it also acts as an area to enjoy views of the outdoors, and functions as a secondary exercise / therapy area.

The layout of the cottages takes as much advantage of the siting as possible, providing an attractive landscaped garden in the void created by the two buildings' "L" shape. Hard and soft surfaces in the courtyards, along with the landscaping, provide visual interest and variety in all seasons. Where the cottages abut the waterway, the site is heavily wooded, giving visual protection from the taller buildings of the remainder of the campus.

The cottages utilize versatile workers who are cross-trained and are responsible for providing holistic care to residents. The staff are empowered to interact with residents on various levels of care and the making of a home. Administration and staff are equally committed to resident-centered care.

Common Spaces: What senior-friendly common spaces are included in the project?

Formal dining; swimming pool / aquatics facilities; dedicated fitness equipment room; dedicated exercise classroom; large multi-purpose room; dedicated conference / meeting space; library / information resource center; religious / spiritual / meditative space; and resident-maintained gardening space.

RLPS Architects

The Village at Orchard Ridge

Winchester, Virginia // National Lutheran Communities & Services

Facility type (date of initial occupancy): Independent Living (May 2013); Assisted Living—dementia / memory support (May 2013); Long-term Skilled Nursing (September 2013); CCRC or part of a CCRC
Target market: Middle / upper middle
Site location: Suburban; greenfield
Project site area (square feet): 5,749,920

Gross square footage of the new construction involved in the project: 399,726
Gross square footage of a typical household: 7,841
Number of residents in a typical household: 10
Ratio of parking spaces to residents: 1.35:1
Provider type: Faith-based non-profit

Below: Orchard Ridge town center
Opposite: Street view of alley homes looking towards clock tower on town center

Overall Project Description

With no room to expand and a growing waiting list, the owner set sights on establishing a second community closer to home for a growing backlog of residents coming from the Shenandoah Valley. Planned to grow incrementally on a 132-acre site in Winchester, Virginia, the Village at Orchard Ridge will unfold in three phases, beginning with a central chapel and town center, known as the Village Green, encircled by a variety of senior living and care options. The Phase I project includes 203 independent living apartments and cottages, as well as 10 skilled care rooms and 18 assisted living memory care rooms, which are both sited in small house neighborhoods. Also included in the first phase was the town center, comprising the dining, cocktail lounge, games room, library, beauty spa, guest rooms and a 100-seat chapel. Eventually, the campus will also include additional dining venues, a wellness center, multipurpose room and fine arts center, walking trails, areas for gardening, and a general store. The Phase II build-out is projected to add up to 340 independent living residences, 70 assisted living residences, and 72 skilled nursing rooms in several independent households.

Historic Old Town Winchester serves as the design inspiration for the town center, which features a clock tower, chapel and the Village Green with fountains, gardens and walking paths. Varied facade treatments and awnings reflect the vernacular of neighboring towns. Regional products, including Virginia brick, help to keep the project in context with western Virginia.

The project is designed to work with the challenging site, leaving acres of wetlands and wooded areas untouched and capitalizing on buildable areas by locating the town center on the high ground of the tract, with patio homes filling in.

Project Goals

What were the major goals?

- A major planning goal was to design a community that was based on neo-traditional design principles and to create a small town neighborhood environment that could grow incrementally through several phases. This planning goal was articulated through the design of a town center and Village Green that form a streetscape, evocative of the neighboring town of Winchester, at the front door. Much like a traditional town, commons areas are on the first floor with apartments above, and feature varied facade treatments and awnings typical of storefronts. Similarly, raised front porches for alley-style homes form a pedestrian-friendly streetscape, with accessible entries and garages accessed via alleys behind the homes.

- To meet the goal of creating an appealing, supportive senior residence while maintaining operational efficiency, careful consideration was devoted to service delivery. A lower level service corridor in the commons area diverts traffic out of public areas and facilitates delivery of services directly to back-of-house areas.

- As a faith-based provider, the owner placed a high priority on including a community chapel that was more like a traditional church building than a designated area in the commons. Phase I of construction included the design solution of locating the chapel in a high-profile position at the front door. Its scale and autonomy from other commons areas signify its importance within the community, as well as provide a resource to the surrounding community.

Challenges: What were the greatest design challenges?

The property for this new CCRC is a challenging site, formerly an orchard, with acres of steep slope, flood plains and wetlands that remain untouched. Sited on the high ground of the tract, the central feature of the community is a Main Street with apartments facing a town center, church and clock tower bounding the Village Green.

The commons building was planned with a phased approach to construction, thus the design had to be carefully planned to be fully functional and feel complete in Phase I, while accommodating future expansion without compromising services to existing residents. A critical aspect of the design response was situating the kitchen in a central location that offers direct access to current needs, while maintaining an exterior exposure to allow for expansion in future phases.

Innovations: What innovations or unique features were incorporated into the design of the project?

The master plan capitalizes on the orchards that are bordering the community, by taking advantage of appealing long-range views, and by incorporating an apple tree grove into the Village Green.

The multiphased design responds to the challenging site by maintaining acres of existing wetlands and wooded area as a campus amenity, while capitalizing on buildable areas to form a vibrant community, inspired by the traditional American small town.

Small homes allow seniors to live in a small group in an environment intentionally designed to look like, feel like, and act like a traditional residential home.

Apartments and patio homes exceed regulations with expanded clearances and considerations for aging in place, such as lower-level kitchen cabinets and larger floor dimensions in kitchens and bathrooms. Details ranging from drawer pulls to temperature controls are designed based on senior end users.

Each skilled care or memory care room in the small houses has a European shower, which has a dramatic positive impact on improving the dignity and quality of life of a nursing resident.

Data / Research: What innovative or unique data collection and / or research was applied during the planning and / or design process?

The market data identified two different markets: the more modest income base of Winchester and the more affluent region of northern Virginia. The result was to provide rental options, as well as a variety of equity return entry fee models, from which prospective residents can choose.

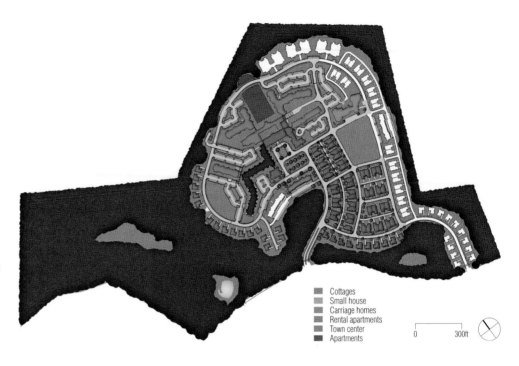

Cottages
Small house
Carriage homes
Rental apartments
Town center
Apartments

0   300ft

Collaboration: How did stakeholders, occupants, the design team, and / or others collaborate during the planning and / or design process?

As with any greenfield site, having the right people involved in the decision-making process is challenging. Staff from the group's existing CCRC in Rockville, Maryland, were critical in developing a CCRC that meshes with the values and culture of the provider.

Green / Sustainable Features: What green / sustainable features had the greatest impact on the project's design?

Energy efficiency, maximized daylighting, and conscientious choice of materials.

What were the primary motivations for including green / sustainable design features in the project?

Support the mission / values of the client / provider, promote good public relations, and lower operational costs.

What challenges did the project face when trying to incorporate green / sustainable design features?

Lack of client knowledge about green design / sustainability.

What program / organization is being used for green / sustainable certification of this project?

Leadership in Energy and Environmental Design (LEED).

For a project with a residential component, what was critical to the success of the project?

Improving common spaces / amenities.

Opposite left: Orchard Ridge commons lobby
Opposite right: Library adjacent to lobby in the commons

Commons floor plan

Right: Pub located in the commons
Below: Private dining room in the commons
Bottom left: Assisted living memory care small house exterior
Bottom right & opposite: Views of great room in a skilled care small house

Photography: Larry Lefever Photography

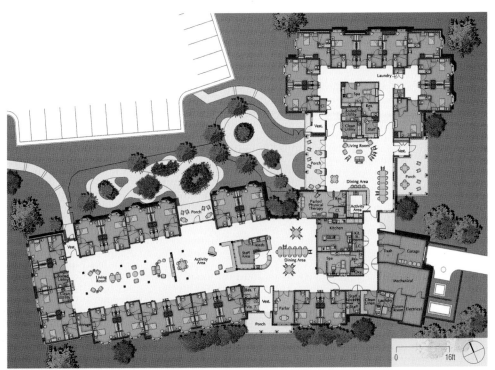

Paired small house floor plan

Households: What is innovative or unique about the households in the project?

This new CCRC is being constructed in three phases. Phase I includes the first of four small houses envisioned by the master plan. The design pairs a 10-bed skilled care house and an 18-bed assisted living memory care house, each with its own distinct living, dining, and core support services. The kitchen, physical therapy, and service areas are positioned between the two for efficient service delivery without compromising the residential scale of living spaces.

Within the skilled care small house, the bedrooms are in a private wing separate from the generously sized, open living room area. All resident rooms are private and include bathrooms with European showers. A great room area with country kitchen and living room looks out onto a covered porch and courtyard area.

Each small house has its own distinct entrance with an outdoor porch. Support areas are located in the center of the plan for each house to maximize natural light and outdoor connections to the resident rooms and living areas, while the memory care house includes skylights to bring natural light into the center core living, and activity areas. The memory care small house also includes a parlor area for family consultations and small meetings. Resident rooms are a mix of private and shared private suites, all including a bathroom with a European shower.

Common Spaces: What senior-friendly common spaces are included in the project?

Formal dining, bistro / casual dining; coffee shop / grab-and-go; dedicated fitness equipment room; salon; large multipurpose room; dedicated conference / meeting space; library / information resource center; club room; and pub.

The Village at Rockville

Rockville, Maryland // National Lutheran Communities & Services

Facility type (date of initial occupancy): Assisted Living (April 2013); Long-term Skilled Nursing (March 2013); Short-term Rehabilitation (February 2012)
Target market: Middle / upper middle
Site location: Suburban
Project site area (square feet): 81,000
Gross square footage of the renovation(s) / modernization(s) involved in the project: 57,405

Purpose of the renovation / modernization: Repositioning
Ratio of parking spaces to residents: 0.3:1
This site is within 1,000 feet of public transportation.
Provider type: Faith-based non-profit

Below: Living room in the new short-term rehabilitation neighborhood
Opposite: Private dining room

Overall Project Description

After more than 100 years providing skilled nursing services, the time had come for this senior care provider to reinvent itself to continue to meet its mission objectives and remain relevant in the marketplace. This project involved health care center renovations to support program objectives that would align services with resident needs. This included a cohesive short-term care rehabilitation program with all private rooms in household configurations, a person-centered long-term care program with all private rooms, and neighborhood common areas, and appealing assisted living residences created through conversion of first floor nursing units.

Multiphased renovations to the original 300-bed, multistory nursing home (constructed in 1980) will ultimately result in 94 extended care nursing rooms, 66 short-term rehabilitation suites, and 50 assisted living apartments, as well as ground-floor dining, and support spaces. The introduction of assisted living

services responds to the need for an intermediate level of care between the existing residential living and skilled nursing programs, and will enable the owner to become a full-service CCRC.

The three different types of care are separated across three levels. The recently completed neighborhood renovations have resulted in 18 assisted living residences on the first floor, a 32-bed neighborhood of skilled nursing on the second floor and a new 33-bed short-term rehabilitation neighborhood on the third floor. Future phases will implement similar renovations to other neighborhoods on all floors, including the creation of an 18-bed dedicated memory care household with its own courtyard garden.

Each reconfigured neighborhood has its own entrance leading into the living areas, providing a comfortable, homelike environment with more privacy, as well as social spaces for family visits and interaction among the residents. The renovations facilitate a decentralized approach

to activities of daily living, with communal living / activity rooms, and country kitchens. The required nurse station, medications, and other service areas are tucked away to allow the resident areas to become the centerpiece of the household. The third-floor rehabilitation neighborhood also has its own dedicated therapy area, focusing on the needs of those residents, while a separate outpatient therapy services area on the ground floor is adjacent to a new, lower-level entrance.

Project Goals

What were the major goals?

The environment needed to support the operational shift to resident-centered care, with specialized services / facilities to meet the specific needs of diverse resident groups. The existing institutional nursing units were reorganized into smaller residential-styled neighborhoods that are reinforced by separate living and dining areas. Neighborhood identities were established through a variety of interior finish material and color selections.

- To align services with resident needs, the project enabled the owner to provide assisted living services. This new residence type filled the void for an intermediate level of care and enabled the owner to become a full-service CCRC. Combining pairs of existing skilled nursing units on the first floor created market-rate studio and one-bedroom assisted living residences that include kitchenettes and bathrooms with accessible roll-in showers. The assisted living neighborhood is located in close proximity to the main entrance and Main Street amenities to support the more active and independent lifestyle expected of residents utilizing assisted living services. Residents also have access to an open country kitchen / dining and living room area, which serves as the focal point within the assisted living neighborhood.

- Realigning services to meet resident needs also required the creation of a dedicated short-term rehabilitation neighborhood that would meet the expectations of independent living residents, as well as members of the community needing these services. The design aesthetic needed to be transformed from clinical hospital to gracious boutique. The transformation is immediately apparent when stepping off the elevator, where the focal point is now a series of LED bubble panels, which set the stage for relaxation and healing. Inside the neighborhood, a soft color palette and natural wood tones reflect the owner's holistic, personalized approach to providing state-of-the-art therapy in a comfortable, supportive setting.

Challenges: What were the greatest design challenges?

Balancing the program goals with budget constraints and existing building infrastructure required careful prioritization. Analysis of the trade-offs between various options helped guide the owner and design team in making complex choices. For example, the small size of the existing bathrooms in resident rooms made them difficult for residents to use, particularly those requiring staff assistance. The design team was able to develop a compact solution, utilizing sliding barn-door-style doors to provide wheelchair accessibility, a modest vanity with curved edges, and a storage cabinet. However, the existing space constraints did not allow for the introduction of showers without negatively impacting the resident living space.

The client objective to introduce assisted living to the community was counterbalanced by the uncertainty of market acceptance for a solution that combined skilled care and assisted living in one building. To overcome a potential market stigma associated with intermingling both under the one roof, the assisted living residences are

on the first floor, enabling the neighborhood to function independently and with easy access to the main lobby and Main Street amenities. These residents also have easy access to the ground-floor dining room that is used by staff, visitors, and independent living residents. Additionally, interior finish upgrades are consistent between the assisted living and nursing floors in a deliberate effort to minimize the traditional differences between them and to reduce the trepidation typically associated with transitioning from one to the other.

Working entirely "inside the box" while maintaining continuous operations required a strategic phased construction approach, ultimately six phases over a period of three and a half years. Carefully orchestrated renovation plans facilitated a gradual census reduction, and enabled residents to continue to live on the floors above and below, as well as in other neighborhoods on the same floor, throughout construction. Further complicating the process was the vertical configuration of the building systems. The design team initiated the reinvention process

with a pre-phase to cut systems connections to the lower floors prior to initiating Phase I work on the third floor, and as the project progressed to the lower floors. All the connected exhaust and make-up air services had to be rerouted, requiring significant above-ceiling work in the occupied resident spaces. Similarly, shutting down the production kitchen for renovations required a temporary kitchen to be set up in an adjacent space, with additional equipment located in a temporary exterior building.

Innovations: What innovations or unique features were incorporated into the design of the project?

Totally replacing old institutional settings with new facilities is often not feasible to providers who are limited by fully built-out campuses, high resident occupancies, and limited financial resources. This total transformation has been accomplished within the constraints of the existing building. The transformation has supported the provider's commitment to bringing culture change in the delivery of care to its residents, while adding specialized services for both short-term

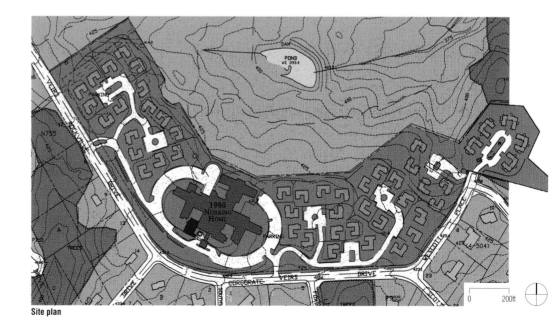

Site plan

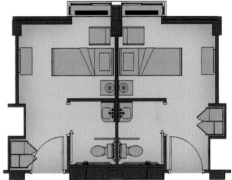

Typical renovated skilled nursing units

Left: Living room in the new assisted living neighborhood
Bottom: View into the assisted living studio

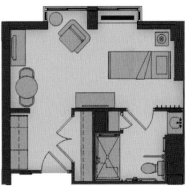

Conversion of two skilled nursing
units into assisted living studio

Ground floor

First floor new assisted living neighborhood

■ New assisted living studios
■ New assisted living one-bedroom units

rehabilitation and assisted living, which had not previously been available. This total nursing home reinvention was accomplished by custom-tailored solutions that prioritized getting the most residential qualities for the construction dollar.

Marketing / Occupancy: What issues were encountered regarding marketing and / or achieving full occupancy?

The owner was able to achieve full occupancy immediately through a combination of in-house transfers and a nonformal waiting list that had accumulated from direct admissions.

Collaboration: How did stakeholders, occupants, the design team, and / or others collaborate during the planning and / or design process?

Input and ideas were solicited through a series of 40-plus focus groups, and concept review sessions with nursing staff, food service, administration, and resident groups. Concept images and renovation scenarios were presented for review and feedback. This culminated in a final presentation to all stakeholders prior to initiating the multiphased census reduction and facility reinvention.

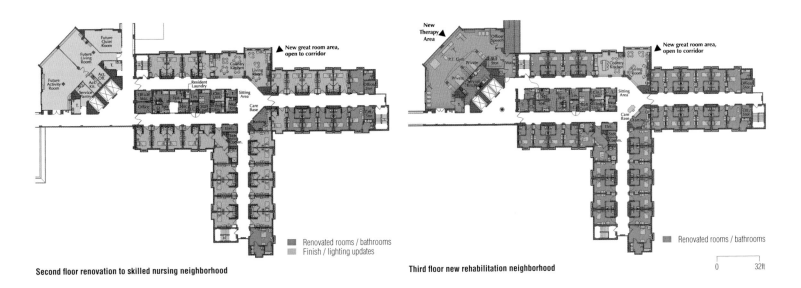

Second floor renovation to skilled nursing neighborhood

New great room area, open to corridor

■ Renovated rooms / bathrooms
■ Finish / lighting updates

Third floor new rehabilitation neighborhood

New great room area, open to corridor

■ Renovated rooms / bathrooms

0   32ft

Green / Sustainable Features: What green / sustainable features had the greatest impact on the project's design?

Energy efficiency, improved indoor air quality, and reuse of existing building structure and / or materials.

What were the primary motivations for including green / sustainable design features in the project?

Support the mission / values of the client / provider, lower operational costs, and improve resident / staff health and well being.

What challenges did the project face when trying to incorporate green / sustainable design features?

Actual first-cost premium.

Common Spaces: What senior-friendly common spaces are included in the project?

Formal dining, bistro / casual dining; dedicated rehabilitation / therapy gym; dedicated conference / meeting space; and dedicated classroom / learning space.

Opposite: LED bubble panels at the entrance to the new rehabilitation neighborhood
Left: Country kitchen design for the new assisted living neighborhood
Photography: Larry Lefever Photography

RLPS Architects

Creekside Homes at Givens Estates

Asheville, North Carolina // Givens Estates

Facility type: Independent Living; CCRC or part of a CCRC
Target market: Middle / upper middle
Site location: Suburban
Project site area (square feet): 39,204
Gross square footage of the new construction involved in the project: 69,044

Ratio of parking spaces to residents: 1 sheltered space and 1 open space per unit
Provider type: Faith-based non-profit

Below: Street view rendering of new hybrid homes
Opposite: Rear unit elevation showing underground parking

The four-story hybrid homes take advantage of the steep terrain to provide sheltered parking on the lower level while maintaining a three-story facade with an inviting front porch on the street side.

Innovations: What innovations or unique features were incorporated into the design of the project?

The hybrid homes blend the benefits of cottage and apartment living. Multiple exposures, sheltered lower level parking, outdoor living, and an absence of corridors are among the cottage-like benefits. Apartment-like features include indoor access to common and service areas and opportunities for social connections in a multistory building that requires less site area. The hybrid homes foster a sense of community between the 12 occupants in each house with shared living areas including a social space on the ground floor.

Marketing / Occupancy: What issues were encountered regarding marketing and / or achieving full occupancy?

As the project begins construction, 19 of the 24 units have been reserved. One possible marketing challenge is that many potential residents are familiar with apartment or cottage living; since hybrids are a new type of housing, many are having trouble visualizing the homes. This concept feels different inside with multiple exposures, outdoor living areas, and the absence of corridors.

Data / Research: What innovative or unique data collection and / or research was applied during the planning and / or design process?

At the conclusion of each construction project, the architects conduct a thorough post-occupancy evaluation. This information is used to update standard practices and project checklists to avoid any problems that might occur in other projects. Data from a previous hybrid design project was used to shape some of the planning details for these hybrid homes.

Overall Project Description

These homes blend the amenities of both cottage and apartment living to provide a new independent living model for the community. They are replacing outdated and under-utilized apartments located on steep terrain adjacent to a creek. The owner was strategic about their desire to diversify the types of housing inventory on their campus and identified the price point, amenities, location, square footage, and connectivity to commons. As part of an existing CCRC, areas of the campus not included in this project include the health center, assisted living center, commons, and independent living cottages.

Project Goals

What were the major goals?

- To provide a new independent living option on the campus by integrating hybrid homes. Previously, these were villa apartments, duplexes, and cottages.

- To replace, on an incremental basis, outdated villa apartments: gradually replacing the villas will use the prime real estate on the campus for a more desirable product.

Challenges: What were the greatest design challenges?

The existing villas needed to be vacated prior to commencing construction. This process became protracted and delayed construction.

The hybrid homes will offer commanding views of the adjacent creek, which requires stringent protection throughout the construction process. All site work needed to occur with a gentle hand so as not to disturb or dump sediment into the existing creek.

At three and four stories in height (from creek-side to street-side), the homes are considerably taller than the two-story villas that they replace. To allay the owner's concern about the height of the homes, the architect provided photorealistic computer-generated renderings of the homes nestled in the existing trees and terrain.

Collaboration: How did stakeholders, occupants, the design team, and / or others collaborate during the planning and / or design process?

A series of face-to-face and web-based meetings were held with prospective residents to introduce the concept and solicit reactions. The comments were documented and incorporated into the design process and considerations.

Green / Sustainable Features: What green / sustainable features had the greatest impact on the project's design?

Site design considerations, maximized daylighting, and the conscientious choice of materials.

What were the primary motivations for including green / sustainable design features in the project?

Support the mission / values of the client / provider, stay competitive against other similar / local facilities, and lower operational costs.

For a project with a residential component, what was critical to the success of the project?

Improving units / private spaces.

Common Spaces: What senior-friendly common spaces are included in the project?

Dedicated social lounge space on each floor.

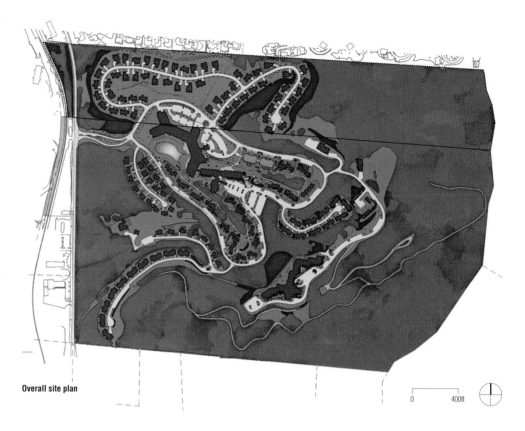

Overall site plan

0   400ft

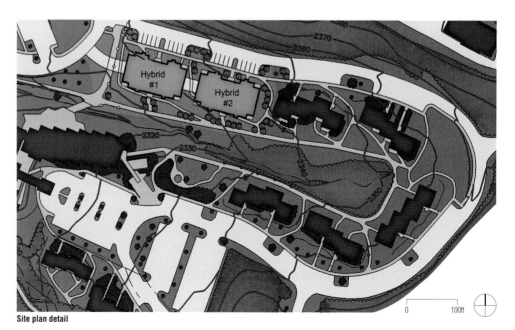

Site plan detail

0   100ft

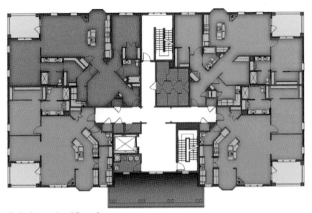

Typical upper level floor plan

One-bedroom plus den unit floor plan (1,400 sq ft)

First floor plan

Two-bedroom plus den unit floor plan (1,550 sq ft)

Garage floor plan

0   32ft

Two-bedroom plus den unit floor plan (1,700 sq ft)

0   16ft

RLPS Architects

Rose Villa Pocket Neighborhoods & Main Street

Portland, Oregon // Rose Villa

Facility type: Independent Living; CCRC or part of a CCRC
Target market: Middle / upper middle
Site location: Suburban
Project site area (square feet): 280,379
**Gross square footage of the new construction
involved in the project:** 128,263

Ratio of parking spaces to residents: 1.2:1
This site is within 1,000 feet of public transportation.
Provider type: Non-sectarian non-profit

Below: Pocket Neighborhood Pedestrian
  Friendly Pathways
Opposite: Pocket Neighborhood Courtyard

Renderings: Myhre Group Architects

Overall Project Description

A garden community in Portland, Oregon, which originally opened in 1960, faces several challenges contributing to declining occupancy. The community, known for its lush landscaping and relaxed garden lifestyle, consists of linear, one-story garden apartments that are increasingly failing to meet current market standards for independent living. In addition, navigating the steep 22-acre hillside site is challenging for senior residents. The goal is to replace all 263 apartments, over a phased approach, with pocket neighborhoods organized around gardens stepping down the hillside. Each pocket neighborhood comprises seven cottage homes overlooking an intimate courtyard setting to promote socialization through small-scale living. The result creates smaller, pedestrian-friendly neighborhoods within the larger community which capitalize on garden connections and outdoor views. The over-under cottages in each pocket neighborhood maximize site utilization while providing compact floor plans that are affordable, yet maintain open and livable spaces with appealing views in multiple directions.

The pocket neighborhoods transition up to a new main street and town center with resident amenities at street level and loft apartment living on the upper levels. The loft apartments provide a new option for residents who find the travel distance from the cottages difficult, or those who prefer a sense of downtown living. Situated at the site's highest point, overlooking the Willamette River, the main street provides a unique and appealing first impression to the campus, as well as providing a sense of place within the community. Once completed, this garden setting, as it was originally conceived, will offer an open, relaxed, and communal lifestyle for seniors.

Project Goals

What were the major goals?

- The goal to replace aging housing stock while creating a smaller "community within a community" resulted in the introduction of pocket neighborhoods. Each pocket neighborhood consists of seven cottage

homes organized around an intimate garden setting which promotes a close knit sense of community and neighborliness through an increased level of contact. Neighbors are naturally acquainted through the daily flow of life, by the simple fact of shared space and small scale living. The courtyard provides a natural setting for outdoor picnics and group gatherings. Multiple clusters of pocket neighborhoods form a larger aggregate community, all contributing to the character and life of the overall CCRC, and connected via walking paths leading up the site to the main street town center and housing.

- Another goal was improving campus amenities and providing spaces where people could casually gather and interact on a regular basis. This led to the creation of the new main street and town center, with loft-style housing above common areas. The street-level resident amenities include a bistro, coffee shop, garden center, art studio, wellness center, and auditorium that are open both from the street and from internal corridors. A wine bar is being proposed for the rooftop garden overlooking Main Street and the Willamette River.

The cottages are sized to be affordable, while open floor plans maximize daylight and views in multiple directions. The active rooms of the homes, including the main living areas and front porches, face the common courtyards rather than turning their back to neighbors. Layering of public-to-private space and using landscape strategies along with the careful placement of windows facilitates privacy for each dwelling. For residents who find the travel distances from the pocket neighborhoods undesirable, loft apartments located directly above the new common areas along Main Street provide a sense of downtown living.

Challenges: What were the greatest design challenges?

The primary challenge was addressing the declining occupancy that resulted from aging housing stock and a lack of social spaces and amenities, with little available property for new construction. This required the careful development of a multiphased approach to reinvent the campus where, ultimately, 70+ existing buildings will be replaced. To initiate the first phase of demolition and construction, 71 of the existing 260 villa units have been taken out of inventory, some held open for redevelopment with others converted for alternate uses. Those units, combined with additional unoccupied units, will allow for resident relocations to implement the improvements envisioned by the master plan.

To achieve financial viability, the planning and design team developed a housing model that addressed the steep slopes while maintaining the necessary density. An over-under cottage plan was developed where each cottage has both a front and back door, with an abundance of natural light in a garden setting. The buildings act as retaining walls to address the steeply sloping site, but maintain level gardens throughout.

Another challenge was creating a senior-friendly design solution that maintains and reinforces the garden community lifestyle that this provider is known for, on a site that includes a 40-foot grade change. Stepped pocket neighborhoods allow for the organizing gardens to be level while still interconnected through accessible walkways. The over-under cottage plans make full use of the site while maintaining one-story living for residents.

To reinvent the entry experience, promote a sense of arrival, and create a community with a center, the design envisions a new main street and town center. New flanking buildings with common areas at the ground level and loft apartments above define the main street, ending in a town square plaza where street fairs, art shows, concerts, and movie nights will be commonplace. The town

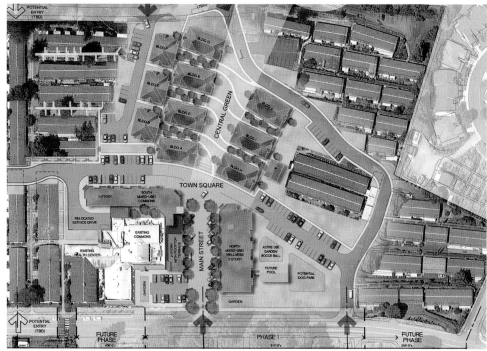

Site plan for pocket neighborhoods, main street and town center

One bedroom (820 sq ft)
One bedroom plus den (996 sq ft)
One bedroom plus den (1,205 sq ft)
Two bedroom (1,222 sq ft)

0   16ft

Pocket neighborhood plan

square sits at the precipice of the site looking down through the linear gardens and pocket neighborhoods to the Willamette River.

Innovations: What innovations or unique features were incorporated into the design of the project?

Introducing a pocket neighborhood concept in combination with an over-under cottage design was instrumental in achieving the provider's programming and marketing goals within the constraints of a built-out site with steep grade level variations. The stacked design—in which the lower level cottage overlooks a courtyard in one pocket neighborhood, while the adjacent upper level cottage takes advantage of the grade to form another neighborhood with its own courtyard—provides a gradual and pedestrian-friendly transition up the hillside to Main Street and the town center.

Marketing / Occupancy: What issues were encountered regarding marketing and / or achieving full occupancy?

Although the facility is not yet occupied, marketing is proceeding as anticipated with 40 percent of units sold to date.

Data / Research: What innovative or unique data collection and / or research was applied during the planning and / or design process?

In addition to traditional marketing studies, the design team conducted five separate focus groups comprising senior management, staff members, independent living residents, the adult children of residents, and family members. Each group responded to a series of open-ended questions regarding the existing facilities and programs, as well as potential areas of improvement, utilizing the owner and design team's shared interest in the pocket neighborhood concept as a guide. A review

Top: Diagram illustrating how pocket neighborhoods step up to main street
Above: Diagram of rooftop garden on south building

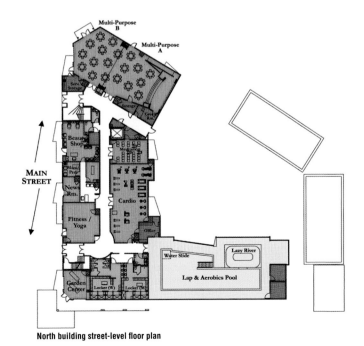

North building street-level floor plan

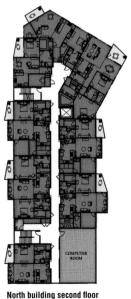

North building second floor

North building third floor

of publications (including Ross Chapin's Pocket Neighborhoods: Creating Small Scale Community in a Large Scale World and The Great Good Place by Ray Oldenburg) along with the tabulated focus group results helped the development team prioritize and refine programming goals.

Collaboration: How did stakeholders, occupants, the design team, and / or others collaborate during the planning and / or design process?

In addition to the focus groups, the development team (including the owner, development consultant, civil engineer, project architect, and local architect consultant) collaborated throughout a four month master planning process. This included a two-day, on-site design charette. The collaborative, interactive process provided an efficient and cost-effective forum for debate, clearly defined relevant design and development issues, structured alternative solutions, and concluded with a graphic presentation of preliminary project designs. Following subsequent refinement culminating in the final master plan, the team continued to advance the design concepts though a series of collaborative review sessions both on-site and utilizing web conferencing technology for real-time reviews from multiple locations.

Green / Sustainable Features: What green / sustainable features had the greatest impact on the project's design?

Energy efficiency, maximized daylighting, and recycling construction waste and / or diversion from landfills.

What were the primary motivations for including green / sustainable design features in the project?

Support the mission / values of the client / provider, stay competitive against other similar / local facilities, and lower operational costs.

For a project with a residential component, what was critical to the success of the project?

Improving units / private spaces.

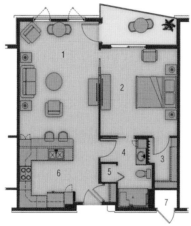

One-bedroom loft apartment

1	Living room	5	Closet
2	Bedroom	6	Kitchen
3	Walk-in closet	7	Mechanical area
4	Bathroom		

One-bedroom with den loft apartment

1	Den	4	Walk-in closet	7	Kitchen
2	Living room	5	Bathroom	8	Closet
3	Bedroom	6	Powder room	9	Mechanical area

Common Spaces: What senior-friendly common spaces are included in the project?

Formal dining, bistro / casual dining; coffee shop / grab-and-go; marketplace / convenience store; swimming pool / aquatics facilities; dedicated fitness equipment room; dedicated exercise classroom; salon; large multipurpose room; library / information resource center; art studio / craft room; religious / spiritual / meditative space; resident-maintained gardening space; and garden center.

Top: Main street town center
Opposite: Main street

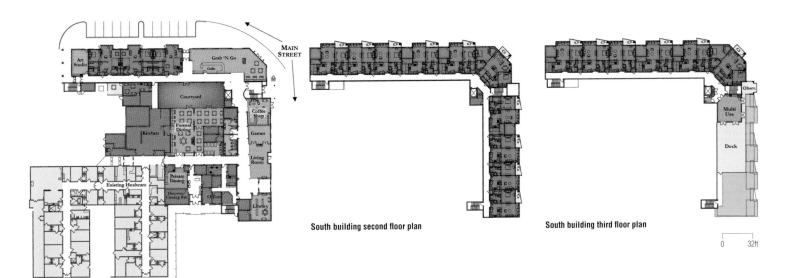

South building second floor plan

South building third floor plan

0   32ft

South building street-level floor plan

Asbury Place at Arbor Acres

Winston-Salem, North Carolina // Arbor Acres United Methodist Retirement Community

Facility type (date of initial occupancy): Assisted Living (February 2012); CCRC or part of a CCRC
Target market: Middle / upper middle
Site location: Suburban; greenfield
Project site area (square feet): 189,602
Gross square footage of the new construction involved in the project: 117,277

Ratio of parking spaces to residents: 0.5:1
This site is within 1,000 feet of public transportation, and within 1,000 feet of at least 10 basic services with pedestrian access to those services.
Provider type: Faith-based non-profit

Below: Exterior at dusk
Opposite: Entry lobby

Overall Project Description

This new three-story assisted living building comprises 60 residential apartments, activity and recreational space, a rehabilitation center, and spa therapy and administrative spaces. The owner challenged the design team to develop a discreetly supportive senior care residence that embraces both the arts and technology, and to create an environment rich in amenities and beauty. The resulting assisted living residence includes an atrium dining room, library / commissary, therapy center, multipurpose room, day spa, and courtyard area. Each floor includes its own lobby space and living room / activity areas. In-room medication management is one of many built-in measures that allow services to be rendered discreetly and gracefully. The fully accessible, predominately one bedroom apartments feature a living room with a walk-out bay window, a kitchenette, a master suite with a walk-in closet and a bathroom with an accessible shower and provisions for a washer and dryer. The six two-bedroom apartments, expected to accommodate couples, were designed to be convertible into smaller apartments providing future flexibility to respond to market needs.

The therapy / fitness center includes areas for occupational and physical therapy, as well as private treatment rooms and a state-of-the art therapy pool with an underwater treadmill. The tranquil 2,000 square-foot spa features European showers and spa tubs. A telecoil hearing loop in the multipurpose room provides a clear signal to residents' hearing aids from the public address system's microphone without any background noise.

The building facade takes on the appearance of attached buildings along the traditional streetscape. The varied color palette and building materials reflect the regional vernacular of Winston-Salem. The new assisted living building is physically connected to the existing health center allowing for shared production, kitchen functions, and ease of movement between buildings for residents, family, and staff members. The building is heated and cooled using a geothermal system and includes automatic lighting controls in office and service areas for operational efficiency.

Project Goals

What were the major goals?

- The owner's vision was to feed the senses with a gracious environment featuring a beautiful collection of local artwork and interior detailing, on par with independent living residences on campus. The oval garden at the entrance features a locally designed rock sculpture suggestive of human forms, each of which represents one of the fundamental aspects of human wholeness. The design inside emphasizes vibrant color, texture, and emotion, with staffing functions kept behind the scenes. Rich with offerings for activities, social interaction, physical therapies, and rejuvenation, Asbury Place encourages residents to remain active from the holistic perspective of body, mind, and spirit.

- To actively promote an atmosphere of wellness and resident well-being, the design aesthetic is supported by various technologies, social spaces, and support services. The therapy suite, beauty shop and spa help maintain and improve mobility, balance, stamina, and well-being. Diverse activity, recreation, and cultural programs are available in three 400-square-foot activity rooms on each floor, as well as the multipurpose room and promenade on the second floor. The design includes a two-bedroom apartment option allowing couples to remain together—and have privacy—when one spouse requires assisted living services. The dining room is open to all residents on campus helping to maintain existing relationships with residents from other campus areas.

- To empower each resident and promote independence, all residences include a kitchenette so that the residents can prepare a snack or simple meal when they wish. Each residence also includes a barrier-free bathroom with a zero threshold European shower to easily accommodate supportive devices, as needed. To assist residents in easily navigating the building, colors vary from floor to floor, and

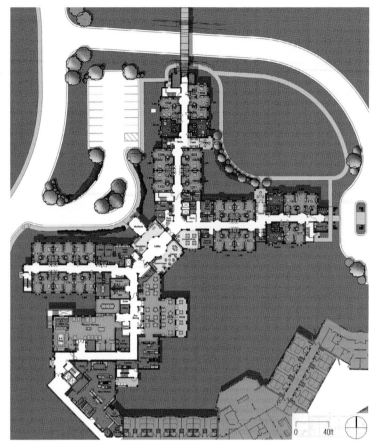

First floor plan

the wall facing the elevators on each floor feature a unique and distinctive design element. Comfortable and varied seating nooks provide opportunities for residents to rest as needed while making their way to the dining room, the beauty shop, a performance in the multipurpose room, or other locations without assistance.

Challenges: What were the greatest design challenges?

The distance residents have to travel to the dining room is a challenge with any assisted living program, but even more so when all 66 apartments are at least one bedroom dwellings of 560 square feet. The owner's desire to have the residents enjoy at least one daily meal in a common dining room

required a solution that minimized walking distances. Staff intervention during the design process re-directed a two-prong floor plan solution to a three-prong solution with shorter distances to elevators and the dining room. Each floor is also equipped to support dining areas for intermediate meals while comfortable seating nooks and program areas along the way enable residents to relax as needed.

Resident safety is of paramount concern in assisted living environments, especially in personal bathrooms. Each apartment is equipped with a three-fixture, barrier-free bathroom including a zero threshold European shower. The challenge with any European shower is containing the water.

The solution called for the introduction of a tiled shower with a linear drain to maintain the desired residential design aesthetic while providing a safe and comfortable experience whether bathing independently or with staff assistance.

The owner was committed to including two-bedroom apartments in the unit mix, recognizing that couples who had been together for decades typically had to face the prospect of separation when one or both required assisted living services. However, there was concern that economic conditions or census levels would not support these units. The response was building flexibly so that the two-bedroom units could be converted into a studio and one-bedroom

unit in the future, if needed. One of the bedroom suites could simply be converted into its own studio unit with the addition of a kitchenette.

Innovations: What innovations or unique features were incorporated into the design of the project?

Embracing the philosophy that aging is a series of celebrations, the owner consciously infused the elements of surprise and reward into the programming and physical design. The introduction of a five-star personal day spa into assisted living was not only bold, but highly innovative. The owner's goal was to provide a transformational experience. Touching upon the five senses of sight, sound, smell, touch, and taste, the spa offers subdued lighting, soothing aromas, soft music, tactile surfaces, and refreshments. Day spa services include massage therapy, guided imagery, and aromatherapy. Attention to detail is evident throughout, from the LED bubble panels in the tranquil waiting areas to special touches that maximize comfort and tranquility, like towel warmers.

Marketing / Occupancy: What issues were encountered regarding marketing and / or achieving full occupancy?

The facility achieved full occupancy earlier than expected. Existing residents were relocated from two other locations on campus with the remaining residences (resulting from the provider increasing its license) occupied within two months of opening.

Data / Research: What innovative or unique data collection and / or research was applied during the planning and / or design process?

During the initial planning and programming phase, the design team toured the existing assisted living facilities to identify current conditions and operational issues to be addressed in the new building. An important part of this process was meeting with administrative,

Opposite top: Second-floor promenade
Opposite bottom: Community Life Center – large multipurpose space
Top left: Dining
Top right: Spa massage / aromatherapy room
Bottom right: Hydroworx therapy pool

Photography: Larry Lefever Photography

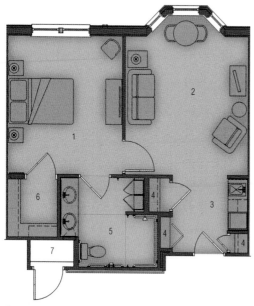

One-bedroom residence

1	Bedroom	5	Bathroom
2	Living room	6	Walk-in closet
3	Kitchenette	7	Mechanical area
4	Closet		

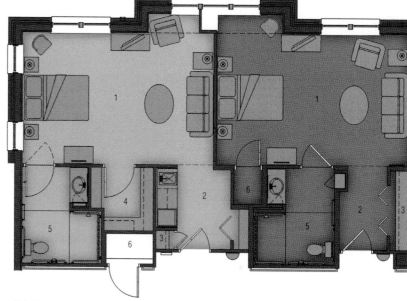

Unit plan to convert two-bedroom residence to two studio residences

1	Bedroom / living room	4	Walk-in closet
2	Foyer	5	Bathroom
3	Closet	6	Mechanical area

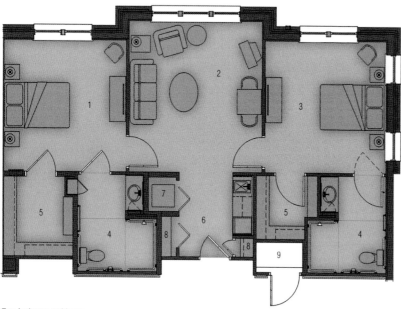

Two-bedroom residence

1	Master bedroom	6	Kitchenette
2	Living room	7	Washer / dryer
3	Bedroom	8	Closet
4	Bathroom	9	Mechanical area
5	Walk-in closet		

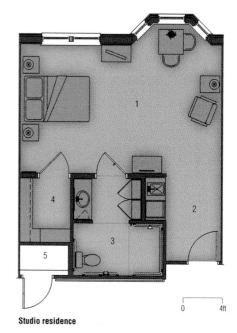

Studio residence

1	Bedroom
2	Foyer
3	Bathroom
4	Walk-in closet
5	Mechanical area

0   4ft

nursing, maintenance, therapy, and food service staff members to brainstorm ideas, define objectives, set priorities, and resolve existing operational or facility issues. One example was a recurring problem with shower overflows in the previous assisted living building. The design team explored options for resolving the issue without compromising the desired design aesthetic or full accessibility. The introduction of a linear drain in European-style tile showers successfully merged the desired form with the required functionality.

Collaboration: How did stakeholders, occupants, the design team, and / or others collaborate during the planning and / or design process?

The first step was master planning, including resident / staff focus groups and a design charette to provide a forum in which all voices could be heard and future options considered within the context of financial capacity and land

development constraints. This resulted in a multiphased master plan that defined phasing strategies for future development opportunities. The subsequent pre-design process for Asbury Place was an inclusive process that also involved all the vested stakeholders: residents, operations, senior management, activities, physical therapy, nursing, board of directors, finance, social workers, marketing, physical plant, housekeeping, and dining services. Through a series of meetings spanning four months, the development team met twice a month to shape the program and evaluate various models to determine the best solution.

Green / Sustainable Features: What green / sustainable features had the greatest impact on the project's design?

Energy efficiency, improved indoor air quality, and maximized daylighting.

What were the primary motivations for including green / sustainable design features in the project?

Support the mission / values of the client / provider and the design team, and lower operational costs.

For a project with a residential component, what was critical to the success of the project?

Improving units / private spaces.

Common Spaces: What senior-friendly common spaces are included in the project?

Formal dining; coffee shop / grab-and-go; dedicated rehabilitation / therapy gym; massage / aromatherapy room; salon; large multipurpose room; dedicated conference / meeting space; library / information resource center; and art studio / craft room.

Top left: Typical residence living room with bay window
Top right: European shower in typical residence

Todd & Associates, Inc.

The Friendship House at Royal Oaks

Sun City, Arizona // Royal Oaks Retirement Community

Facility type: Assisted Living; Assisted Living—dementia / memory support; CCRC or part of a CCRC
Target market: Middle / upper middle
Site location: Suburban
Project site area (square feet): 74,967
Gross square footage of the new construction involved in the project: 59,038

Gross square footage of a typical neighborhood: 9,921
Number of residents in a typical neighborhood: 14
Ratio of parking spaces to residents: 0.25:1
Provider type: Non-sectarian non-profit

Below: Street view
Opposite: Garden view

Overall Project Description

In mid-2011, discussions began regarding how to improve the environment in a secure area of a care center servicing dementia residents. This wing includes two halls of resident rooms: one being part of the original 1983 build, the other an addition in 1994. In 2006, a renovation was completed merging the two halls to make an enlarged 50-bed secure wing. The need for this type of special care was increasing in the community; nearly 50 percent of residents occupying a healthcare bed have a diagnosis of dementia and thus increased need for memory and physical support. Even with the extensive renovation of the care center in 2006, this wing suffers from a lack of natural light. In September 2011, consultants identified common areas where lighting could be improved. A larger problem with the current wing is double-occupancy rooms. Research has shown that residents greatly benefit from a personal space of their own, to display mementos collected in their lifetime that trigger the recall of a fun / memorable time from the past.

Privacy and solitude provides time for reflection and rejuvenation, peace and serenity. Semi-private rooms do not facilitate these experiences and feelings, resulting in increased anxiety and confusion. They also create challenges in the care of the residents when equipment is used for personal care. Additionally, the congestion in corridors caused by service carts, equipment storage, and people impede safe ambulation. The increased noise levels associated with the traffic flow cause confusion and agitation in residents who do not understand the commotion. Shift changes are huge interruptions in the residents' day since the entry and exit doors are adjacent to the nurse station fronting the residential congregation area. Residents see staff leaving and want to leave too. The secure patio is non-visible, meaning residents require a staff escort to and from the outdoor space; even though the patio is monitored, the design does not encourage residents to engage in outdoor activities. The solution is to build a 56-bed center (with private rooms) and re-license it for assisted living — dementia / memory support.

Project Goals

What were the major goals?

- Improve the quality of life for dementia residents by providing care in an intimate residential setting. This project includes a private, roomy suite for each resident and a centralized common space for activities and socialization. Another goal was to improve the quality of lighting and provide more natural light: floor plans were designed to allow natural light to cascade through the common living space from either side, while a large NanaWall allows natural light to enter from outdoor gardens. Each residence also has large windows with operable wooden shutters.

- Centralize and open up dining: resident rooms wrap around large, open, and centralized dining / living / activity spaces within each household wing.

- Visible, usable, and quality outdoor space. The centralized fireplace within each household separates different scale living / activity spaces creating a unique open floor plan that includes secure outdoor gardens (with NanaWalls) as an extension of the interior spaces.

- Design a flexible building that accomodates aging-in-place: the building is designed to meet the physical requirements for skilled care and can be converted into a total care facility if required.

- Decrease overall staffing needs: by relocating nearly 50 percent of the residents from a skilled care model into an assisted living—dementia / memory support model, overall staffing needs will potentially decrease. Licensed practical nurse (LPN) slots will be replaced by 4-6 certified nursing cssistant (CNA) / certified caregiver (CCG).

- Create private rooms in the health care center: the relocation of 56 memory care beds from the existing health care center allows for a second phase that will re-license the existing health care center to accommodate 57-64 private rooms (with the ability to create semi-private rooms when desired for couples who may both require this level of care).

Challenges: What were the greatest design challenges?

Creating four individual households for 56 resident rooms (14 each) with an intimate / residential feel while providing appropriately scaled living spaces and support spaces: this was addressed through centralized support spaces for staff (for easy access / efficiency, yet removed from the residential wings); creating resident rooms wrapped around living / dining / activity spaces within the household wing; breaking resident spaces up within the household (fireplaces separating different scale living / activity spaces); and, creating an open floor plan, including the secure outdoor garden. This allows staff to be a part of the individual household and easily view the entire space.

Appropriately integrating the new assisted living—dementia / memory support facility into the existing campus: this was addressed by creating a stronger relationship to the existing assisted living program by locating the new building directly adjacent. The location was strategically selected to eliminate the fewest number of existing garden homes, while providing a buffer to the remaining existing garden homes.

Innovations: What innovations or unique features were incorporated into the design of the project?

Outdoor garden courtyards with an emphasis on visibility and year-round use promote "fun" therapy: in lieu of going to a therapy room, residents are encouraged to take a walk in the garden which incorporates specific therapy elements such as changes in surface materials, steps, and other associated activities.

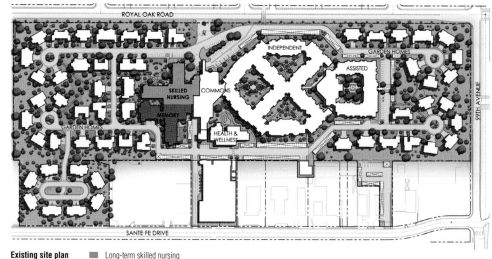

Existing site plan ▪ Long-term skilled nursing
▪ Long-term skilled nursing—dementia / memory support

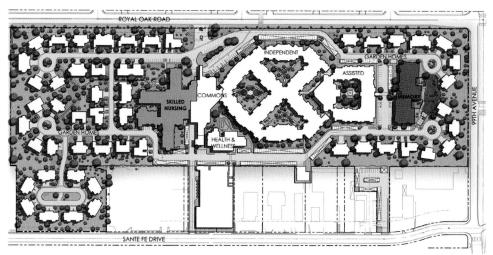

Proposed site plan ▪ Long-term skilled nursing
▪ Long-term skilled nursing—dementia / memory support

0   160ft

Households are designed with 14 private suites— each with a private bathroom—surrounding a 2,300+ square-foot common living space. All staff support spaces and equipment areas are removed from the resident household to create a residential feel. In lieu of nurse stations, staff work areas (LPN, CAN, and CCG) are located among the furnishings within the open living areas, resulting in full engagement with the residents.

Behind the scenes, full-service kitchens on each floor allow the country kitchen to remain highly accessible, residential in nature, and open to the resident living / activity space. The mechanical system is designed to provide continuous air flow, maintaining a constant level of fresh air throughout the building.

Data / Research: What innovative or unique data collection and / or research was applied during the planning and / or design process?

An outside consultant was hired to complete a market study to evaluate other communities and to make recommendations based on the findings. The design team toured three existing communities, interviewing and discussing the pros and cons with staff members.

Collaboration: How did stakeholders, occupants, the design team, and / or others collaborate during the planning and / or design process?

The initial premise was not to build a new memory care building, but began as an effort to renovate the existing health center and continue to provide memory and long-term care within the same facility. Through staff, community, and consultant input, Royal Oaks' leadership exhausted all avenues before realizing that the existing health center model with small, shared resident rooms and segregated common areas could not

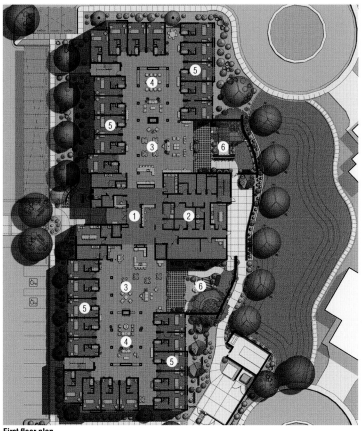

First floor plan

1 Reception area
2 Staff support space
3 Activity / dining area
4 Living space
5 Resident rooms
6 Therapy garden

Second floor plan

1 Reception area
2 Staff support space
3 Activity / dining area
4 Living space
5 Resident rooms
6 Balcony

0   40ft

accommodate the goals and market demand of a smaller, more residential neighborhood model with private rooms. This led to the solution: to build a new 56-private room assisted living—dementia / memory support structure.

Green / Sustainable Features: What green / sustainable features had the greatest impact on the project's design?

Energy efficiency, improved indoor air quality, wet blown cellulose (fire and microbial retardant), insulated building envelope, exhaust energy recovery system, dual pane, high performance, low-E window glazing with laminated glass at resident rooms, highly efficient LED-based lighting including energy management systems, and high efficiency heat pump A / C units throughout.

What were the primary motivations for including green / sustainable design features in the project?

Support the mission / values of the client / provider, stay competitive against other similar / local facilities, and lower operational costs.

What challenges did the project face when trying to incorporate green / sustainable design features?

Determine real / long-term sustainable solutions versus perceived.

What program / organization is being used for green / sustainable certification of this project?

Designed to Earn the ENERGY STAR (DEES) program. The building is being designed to be at least 15 percent more energy efficient than a home built to the 2009 International Residential Code (IRC) and will include additional energy-saving measures that could result in a 35 percent savings relative to ASHRAE 2007 standards.

For a project with a residential component, what was critical to the success of the project?

Improving units / private spaces.

Households: What is innovative or unique about the households in the project?

There are no resident corridors: private resident suites are designed around living / dining / activity spaces. There are also no nurse stations in the resident wing: staff spaces in the living area are tucked out of sight and disguised as a workstation armoire. Resident laundry is incorporated into the open activity space and finished to complement the adjacent country kitchen with an island for clothes folding. Indoor common areas blend into outdoor garden spaces through the use of NanaWalls, an operable glass wall system custom designed for large openings.

Typical household plan

1	Main entry	7	Life enrichment workspace
2	Nurse / external provider work area	8	Country kitchen
3	Staff support area	9	Resident laundry
4	Full-service kitchen	10	Fireplace
5	Typical resident room	11	Media wall
6	Staff armoire workspace	12	Therapy courtyard

0   20ft

Opposite: Household country kitchen and resident laundry
Top: Household living area
Above: Household view from garden therapy

Common Spaces: What senior-friendly common spaces are included in the project?

Bistro / casual dining; salon, large multipurpose room; small-scale cinema / media room; dedicated conference / meeting space; religious / spiritual / meditative space; and resident-maintained gardening space. The building is sectioned into four neighborhoods contained in a energy-efficient building with therapy gardens, and is completely secure to ensure the safety of residents who have a tendency to wander. Abundant outdoor garden spaces, with an emphasis on visibility and therapeutic components, are included. Each of the neighborhoods will comprise 14 private rooms with private bathrooms and each will surround 2300+ square-foot living areas. Within each of the open living areas there are defined spaces for the following: cinema / media, meditative / spiritual, dining, activities, cooking, laundry, spa, and beauty salon. Residents will have a comfortable and quiet place for uninterrupted sleep and a place to carry out their morning routines with all of their own personal items in easy access.

Legacy Place

Allentown, Pennsylvania // Jah-Jireh Homes of America

Facility type: Assisted Living; Assisted Living—dementia / memory support
Target market: Middle / upper middle
Site location: Suburban; greenfield
Project site area (square feet): 106,358
Gross square footage of the new construction involved in the project: 22,223

Gross square footage of a typical household: 9,108
Number of residents in a typical household: 12 in assisted living memory care; 10 in assisted living
Ratio of parking spaces to residents: 15 for staff and visitors; residents won't drive
This site is within 1,000 feet of public transportation.
Provider type: Faith-based non-profit

Below: Artist's rendering depicting exterior perspective of paired assisted living small houses
Opposite: Interior rendering of family-style dining room

room sizes include small studios, large studios, and one-bedroom units that are fully accessible so that residents can remain in their apartments as they age further and need additional support.

Project Goals

What were the major goals?

- To provide a place for Jehovah's Witness members in the Allentown, Pennsylvania area to reside when they require assisted living or assisted living memory care where they will be cared for by, and reside with, members of their own faith (frequently referred to as brothers and sisters), and where they will remain in a familiar and comfortable environment. This was accomplished by local Jehovah's Witness members spearheading the project, and will be designed and built with funds donated by members of the Jehovah's Witness community.

- To create a Jehovah's Witness–style care community similar to those successfully functioning in Great Britain. This is being accomplished by area-based Jehovah's Witnesses spearheading the effort with guidance from the individuals running the original facilities in Great Britain. Funding for this yet-to-be-built project comes exclusively from private donations from members of the church.

- To keep a residential scale and feel to the residences. This was accomplished by creating small houses and locating the community in an already established residential neighborhood.

Challenges: What were the greatest design challenges?

Stormwater management on a tight sloping site: underground stormwater storage tanks are positioned under the parking areas and are part of an irrigation system that gradually distributes water back over the site.

Overall Project Description

This project was borne from the desire of a group of Jehovah's Witnesses to create a senior living community based on the example of the Jehovah's Witness homes in Great Britain. Thus began the process of designing the first Jehovah's Witness senior living homes in the United States: a pair of small houses on a 2.4 acre site located in a residential neighborhood in Allentown, Pennsylvania.

These houses are designed to reflect the look and feel of a traditional residential home and will only be inhabited by a small group of residents. Two buildings are strategically situated on the site—one for assisted living, the other for assisted living memory care residents. The assisted living house pairs two small homes of 10 beds each with their own distinct living, dining, and core support services. The kitchen and service areas are positioned between the two for efficient service delivery without compromising the residential scale of living spaces. The 12-bed assisted living memory care house is located across the drive from the assisted living house. It includes a daylight basement which was facilitated by the sloping site.

Both small houses are designed to separate the public living and dining areas from the private bedroom and bathing areas. Service and staff areas are further removed and screened from sight. The open great room includes a living room with a fireplace, a dining room, and a kitchen, and is organized to allow daylight to enter the space from both sides. This encourages residents to access the gardens on either side via shaded porches, and helps alleviate sun-downing issues with the spaces remaining bright all day. Parlors in each house provide a flexible space that serves as a quiet den, TV room, private function room, and a respite overnight room for guests. As with most small-house designs, corridors are minimized and organized in a simple loop ending at the great room. This design provides a simple path for residents with cognitive issues and also avoids dead-end corridors. Resident

To locate the small houses in an existing residential community: to alleviate neighbors' concerns about a senior living community changing the look and feel of the neighborhood, 3D renderings were employed to show how the buildings would look from neighboring lots. Screening, such as landscaping, will also be employed to mitigate the views from existing neighboring lots.

Situating three small houses on a tight site in a residential community: the two assisted living houses were paired together, sharing service areas so that they take up less area on the site and to reduce cost. This does not diminish the small house concepts because the two assisted living homes will still function independently.

Innovations: What innovations or unique features were incorporated into the design of the project?

Small house design concept: each household is located within its own small house, functioning much like a traditional residential family home. The organization of public versus private areas is consistent with a traditional home where residents and visitors enter into the more public living and dining areas, then move through the more private areas. Service areas are further removed and out of sight. The common living and dining room areas are organized so that daylight enters from both sides, ensuring that both areas remain bright and full of natural light.

Data / Research: What innovative or unique data collection and / or research was applied during the planning and / or design process?

A small house design consultant was commissioned for the project to help set the theme and to ensure that the lessons learned from existing small houses for Jehovah's Witnesses in Great Britain were incorporated.

Collaboration: How did stakeholders, occupants, the design team, and / or others collaborate during the planning and / or design process?

A design charette was introduced early in the process, including the owner, board members, design consultant, architect, civil engineer, and contractors. They collectively agreed on the approach and design for the project. All parties came away with a greater understanding of the thought that went into the design and were able to buy in to the concept moving forward.

Green / Sustainable Features: What green / sustainable features had the greatest impact on the project's design?

Site design considerations, energy efficiency, and maximized daylighting.

What were the primary motivations for including green / sustainable design features in the project?

Support the mission / values of the client / provider, promote good public relations, and lower operational costs.

What challenges did the project face when trying to incorporate green / sustainable design features?

Perceived first-cost premium.

For a project with a residential component, what was critical to the success of the project?

Improving common spaces / amenities.

Households: What is innovative or unique about the households in the project?

The households in this project are set up as small homes: each household resides in its own small house that functions just as a private residence would. The space is divided into private, common, and behind-the-scenes service areas, while the resident rooms sit in a private area (mirroring that of a traditional house). The common area is a great room with a traditional family room, dining, and kitchen areas shared by the residents. The two 10-bed assisted living small houses are paired to share common service areas but the private and common spaces are still separated and operate as their own small homes, staying true to the small house concept. The 12-room assisted living memory care house is a single household.

Common Spaces: What senior-friendly common spaces are included in the project?

Bistro / casual dining; dedicated fitness equipment room; salon; dedicated conference / meeting space; resident-maintained gardening space; and a parlor that can function as a conference room, quiet room, TV room, or guest quarters.

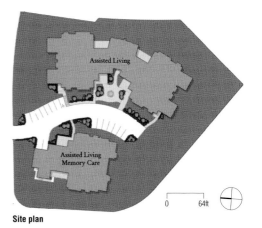

Site plan

Pair of 10-bed assisted living small houses

12-bed assisted living memory care small house

BAR Architects

Sun City Tower Kobe

Kobe, Kansai, Japan // Half Century More

Facility type: Independent Living; Long-term Skilled Nursing; CCRC or part of a CCRC
Target market: Upper
Site location: Urban; greyfield
Project site area (square feet): 135,000
Gross square footage of the new construction involved in the project: 508,000

Ratio of parking spaces to residents: 1 parking space for every 4 units
This site is within 1,000 feet of public transportation.
Provider type: For-profit

Below: Courtyard perspective
Opposite: Overall perspective

Renderings: BAR Architects

Overall Project Description

The design of this CCRC was intended to bring the high standards of design, care, and service for seniors to the Kansai region of Japan. Creating a large yet integrated urban community in this redevelopment district—that was rapidly transitioning from industrial to residential use—was of paramount importance. The commission provided a unique opportunity to design a landmark property for the client that emphasized community, care, and comfort. After being awarded the full commission, the integrated team of architects, interior designers, and landscape architects collaborated closely with the client to design an urban solution that fosters community, internally and externally. With the 35-story tower anchoring the northwest corner of the site, a complement of ground floor public spaces are used to surround and enclose a large, richly landscaped central courtyard providing controlled views and access from a residential promenade. Public amenities such as reception, an auditorium, and a tea lounge are placed on the south side of the site.

Project Goals

What were the major goals?

- Site planning: as a high-rise residential tower, the first goal was to distinguish the building from other residential and waterfront blocks in Kobe while maintaining a sense of community among residents. This is achieved by maximizing corner units and views, stepping back the primary south and north elevations, and lastly, by creating a signature glassy lantern at the top southwest corner. The lantern element houses larger premium units as well as intimate city-view and unobstructed water-view dining on the 34th floor, along with the sky-view lounge located on the 35th floor.

- Community: to create a rich diversity and identity of public amenities at lower levels. Placing the tower on the corner of the lot allows for a large courtyard that takes advantage of light, sun, and a more expansive central courtyard. Surrounding the courtyard is a public promenade that promotes interaction and offers a variety of amenities, including a lobby lounge, library, full fitness facility, pool and spa (ofuro), tea lounge, billiards, club, mahjong, karaoke, and a 500-seat auditorium / multipurpose room.

- To provide quality continuing care facilities which are integrated with the community. Skilled nursing functions are located on the second, third, and fourth floors at the east side of the central court, adjacent to the tower. Nursing care facilities can be accessed from ground floor public spaces or from the tower core. A private nursing care garden is accessible from public spaces on the second floor providing outdoor dining and rehabilitation.

- Integration into the surrounding community and sustainable transport. This is a high density project on a transit hub including two city bus lines. The provider offers hourly daytime shuttles to cultural and commercial areas and the nearby train station.

- Seamless integration of architectural design, landscape architecture, and interior design. These disciplines collaboratively designed the project to achieve this integration, as well as an indoor-outdoor garden feel, which is culturally significant to the targeted population. For example, the gardens in the center courtyard were closely integrated with the architecture so each associated internal room (auditorium, entry pavilion, library, and recreation areas) has its own unique outdoor space and garden view. In addition to coordinating the palette of materials and finishes, the team also extended the interior flooring to the outside patios to maximize the indoor-outdoor feel.

Challenges: What were the greatest design challenges?

The greatest challenge was maintaining a sense of community despite the inherently detached nature of a tower. Bringing the pool and bath facilities, which are an important community space, to the sixth floor and providing direct access from the tower with a glassy bridge creates a unique experience for residents. The dining and sky lounge spaces at the top of the tower are designed to be reached quickly and easily by residents to promote more social activity outside of their units. Similarly, the large and inviting ground floor public promenade, gardens, and circulation allows residents to reach a variety of spaces and increases their interaction with one another on a daily basis.

The strict building code (requiring wrap-around balconies) has a great impact on the towers designed in this area. Careful studies of massing, materials, and views resulted in a highly varied exterior with interlocking masses and strong verticality. Subtle changes in the material palette also help differentiate the massing of the tower.

Innovations: What innovations or unique features were incorporated into the design of the project?

The most unique feature of the project is the arrangement of the major architectural program elements and the development of a significant garden space in a high density urban context. Culturally, gardens of this nature are important to this user group. The tower is moved to the rear of the site to emphasize its residential nature; it stands away from the major public boulevard, has reduced-impact shadowing, and is positioned for the best access to public transportation. Public amenities such as reception, the auditorium, and tea lounge are placed on the south side of the site as the public face of the community, and also to allow a maximum amount of sunlight into the central courtyard. The care facilities are placed to the east overlooking the courtyard, with their back to the big-box retail next door.

Sun orientation and views are both extremely important in the marketing of independent living units. South and east residential units command a notable premium, as do corner units. Consequently floor plates are arranged with the larger units at the corner and to the south.

Resident incomes are in the upper 70 percent of the Japanese senior population. Because of the scale of the project and the target market (high net worth seniors), a large amount of common space is provided (15 percent of the gross building area). The perception of both the quantity and diversity of common space is particularly important. The first major experience is the entry pavilion. The entry into the lobby lounge is highlighted by tall windows, a garden view of the central courtyard, and a glimpse of the tower beyond.

Data / Research: What innovative or unique data collection and / or research was applied during the planning and / or design process?

The team worked closely with the local welfare office to size the nursing and health facilities appropriately for the neighborhood. Clients conducted current and post-occupancy reviews of their other facilities to refine the public space program.

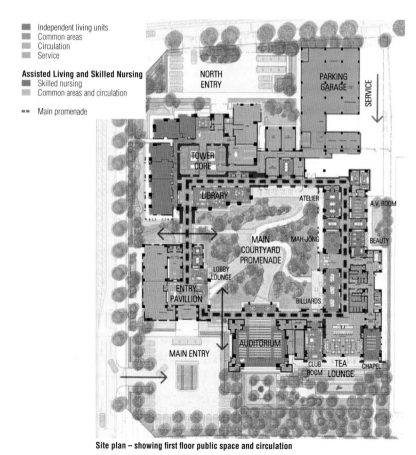

Site plan – showing first floor public space and circulation

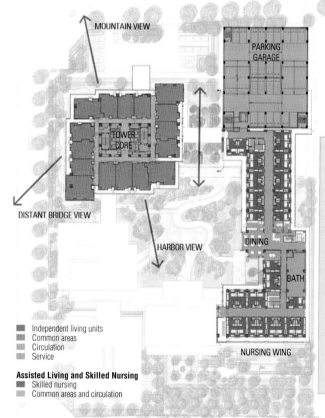

Third floor plan – showing nursing wing and typical tower plan

Collaboration: How did stakeholders, occupants, the design team, and / or others collaborate during the planning and / or design process?

There was a constant feedback loop from the facility managers in existing facilities about the residents' preferred activities, what was being used the most, what programs contributed to health and wellness, and general sizing of the various program elements. This allowed the team to constantly update the program throughout the design so that the project will have an efficient and enjoyable mix of features and amenities. Similar feedback has been provided regarding unit design.

Outreach: What off-site outreach services are offered to the greater community?

The pharmacy and clinic will be open to the greater community, as needed.

Green / Sustainable Features: What green / sustainable features had the greatest impact on the project's design?

Reduced solar gain / heat island–effect sunshades, planting, maximized daylighting, and rideshare, carpooling, Zipcars.

What were the primary motivations for including green / sustainable design features in the project?

Support the mission / values of the client / provider and the design team, and lower operational costs.

What challenges did the project face when trying to incorporate green / sustainable design features?

Actual first-cost premium.

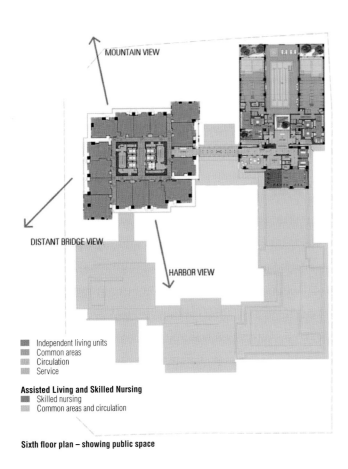

Independent living units
Common areas
Circulation
Service

Assisted Living and Skilled Nursing
Skilled nursing
Common areas and circulation

Sixth floor plan – showing public space

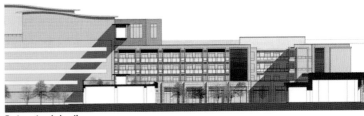

East courtyard elevation

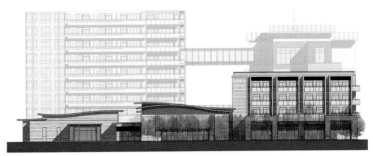

South elevation

For a project with a residential component, what was critical to the success of the project?

Improving common spaces / amenities.

Common Spaces: What senior-friendly common spaces are included in the project?

Formal dining, bistro / casual dining; marketplace / convenience store; swimming pool / aquatics facilities; dedicated fitness equipment room; dedicated exercise classroom; dedicated rehabilitation / therapy gym; massage / aromatherapy room; salon; large multipurpose room; small-scale cinema / media room; dedicated conference / meeting space; dedicated classroom / learning space; library / information resource center; art studio / craft room; and religious / spiritual / meditative space.

Opposite top: Sky lounge city salon
Opposite bottom: Lobby lounge
Left: Dining area overlooking water views
Below: Dining area overlooking city views

Renderings: BAMO

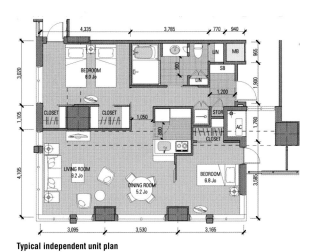

Typical independent unit plan

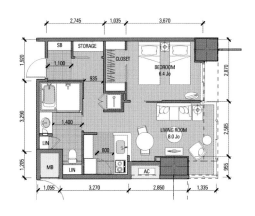

Typical independent unit plan

Typical independent unit plan

Brown Craig Turner

Worman's Mill Village Center

Frederick, Maryland // The Wormald Companies

Facility type: Independent Living; Assisted Living; Assisted Living—dementia / memory support
Target market: Middle / upper middle
Site location: Suburban; greenfield
Project site area (square feet): 485,000
Gross square footage of the new construction involved in the project: 288,000
Number of residents in a typical household: 11, 11, 14 (if approved)

Ratio of parking spaces to residents: 1.5:1 (counting 50 percent of 2-bedroom units with 2 residents)
This site is within 1,000 feet of public transportation, and within 1,000 feet of at least 10 basic services with pedestrian access to those services.
Provider type: For-profit

Below: Bird's-eye view looking south showing the town square with restaurant pavilion in the foreground. Interior public amenity spaces occupy the ground floor of the large civic buildings comprising the south side of the square, with intergenerational apartments above.
Opposite: View from within the town square looking west past the gazebo. Retail and dining venues on the left, and dining and retail with intergenerational apartments above on the right.

The senior-friendly housing is conceived as including the following:

Fully compliant with the Fair Housing Act (FHA) and fully accessible where units were to be designed to meet handicapped guidelines.

In the fully compliant FHA units, unit plans include, but are not limited to:

Amply sized living and sleeping areas; low-sheen, matte finish, slip-resistant floor surfacing, including low pile carpet; acoustical treatment of party walls and floors; lever hardware on all doors, faucets, and cabinets; wide doorways; senior-friendly HVAC controls and electric-device mounting heights; large, easily opened windows, with low sills and sunshading; senior-friendly toilet height; accessible shower, with assist bars and continuous trench drain; security access systems; accessible, stacked washer / dryers; side-by-side refrigerator / freezer; and, front control electric range.

Under consideration are:

Options and rough-in for a wall oven, slide-out cabinet shelves, and slide-out drawer dishwashers; and, rough-in for technology for medical, security, and other monitoring.

Project Goals

What were the major goals?

- The enduring planning and design goal of this complex of buildings is that it serve as the Village Center. When conceived well over 20 years ago, a retail center was envisioned. However, because two intersecting roads at this village center are essentially collector roads, not arteries, a large retail center became infeasible. With the emergence of the virtual CCRC concept, and its array of restaurants, retail, and services available to anyone in the community at large, the retail / commercial size of the Village Center was reduced, and housing was added and appropriately scaled to the retail in a walkable setting. To reinforce the critical mass (the correct number of units to its walkable setting) all remaining unbuilt density units were transferred to this site.

Overall Project Description

This is a virtual CCRC; it is also, in effect, a naturally encouraged retirement community. It is a collaboration between a for-profit developer and an architect who shared the same vision of the future of senior living.

Over two decades ago, the developer's father created a planned, walkable, non-senior housing community composed of single-family homes tightly clustered to preserve open space, town homes, and elevator condos. Originally, a recreational / activity clubhouse and a shopping center were planned to be built at the community's center, within a walkable distance. It was a precursor to what is now called a TND: traditional neighborhood development.

What is unique—especially for the time it was built—is that all homes are physically accessible, and all homes and town homes have ground floor master bedrooms and baths. Now, some 20 plus years later, the community is nearly completed and built out (however the retail center was never built). Many original residents have elected to stay and would like to remain in the community they have come to love.

With the developer now retired, his sons realized that many older life-long residents were moving to CCRCs. They held a community-wide meeting to discuss what they could do to offset this migration out of the neighborhood (despite the newer residents moving in). After surveying the entire neighborhood, they realized that most of what the residents sought in traditional CCRCs were senior-friendly housing, retail services, and amenities. When paired with assisted living and in-home services, these needs could be accomplished on the 11-acre village retail center that had never been constructed.

What transpired was the vision of a virtual CCRC: accessible, senior-targeted housing, with à la carte access to a range of retail services, amenities, and care, available right outside their doors. In fact, via technology, a form of "village network" could serve everyone in the surrounding 1,500 homes.

Challenges: What were the greatest design challenges?

The neighborhoods closest to the construction objected despite the well-meant, visionary direction. One neighborhood street was originally planned to be closed to permit a larger apartment building with ground floor in-building retail. After multiple formal and informal meetings, the plan to keep the street and building size was modified, yielding a signature restaurant on the Village Green with retail arranged on both sides of the street to emulate traditional town center developments.

Another example was the preference for multistory assisted living by the planning and zoning staff. At this point in the plan's evolution, the exact nature of the assisted living facilities is undetermined. Hence, the original assisted living concept remains illustrated.

Site plan

What challenges did the project face when trying to incorporate green / sustainable design features?

Perceived first-cost premium.

For a project with a residential component, what was critical to the success of the project?

Improving common spaces / amenities.

Households: What is innovative or unique about the households in the project?

The original plan included three households: two for memory care and one for assisted living. The two memory care households had a shared core for night shift staff efficiency. All shared the same secure garden. During the planning and zoning review process, the city officials favored a multistory building for traditional assisted living.

Common Spaces: What senior-friendly common spaces are included in the project?

Formal dining, bistro / casual dining; coffee shop / grab-and-go; marketplace / convenience store; dedicated fitness equipment room; dedicated exercise classroom; dedicated rehabilitation / therapy gym; massage / aromatherapy room; salon, large multipurpose room; dedicated conference / meeting space; dedicated classroom / learning space; and library / information resource center.

Innovations: What innovations or unique features were incorporated into the design of the project?

The buildings were intentionally arranged to respect an existing community square with a gazebo and landscaped open space. To reinforce the Village Center concept, the buildings were to be designed to resemble the texture, scale, style, and materials of the historic downtown of Frederick, Maryland.

Data / Research: What innovative or unique data collection and/or research was applied during the planning and / or design process?

The concept of this virtual CCRC was born of a community survey conducted by the developer, which resulted in about 72 potential uses for the Village Center. The majority of these paralleled that of a CCRC once assisted living and outreach care were added. These 72 potential uses, prioritized by frequency of request, were listed and discussed in community neighborhood meetings organized by neighborhood captains.

Collaboration: How did stakeholders, occupants, the design team, and / or others collaborate during the planning and / or design process?

The developer retained the majority vote to control overall community continuity but conducted multiple community input meetings to try to reach an understanding of community needs and garner support from a majority of neighbors. This planning process then became a completely public process, because a transfer of master-planned community-wide density had to be approved by the city's planning and zoning board—this was ultimately approved. In the process, the developer used mailers, emails, websites, and in-person meetings to increase the level of community / resident understanding.

Outreach: What off-site outreach services are offered to the greater community?

The concept is to ultimately offer outreach in-home services to residents of the entire community and beyond: some 5,000 households within less than one mile. Ultimately smart-house technology will be implemented if the client does not wish to move from their home.

Green / Sustainable Features: What green / sustainable features had the greatest impact on the project's design?

Site selection, site design considerations, and energy efficiency.

What were the primary motivations for including green / sustainable design features in the project?

Support the mission / values of the client / provider, make a contribution to the greater community, and promote good public relations.

Opposite: Street-level view looking northeast along the side of the town square. The brick building on the right houses another restaurant.
Top: View into the town square with the restaurant pavilion in the foreground and intergenerational apartments beyond.

Appendix

The 10-Year Award

For this cycle of *Design for Aging Review*, the AIA Design for Aging (DFA) Knowledge Community presents the 10-year award to Dr. William Thomas for his leadership in improving environments for the elderly. Dr. Thomas's beliefs and philosophy pioneered programs that were designed to improve the lives of elders and their care providers. His passion and vision made him a profound innovator and leader in the culture change movement, ultimately leading to household models that de-institutionalized environments for the elderly and transformed the nursing home industry.

Dr. Thomas founded the Eden Alternative, a philosophy and program of culture change the goal of which was to alleviate the "three plagues" of the elderly in traditional nursing homes—loneliness, helplessness, and boredom. The Eden Alternative called for fundamental changes in the relationship between the resident, frontline staff, and management, focusing care on the resident and giving them greater control over their daily lives. Dr. Thomas took the Eden Alternative one step further and created the Green House®, a proprietary model that has spurred the long-term care industry to change.

Throughout his work in bringing culture change to residents, Dr. Thomas recognized the importance of the built environment to the residents' quality of life, emphasizing a residential environment as a critical component of resident-centered care. He is credited with contributing to the creation of the household model nursing home, one in which residents have private rooms, access to the outdoors and natural light, and common spaces similar to one's home in a familial setting. The household model continues to be the cornerstone of new nursing home and assisted living environments.

To recognize Dr. Thomas for his passion, vision, and the significance of his work in improving the nursing home environment, the AIA DFA is pleased to award Dr. Thomas with the 10-year award.

Joyce K. Polhamus, AIA
2013 DFA Chair

Photography: Courtesy of THE GREEN HOUSE® Project

DFAR12 Insights and Innovations

by Emily Chmielewski, Perkins Eastman Research Collaborative

About the Design Competition and Insights Study

In the summer of 2013, the American Institute of Architect's Design for Aging Knowledge Community (DFA) conducted its 12th biennial Design for Aging Review design competition (DFAR12). In total, there were 64 submissions, 34 of which were recognized by the jury for an award or publication. Eleven projects received an award of merit; 7 projects were given a citation award; and 16 projects were recognized for publication within this book.

Projects submitted to DFAR12 and recognized by the jury include:

Merit award winners:
- Atria Valley View
- Brandman Centers for Senior Care
- Camphill Ghent
- Cosby Spear Highrise
- Marian's House
- The Mather
- Moorings Park
- Rockhill Mennonite Community
- The Summit at Central Park
- The Townhomes on Hendricks Place
- White Oak Cottages at Fox Hill Village

Citation award winners:
- Armed Forces Retirement Home
- Cohen Rosen House
- Creekside Homes at Givens Estates
- Good Shepherd Cottage, Santa Teresita, Inc.
- Mather More Than a Cafe
- Rose Villa Pocket Neighborhoods & Main Street
- Tohono O'odham Elder Home

Published:
- Asbury Place at Arbor Acres
- The Deupree House and Nursing Cottages
- The Friendship House at Royal Oaks
- Haven Hospice Custead Care Center
- Laclede Groves
- Legacy Place
- Mary Helen Rogers Senior Community
- Merritt Crossing
- Orchard Cove
- Rydal Park Repositioning
- Sharon Towers Dining Renovation
- St. Ignatius Nursing & Rehab Center
- Sun City Tower Kobe
- The Village at Orchard Ridge
- The Village at Rockville
- Worman's Mill Village Center

Categories for submission included: Built (with 46 submissions, 21 of which were recognized by the jury); Planning / Concept Design—formerly called Not Built (with 9 submissions, 7 of which were recognized by the jury); and Small Projects, for those with $3 million or less in total construction costs (with 9 submissions, 6 of which were recognized by the jury). Note that the Research / POE category included in previous DFAR cycles was eliminated this year due to low submission rates since its introduction.

Project Statistics

The following graphs are derived from all 64 projects submitted to DFAR12, with comparisons to 3 previous design competition cycles (DFAR9, 10, and 11) where possible.

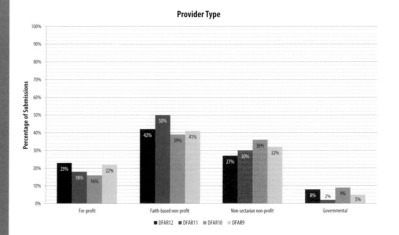

Provider Type

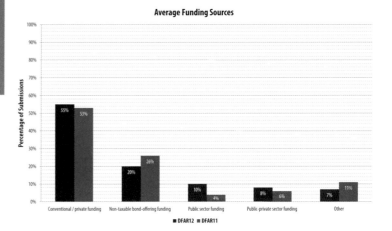

Average Funding Sources

Target Market

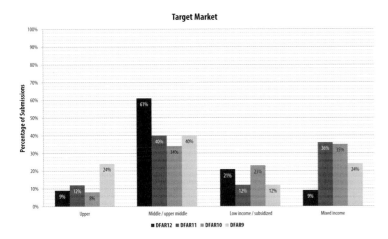

Site Location

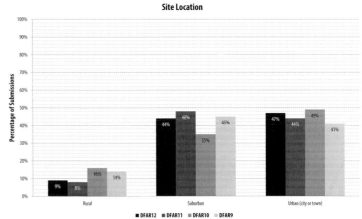

Median Site Area, by Site Location

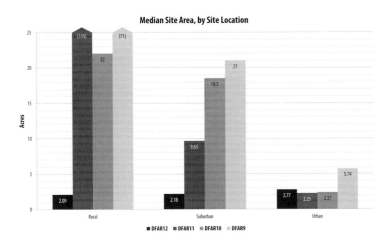

Average Number of Parking Spaces Per Resident, by Site Location

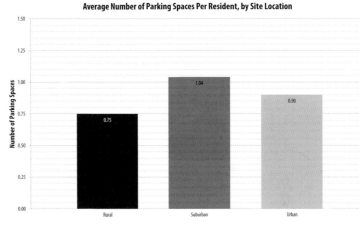

CCRC / Part of a CCRC

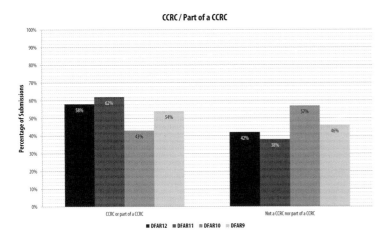

Facility Types

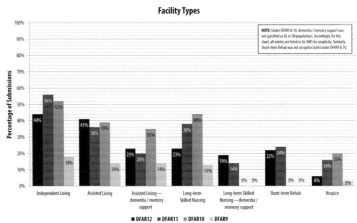

Projects by Construction Type

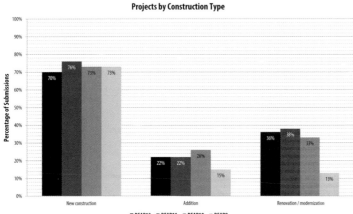

Project Costs

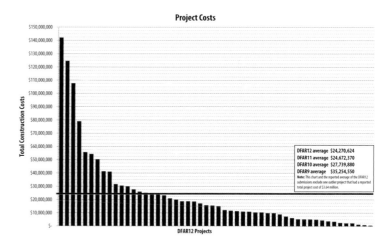

DFAR12 average $24,270,624
DFAR11 average $24,672,370
DFAR10 average $27,739,880
DFAR9 average $35,254,550

Note: This chart and the reported average of the DFAR12 submissions exclude one outlier project that had a reported total project cost of $3.64 million.

Project Size, by Construction Type

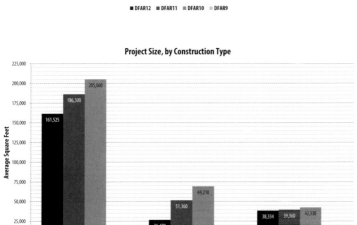

Median Cost Per Gross Square Foot, by Facility Type and Site Location

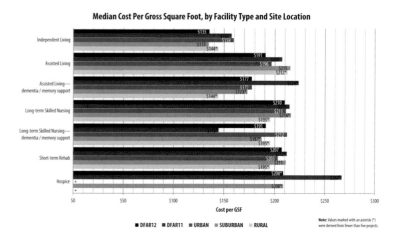

Note: Values marked with an asterisk (*) were derived from fewer than five projects.

Purpose of the Renovation

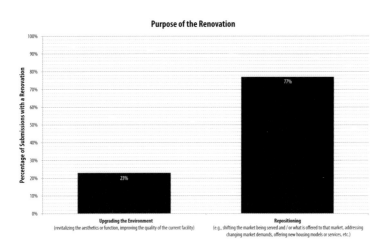

Residential to Common Space Ratios, by Facility Type

Facility Type	Residential to Commons Ratio (based on average net square footages)	
	DFAR12	DFAR11
Independent Living	2.78 : 1	2.71 : 1
Assisted Living	1.41 : 1	1.65 : 1
Assisted Living—dementia / memory support	1.26 : 1	1.26 : 1
Long-term Skilled Nursing	0.95 : 1	0.93 : 1
Long-term Skilled Nursing—dementia / memory support	1.26 : 1	0.69 : 1
Short-term Rehab	0.74 : 1	0.67 : 1
Hospice	0.60 : 1*	1.30 : 1

*Note: Data from only two Hospice projects were available for this calculation

Residential Unit Space Breakdowns, by Facility Type

UNIT TYPE	DFAR12 UNIT DISTRIBUTION	DFAR12 AVERAGE UNIT SIZE	DFAR11 UNIT DISTRIBUTION	DFAR11 AVERAGE UNIT SIZE	DFAR10 UNIT DISTRIBUTION	DFAR10 AVERAGE UNIT SIZE	DFAR9 UNIT DISTRIBUTION	DFAR9 AVERAGE UNIT SIZE
Independent Living								
Studio	22%	441 NSF	4%	400 NSF	20%	658* NSF	5%	508* NSF
One bedroom	34%	645 NSF	41%	629 NSF	28%	769 NSF	45%	844 NSF
One bedroom plus den	13%	838 NSF	8%	983 NSF	0%	---	0%	---
Two bedroom	19%	1,192 NSF	30%	1,069 NSF	36%	1,183 NSF	37%	1,184 NSF
Two bedroom plus den	12%	1,629 NSF	15%	1,791 NSF	13%	1,515 NSF	13%	1,465 NSF
Three bedroom+	0.3%	2,640* NSF	2%	1,929 NSF	4%	1,682* NSF	1%	2,259 NSF
Assisted Living								
Studio	50%	394 NSF	48%	354 NSF	11%	385* NSF	20%	358 NSF
One bedroom	28%	528 NSF	38%	594 NSF	49%	589 NSF	63%	581 NSF
One bedroom plus den	18%	650* NSF	0%	---	0%	---	0%	---
Two bedroom	4%	682 NSF	14%	828 NSF	30%	1,178 NSF	17%	877 NSF
Two bedroom plus den	0%	---	0%	---	0%	---	0.3%	1,464* NSF
Three bedroom+	0%	---	0%	---	10%	N/A	0%	---
Assisted Living—dementia / memory support								
Private room	87%	445 NSF	84%	348 NSF	80%	316 NSF	80%	351 NSF
Semi-private room	5%	497* NSF	8%	591* NSF	20%	451 NSF	20%	795* NSF
Shared room	8%	348* NSF	9%	400* NSF	0%	---	0%	---
Long-term Skilled Nursing								
Private room	92%	264 NSF	91%	274 NSF	78%	297 NSF	97%	293 NSF
Semi-private room	8%	428 NSF	8%	327 NSF	22%	369 NSF	3%	423* NSF
Shared room	0.3%	274* NSF	1%	506* NSF	0%	---	0%	---
Long-term Skilled Nursing—dementia / memory support								
Private room	83%	299 NSF	100%	285 NSF	N/A	N/A	N/A	N/A
Semi-private room	16%	396* NSF	0%	---	N/A	N/A	N/A	N/A
Shared room	1%	339* NSF	0%	---	N/A	N/A	N/A	N/A
Short-term Rehab								
Private room	85%	269 NSF	88%	249 NSF	N/A	N/A	N/A	N/A
Semi-private room	13%	455* NSF	12%	474* NSF	N/A	N/A	N/A	N/A
Shared room	2%	413* NSF	0%	---	N/A	N/A	N/A	N/A
Hospice								
Private room	51%	384* NSF	100%	311 NSF	N/A	N/A	N/A	N/A
Semi-private room	49%	475* NSF	0%	---	N/A	N/A	N/A	N/A
Shared room	0%	---	0%	---	N/A	N/A	N/A	N/A

Notes:
- Values marked with an asterisk (*) were derived from fewer than five projects.
- "Private room" consists of a single occupant.
- "Semi-private room" consists of two occupants with separate bed areas but a shared bathroom.
- "Shared room" consists of two occupants with a shared bed area and a shared bathroom.
- Under DFARs 9&10, Skilled Nursing was not distinguished between semi-private and shared rooms. Accordingly, for this chart, all entries have been listed under semi-private.
- Under DFARs 9&10, dementia / memory support was not distinguished between Assisted Living and Long-Term Skilled Nursing. Accordingly, for this chart, all entries have been listed under Assisted Living—dementia / memory support.

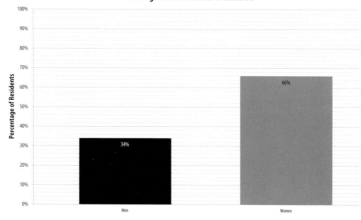

Average Resident Gender Breakdown

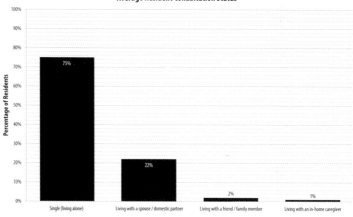

Average Resident Cohabitation Status

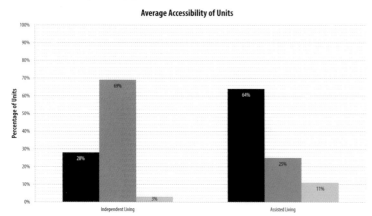

Average Accessibility of Units

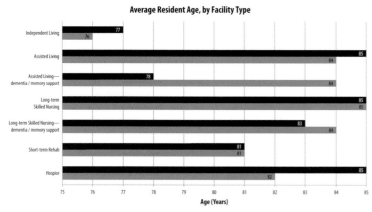

Average Resident Age, by Facility Type

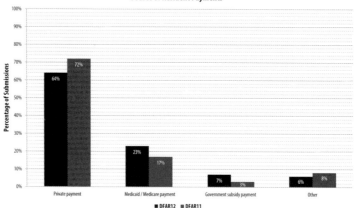

Source of Resident Payments

Project Themes

Though the 34 DFAR12 projects recognized by the jury are quite diverse, several common and often interrelated project themes were identified based on the similarities among the submissions' building components, project descriptions, and goals. The following describe the jury-recognized DFAR12 projects' common themes.

The common themes described by the jury-recognized DFAR12 projects include:

- Ecological sustainability (97% of the projects recognized by the jury)
- Using research in the design process (79%)
- Collaborative designing (76%)
- Connection to nature (65%)
- Contemporary (56%) vs. traditional (44%) interior aesthetics
- Household model and person-centered care (50%)
- Extensive amenities (41%)
- Connecting to the greater community (29%)
- Promoting a sense of community (26%)
- Fitting the local context (26%)
- Flexibility (24%)
- Holistic wellness (15%)

Ecological Sustainability

Ninety-seven percent of the jury-recognized DFAR12 projects (and 91% of all submissions) report having green / sustainable features. However, only 8 of the jury-recognized DFAR12 projects (24%) actually discussed ecological sustainability within their project description text.

DFAR12 projects recognized by the jury that specifically described how their submission is ecologically sustainable include:

- Armed Forces Retirement Home
- Atria Valley View
- Cohen Rosen House
- The Deupree House and Nursing Cottages
- Good Shepherd Cottage, Santa Teresita, Inc.
- The Mather
- Merritt Crossing
- The Summit at Central Park

Thirty-eight percent of the jury-recognized DFAR12 projects (and 33% of all submissions) are, or are registered to be, certified as ecologically sustainable by an independent organization (e.g., LEED). This percentage of projects is slightly higher than the previous cycle, where 32% of all DFAR11 projects

were green certified. However, these rates are up from DFAR10's 19% of submissions. Of the certified jury-recognized DFAR12 projects, 12 out of 13 pursued LEED ratings. One project pursued the "Design to Earn the ENERGY STAR" (DEES) program.

The green features with the greatest impact on the jury-recognized DFAR12 projects' designs include: maximized daylighting (64% of the green DFAR12 projects recognized by the jury); energy efficiency (61%); and site design considerations (42%)—the same top 3 influencers as for DFAR11.

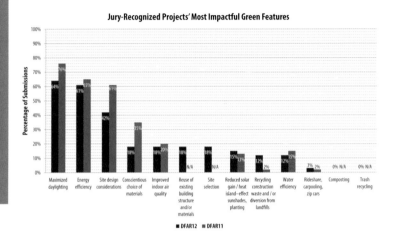

In addition, for the jury-recognized DFAR12 submissions, 26% are built on greenfield sites (no previous development other than agricultural or natural landscape); 18% are on greyfields (an underused real estate asset or land, such as an outdated / failing retail and commercial strip mall); and 9% are on brownfields (land previously used for industrial or commercial use, often requiring remediation of hazardous waste or pollution).

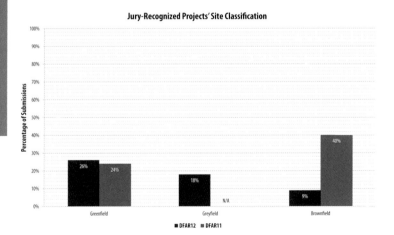

When asked about the primary motivation for including ecologically sustainable features, responses were similar to those from DFAR11. Supporting the mission / values of the client / provider was the most popular response among all jury-recognized DFAR12 submissions. Other common responses included: lowering operational costs, making a contribution to the greater community, and supporting the mission / values of the design team.

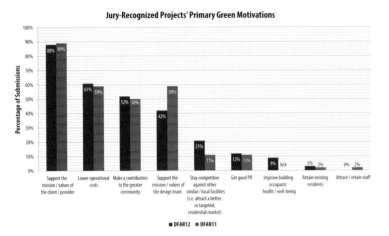

Jury-Recognized Projects' Primary Green Motivations

The DFAR12 submission form also asked about the challenges faced by the projects when the design team attempted to incorporate green features. Seventy percent of the green jury-recognized DFAR12 projects reported that they had difficulties. Perceived first-cost premiums were the greatest deterrent, followed by actual costs—a reversal from DFAR11, where actual costs had a greater impact than perceived costs.

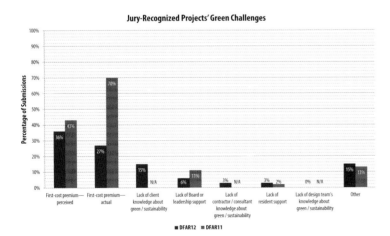

Jury-Recognized Projects' Green Challenges

In Their Own Words

Cohen Rosen House

"To achieve LEED Silver certification, many parts and pieces of the home, from concept to construction to operation, come together. Innovations in design (green roofs) and thoughtful follow through during construction (recycling materials) are just as integral as the staff's cleaning and maintenance methods (low VOC products). This commitment to sustainability further paints the picture of a priceless whole in view of its parts."

From green roofs to clerestory windows for extensive natural light indoors, the LEED Silver Certified Cohen Rosen House incorporates many green design features. Photography: Alain Jaramillo

Using Research in the Design Process

Based on past submissions and the growing practice of evidence-based design, DFA decided that for this cycle of the design competition, applicants should be asked specifically about how their projects use research. We found that 79% of the jury-recognized DFAR12 submissions reported using some form of research during the design process.

Of those that conducted research (formally or informally) during the design process: 89% incorporated building occupant feedback, from existing and / or prospective users; 22% created 3D views or computer models to better explore the proposed design; 22% made observations of existing spaces to understand operational issues and / or building users' needs, desires, and expectations; 19% made use of existing data (i.e., post-occupancy evaluation findings or benchmark data); 7% built full-scale mock-ups so that design details and actual layout could be assessed prior to construction; 4% performed sun-angle computer modeling to better understand how daylight could permeate the building; and 4% piloted a built environment by building a case study setting and allowing it to function, while recording associated outcomes to inform the final design and replication of the setting.

DFAR12 projects recognized by the jury that described using research in the design process include:

- Armed Forces Retirement Home
- Asbury Place at Arbor Acres
- Brandman Centers for Senior Care
- Cohen Rosen House
- Cosby Spear Highrise
- Creekside Homes at Givens Estates
- The Deupree House and Nursing Cottages
- The Friendship House at Royal Oaks
- Good Shepherd Cottage, Santa Teresita, Inc.
- Laclede Groves
- Legacy Place
- Marian's House
- Mary Helen Rogers Senior Community
- The Mather
- Mather More Than a Cafe
- Moorings Park
- Orchard Cove
- Rockhill Mennonite Community
- Rose Villa Pocket Neighborhoods & Main Street
- Rydal Park Repositioning
- Sharon Towers Dining Renovation
- St. Ignatius Nursing & Rehab Center
- Sun City Tower Kobe
- Tohono O'odham Elder Home
- The Townhomes on Hendricks Place
- The Village at Rockville
- Worman's Mill Village Center

In Their Own Words

Creekside Homes at Givens Estates

"We hosted a series of face-to-face and web-based meetings with prospective residents to introduce the concept and solicit reactions… [In addition, to] allay the owner's concern about the height of the homes, the architect provided photorealistic computer generated renderings of the homes nestled in the existing trees and terrain."

To help the owner of Creekside Homes at Givens Estates understand the scale of the proposed design, the architect provided a rendered image of the project well before anything was built.

Marian's House

"The designers applied 25 years of experience designing special care environments with a recently completed post-occupancy evaluation of 5 buildings built over a 20 year period. [The study] confirmed many powerful findings about the role of outdoor space, the central image of the kitchen, and the importance of sightlines for unobtrusive surveillance of the environment. Just as powerful was seeing how innovative concepts from 20 years ago were either still relevant or [how the] spaces were adapted to new needs as programs evolved."

The Mather

"The entire development of The Mather is a result of market surveys, lifestyle surveys, [and] discussions with existing residents and future prospects to understand their wants and desires for a new community."

Moorings Park

"A digital virtual tour was created in great detail during the design process, not after, to further vet the design and provide the design team, stakeholders, residents, and operational management a clear picture of the space qualities … [The] clinic exam room was mocked-up full scale and then revised upon user input from physician and nurses."

Rose Villa Pocket Neighborhoods & Main Street

"The design team conducted 5 separate focus groups comprised of senior management, staff members, independent living residents, adult children of residents, and family members. Each group responded to a series of open-ended questions regarding existing facilities and programs, as well as potential areas of improvement."

St. Ignatius Nursing & Rehab Center

"Early in the design process, the client researched the decentralization of dining and providing choice for meal options. A small dining room was set up as a study. After a period of time the staff found that residents' health had dramatically improved with significant weight gain with a number of residents able to be taken off of their feeding tubes. This was the encouragement the facility needed to pursue the project with the ultimate goal of decentralizing dining and offering choice throughout the facility."

Collaborative Designing

More than ever, working with collaborators (i.e., those outside of the traditional architectural design team) has become a popular and effective way to improve project outcomes. In fact, 76% of the jury-recognized DFAR12 submissions reported collaborating during the design process (compared to 25% of DFAR11 projects).

Of those projects that used a collaborative process, 92% incorporated feedback from existing and / or prospective building occupants. Forty-two percent worked with the client / owner's senior management team during the design process. Nineteen percent tapped into the expertise of another organization, such as the Marian's House team working with the Alzheimer's Association to expand the offerings of their community-wide resource center, or the Legacy Place team who commissioned a consultant to learn from a similar project in Great Britain that was also designed for a population of Jehovah's Witnesses.

DFAR12 projects recognized by the jury that described a collaborative design process include:

- Armed Forces Retirement Home
- Asbury Place at Arbor Acres
- Brandman Centers for Senior Care
- Camphill Ghent
- Cosby Spear Highrise
- Creekside Homes at Givens Estates
- The Deupree House and Nursing Cottages
- The Friendship House at Royal Oaks
- Good Shepherd Cottage, Santa Teresita, Inc.
- Laclede Groves
- Legacy Place
- Marian's House
- Mary Helen Rogers Senior Community
- The Mather
- Mather More Than a Cafe
- Moorings Park
- Orchard Cove
- Rockhill Mennonite Community
- Rose Villa Pocket Neighborhoods & Main Street
- Rydal Park Repositioning
- St. Ignatius Nursing & Rehab Center
- Sun City Tower Kobe
- Tohono O'odham Elder Home
- The Townhomes on Hendricks Place
- The Village at Rockville
- Worman's Mill Village Center

Asbury Place at Arbor Acres

The project used "an inclusive process that also involved all the vested stakeholders: residents, operations, senior management, activities, physical therapy, nursing, Board of Directors, finance, social workers, marketing, physical plant, housekeeping, and dining services."

The Deupree House and Nursing Cottages

"The project team had the added benefit of a Culture Change Planner, who directed the provider to visit communities where culture change models had been incorporated into the campus."

Laclede Groves

"The project commenced with [a] strategic planning workshop that was structured to help the client determine strategic ways to develop new opportunities and to create, reposition, and reinvent existing services and environments for seniors. Meetings engaged executive teams, board members, and key staff in a process that integrates forward-thinking design, thoughtful economic analysis, and thorough market assessment to create sustainable strategies."

Rydal Park Repositioning

Designing was an "interactive team process involving all stakeholders including administration, architect, development consultant, staff, selected residents, resident committees, and zoning and code officials."

Orchard Cove

"Specifically focused resident committees were formulated by the Orchard Cove administration with the sole purpose of getting [the] participation of respected individuals who had been acknowledged as fair and well informed people, best suited to represent the community in their respective areas of expertise. The committees included: library, dining, acoustics, fitness / wellness, interior design, and artwork. This process resulted in capitalizing upon the excellent ideas and insights that the existing residents already had and allowed us to gain their trust soon after the first phase was completed. By working closely with the various resident committees, the majority of the residents felt that they had been listened to, and the final preferred solution was often close to [being] unanimously embraced."

Incorporating feedback from building occupants, like these residents of Orchard Cove, adds to a collaborative design process—this has become a popular and effective way to improve project outcomes. Photography: DiMella Shaffer

Insights and Innovations

While exploring the ways in which the designers worked with stakeholders, we started to see a trend: Seven projects (21% of the DFAR12 projects recognized by the jury) discussed using a charrette during the design process. The submissions that described using a charrette include: Armed Forces Retirement Home, Asbury Place at Arbor Acres, The Deupree House and Nursing Cottages, Laclede Groves, Legacy Place, Rockhill Mennonite Community, and Rose Villa Pocket Neighborhoods & Main Street.

Charrettes are not an innovative technique per se but the prevalence of these sessions and the effectiveness described by the submissions indicate that charrettes are being used as a powerful tool to improve project outcomes and gain stakeholder buy-in. In addition to the traditional architectural design team, charrette participants included: the client / owner / developer, board members, executives / administrative staff, marketing staff, care team and operational staff, design consultants, civil engineers and contractors, residents (existing and prospective), and / or residents' families.

The submissions described charrettes that allowed the participants to "create a shared vision, understand needs, desires, and trade-offs, and effectively build group consensus" (Laclede Groves). Sessions were held so that participants could "collectively agree on the approach and design for the project" (Legacy Place), and to "clearly define relevant design and development issues, structure alternative solutions, and [create] a graphic presentation of preliminary project designs" (Rose Villa Pocket Neighborhoods & Main Street). The charrettes provided "a forum in which all voices could be heard and future options considered within the context of financial capacity and land development constraints" (Asbury Place at Arbor Acres). The charrette conducted for the Armed Forces Retirement Home project even included the construction of full-scale mock-ups for people to respond to.

Several projects described using a charrette (like the one for Laclede Groves pictured here) during the design process to improve project outcomes and gain stakeholder buy-in. Photography: Daniel Cinelli / Perkins Eastman

Connection to Nature

Sixty-five percent of the jury-recognized DFAR12 projects described a connection to nature. This was similar to DFAR11, both in the percentage of projects (at 67% for DFAR11) as well as the types of natural amenities described. For DFAR12, projects noted views to parklands, oceans, gardens, and orchards. Buildings were planned around natural site features, like wetlands and mature trees. Submissions described providing access to shared gardens as well as private outdoor spaces (i.e., residential unit patios / balconies). Projects include walking paths, raised planter beds, and rooftop gardens. Some submissions even described their use of natural materials, colors, and textures.

Many projects also noted their indoor / outdoor connections, and al fresco dining and social / event spaces. One project, Tohono O'odham Elder Home, even offers outdoor cooking spaces to accommodate the cultural background of its residents, who spent their lives cooking outdoors and wished to continue doing so. Many projects include abundant natural light, both in common spaces and within residential units. Two projects (Cohen Rosen House and Legacy Place) specifically noted the inclusion of daylight to regulate circadian rhythms and minimize the effects of sundowning in their buildings' dementia populations.

DFAR12 projects recognized by the jury that described the theme of connecting to nature include:

- Armed Forces Retirement Home
- Atria Valley View
- Camphill Ghent
- Cohen Rosen House
- The Deupree House and Nursing Cottages
- The Friendship House at Royal Oaks
- Good Shepherd Cottage, Santa Teresita, Inc.
- Haven Hospice Custead Care Center
- Legacy Place
- Marian's House
- Mary Helen Rogers Senior Community
- The Mather
- Merritt Crossing
- Moorings Park
- Rockhill Mennonite Community
- Rose Villa Pocket Neighborhoods & Main Street
- The Summit at Central Park
- Sun City Tower Kobe
- Tohono O'odham Elder Home
- The Village at Orchard Ridge
- White Oak Cottages at Fox Hill Village
- Worman's Mill Village Center

Armed Forces Retirement Home

The project offers "a view of the ocean from every apartment and a balcony that is canted toward the ocean. The balcony is large enough to have a couple of chairs and a small table for eating or socializing."

Atria Valley View

"The building concept incorporates the use of natural materials and introduces details rich with earth-tone colors and textures."

Atria Valley View connects with nature by providing views and access to the outdoors, and through the use of natural materials, colors, and textures.

The Friendship House at Royal Oaks

"Outdoor garden courtyards with an emphasis on visibility promote 'fun' therapy. In lieu of going to a therapy room, residents are encouraged to take a walk in the garden which incorporates specific therapy elements such as changes in surface materials, steps, and other associated activities as deemed necessary for each resident along their walk through the garden."

The Village at Orchard Ridge

"The master plan capitalizes on orchards bordering the community not only by taking advantage of appealing long-range views, but also incorporating an apple tree grove into the Village Green … [The project also] responds to the challenging site by maintaining acres of existing wetlands and wooded area as a campus amenity."

Good Shepherd Cottage, Santa Teresita, Inc.

"The building provides a vibrant and engaging lifestyle by focusing on direct access to social areas that have abundant natural light and multiple connections to the outdoors … The patios and outdoor gardens on the first floor become places for residents to interact. The second floor has accessible common decks with view of the San Gabriel Mountains."

At Good Shepherd Cottage, Santa Teresita, Inc., rooms have indoor-outdoor connections—residents have access to the outdoors on both the ground floor and upper levels, with views to the surrounding landscape.

The Mather

"A rare commodity in an urban setting is the availability of a welcoming garden or outdoor terrace. A truly unique feature of The Mather is the availability of outdoor dining terraces, walking paths in an informal multi-faceted garden with climbing roses, quiet sitting enclaves, and resident planting beds."

Even projects in urban locations can offer outdoor connections, like The Mather's rooftop patio and gardens.

White Oak Cottages at Fox Hill Village

"Natural light is always important in any residential project, but takes on a higher level of importance for those with dementia and Alzheimer's, and is often a struggle on projects employing the Green House® and small house models because of the relatively high ratio of resident rooms to commons. It can be difficult to get multiple exposures in the commons spaces, limiting the quality of natural light in those spaces. In this project, the building was articulated in such a way as to allow large exposures into the main common spaces, and additional skylights were used in those other public or semi-public spaces that otherwise lack access to more conventional sources of natural light."

White Oak Cottages at Fox Hill Village allows daylight to permeate via large windows, bay windows, clerestory windows, skylights, and the careful articulation of the exterior wall.

Contemporary vs. Traditional Interior Aesthetics: What "Home" Looks Like Today

It is now just as common to find a senior living community with a contemporary interior aesthetic, as opposed to a traditional setting, which was the standard not too long ago. Fifty-six percent of the jury-recognized DFAR12 projects were classified as having a contemporary interior aesthetic; 44% had a traditional interior aesthetic. This is slightly different than the jury-recognized DFAR11 submissions, which had slightly more traditional projects (52%) than contemporary (48%).

A contemporary interior aesthetic may be recognized by such features as clean lines, geometric patterns, and minimal details. A traditional interior aesthetic, on the other hand, is more likely to include crown and base molding, rolled arm furniture, pleated curtains, and more ornate details and patterns.

Interestingly, for both DFAR11 and 12, we saw that the aesthetic style tended to vary based on the facility type. Projects aimed at a younger market (i.e., Independent Living residential buildings and community centers / common spaces) were typically designed with a contemporary interior aesthetic. Assisted Living, Skilled Nursing, and Hospice projects, on the other hand, more often had a traditional style. In fact, for the jury-recognized DFAR12 projects, IL / Commons projects had a ratio of 7:3 contemporary to traditional, whereas AL / SN / Hospice projects had an inverse ratio of 3:7.

Not only is the market responding to contemporary interior aesthetics, but these settings are now considered to be as "home-like" as traditional-style projects. In fact, 5 of the jury-recognized DFAR12 projects actually noted in their project descriptions that their submission has a homey feel alongside a contemporary aesthetic (Marian's House, Cohen Rosen House, Legacy Place, Brandman Centers for Senior Care, and The Friendship House at Royal Oaks). It is clear that no matter what a person's personal aesthetic preference is, there are high-quality senior living environments from which to choose.

Laclede Groves

Brandman Centers for Senior Care

DFAR12 projects recognized by the jury that were categorized as having a contemporary interior aesthetic include:

- Brandman Centers for Senior Care
- Camphill Ghent
- Cohen Rosen House
- Cosby Spear Highrise
- The Friendship House at Royal Oaks
- Laclede Groves
- Legacy Place
- Marian's House
- Mather More Than a Cafe
- Mary Helen Rogers Senior Community
- Merritt Crossing
- Moorings Park
- Orchard Cove
- Rockhill Mennonite Community
- Rose Villa Pocket Neighborhoods & Main Street
- Sharon Towers Dining Renovation
- The Summit at Central Park
- Sun City Tower Kobe
- Tohono O'odham Elder Home

Cosby Spear Highrise

Cohen Rosen House

Merritt Crossing

Marian's House

Sun City Tower Kobe

DFAR12 projects recognized by the jury that were categorized as having a traditional interior aesthetic include:

- Armed Forces Retirement Home
- Asbury Place at Arbor Acres
- Atria Valley View
- Creekside Homes at Givens Estates
- The Deupree House and Nursing Cottages
- Good Shepherd Cottage, Santa Teresita, Inc.
- Haven Hospice Custead Care Center
- The Mather
- Rydal Park Repositioning
- St. Ignatius Nursing & Rehab Center
- The Townhomes on Hendricks Place
- The Village at Orchard Ridge
- The Village at Rockville
- White Oak Cottages at Fox Hill Village
- Worman's Mill Village Center

Atria Valley View

The Townhomes on Hendricks Place

The Deupree House and Nursing Cottages

Good Shepherd Cottage, Santa Teresita, Inc.

The Village at Orchard Ridge

Haven Hospice Custead Care Center

St. Ignatius Nursing & Rehab Center

The Mather

The Village at Rockville

Household Model and Person-Centered Care

Because building occupants' mental, social, emotional, and physical wellbeing—and, therefore, quality of life—are affected by operational and design decisions, it is important to provide person-centered care and create physical environments that empower people.[1] Fifty percent of the jury-recognized DFAR12 submissions described a physical environment that supports person-centered care and / or includes a Household in the project. However, only 12 of the jury-recognized DFAR12 projects (35%) actually discussed person-centered care and / or Households within their project description text (comparable to 33% of the jury-recognized DFAR11 projects).

"Person-centered care promotes choice, purpose, and meaning in daily life. Person-centered care means that nursing home residents are supported in achieving the level of physical, mental, and psychosocial well-being that is individually practicable. This goal honors the importance of keeping the individual at the center of the care planning and decision-making process."[2]

DFAR12 projects recognized by the jury that specifically described person-centered care and / or Households include:

- Armed Forces Retirement Home
- Camphill Ghent
- Cohen Rosen House
- The Deupree House and Nursing Cottages
- The Friendship House at Royal Oaks
- Good Shepherd Cottage, Santa Teresita, Inc.
- Haven Hospice Custead Care Center
- Legacy Place
- Rockhill Mennonite Community
- Tohono O'odham Elder Home
- The Village at Orchard Ridge
- White Oak Cottages at Fox Hill Village

Based on plan analysis, 11 of the jury-recognized DFAR12 submissions include a Household, typically defined as 8–12 private residential bedrooms organized around a shared living / dining / kitchen area. Five additional projects were classified as "Neighborhoods," where 2–3 groups of eight to 8–12 private residential bedrooms are organized around a shared living / dining / kitchen area. (One project that indicated they had a Household did not submit a floor plan so, therefore, could not be analyzed.)

In terms of the size of the Households, we found that the average* was 8,693 square feet. The range* was 6,780–11,080 square feet. Regarding the number of residents per Household, we found an average* of 11 people, with a range* of 9–14 residents. The overall average* square footage per resident was 763, with a range* of 484–996 square feet per person. As would be expected, we saw in the larger Households that there typically was a smaller square footage per resident—that Household size does not stay relative (i.e., the building did not necessarily have a larger square footage per resident when there was a greater number of residents).

*Excluding outliers

Legacy Place

"These small houses are designed to reflect the look, feel and scale of a traditional residential home … This was accomplished by creating small houses and locating the community in an already established residential neighborhood."

Legacy Place reflects the feel and scale of a traditional residential home and is located within an existing neighborhood.

Rockhill Mennonite Community

"A small house design for 10 residents in each Household encourages socialization and family living while promoting independence. The [project includes] small Households with gracious living units and an emphasis on community and socialization instead of traditional apartment living with services."

Households like this one at the Rockhill Mennonite Community typically offer 8–12 private residential bedrooms organized around a shared living / dining / kitchen area.

Insights and Innovations

The typical Household floor plan offers short walking distances, opportunities to participate in the day-to-day life of the home (e.g., cooking, folding laundry, etc.), and family-like social interactions. One industry complaint that is sometimes heard, however, is that even though Households are made up of the standard house "kit-of-parts" (i.e., the spaces found in most Western-style homes), their arrangement does not support the traditional public-to-private hierarchies expected in our culture. For instance, in most American homes, bedrooms are not located off of a living room—they are instead clustered with other private spaces, accessed by semi-private hallways. Yet this is often not the case in Household design, where it is not unusual to find a bedroom opening to the living or dining room.

However, this may be beginning to change, as seen in the Households included in the jury-recognized DFAR12 projects: The Deupree House and Nursing Cottages, Legacy Place, Rydal Park Repositioning, and White Oak Cottages at Fox Hill Village. All 4 of these projects arranged their Household floor plan so that "the private areas, such as the bedrooms and spa, [are] separated from [the] more public spaces of hearth room, dining, and kitchen areas" (The Deupree House and Nursing Cottages).

Legacy Place notes that its Household is "consistent with a traditional home where you enter into the more public living and dining area, then move through the more private bedroom area." The Rydal Park Repositioning project is "similar to a well designed home [in that] there is a public to private gradient consisting of an entry 'threshold' adjacent to more public areas such as kitchen, dining and living rooms, proceeding to private bedroom areas." White Oak Cottages at Fox Hill Village similarly aimed to provide a layout that "is more like the arrangement you would find in a typical house, where bedrooms rarely are accessed directly off of the main living spaces."

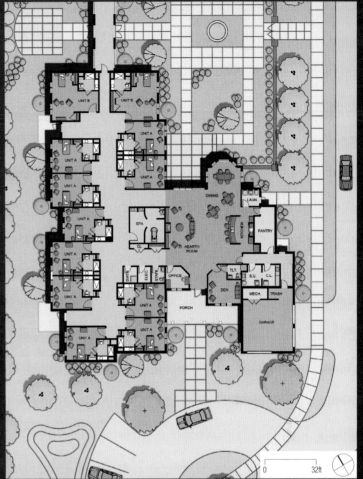

Several DFAR12 projects, like The Deupree House and Nursing Cottages, are reworking the layout of the Household for a better hierarchy of public-to-private spaces. Bedrooms no longer open into common areas, like living or dining rooms.

Extensive Amenities

Forty-one percent of the DFAR12 projects recognized by the jury discussed the extensive amenities offered on-site (comparable to the 38% of jury-recognized DFAR11 projects). Furthermore, when the projects with residential components were asked what was more critical to the success of the project—improving common spaces / amenities or improving units / private spaces—63% stated that the common spaces were more important (again comparable to DFAR11's 59%).

DFAR12 projects recognized by the jury that described extensive amenities include:

- Armed Forces Retirement Home
- Asbury Place at Arbor Acres
- Atria Valley View
- The Deupree House and Nursing Cottages
- Laclede Groves
- The Mather
- Moorings Park
- Orchard Cove
- Rydal Park Repositioning
- Sharon Towers Dining Renovation
- The Summit at Central Park
- Sun City Tower Kobe
- The Village at Orchard Ridge
- Worman's Mill Village Center

Taking an overall look at the amenities described by the jury-recognized DFAR12 projects, we see that 76% specifically described formal and informal dining venues, including: casual dining spaces (e.g., bistros and cafes), formal dining rooms, coffee shop / grab-and-go venues, and marketplace / convenience stores. Several projects also described Household-like dining spaces.

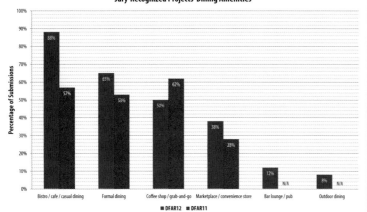

Jury-Recognized Projects' Dining Amenities

Percentage of Submissions

Category	DFAR12	DFAR11
Bistro / cafe / casual dining	88%	57%
Formal dining	65%	53%
Coffee shop / grab-and-go	50%	62%
Marketplace / convenience store	38%	28%
Bar lounge / pub	12%	N/A
Outdoor dining	8%	N/A

■ DFAR12 ■ DFAR11

DINING AMENITY SPACES

Asbury Place at Arbor Acres

Sharon Towers Dining Renovation

Rydal Park Repositioning

Orchard Cove

The Village at Orchard Ridge

Sharon Towers Dining Renovation

Laclede Groves

Sharon Towers Dining Renovation

Orchard Cove

Eighty-two percent of jury-recognized DFAR12 projects described spaces where learning, meetings, activities, and hobbies occur. These learning / activity spaces included: large multi-purpose rooms, dedicated conference / meeting spaces, library / information resource centers, art studios / craft rooms, dedicated classroom / learning spaces; religious / spiritual / meditative spaces; and small-scale cinema / media rooms. Several projects also described Household-like community / activity spaces.

Jury-Recognized Projects' Learning / Activity Amenities

	DFAR12	DFAR11
Large multipurpose room	79%	79%
Dedicated conference / meeting space	79%	68%
Library / information resource center	64%	68%
Art studio / craft room	46%	51%
Dedicated classroom / learning space	43%	36%
Religious / spiritual / meditative space	32%	57%
Small-scale cinema / media room	32%	30%
Outdoor event / activity space	14%	N/A
Community / activity kitchen	7%	N/A

Percentage of Submissions

Atria Valley View

LEARNING / ACTIVITY AMENITY SPACES

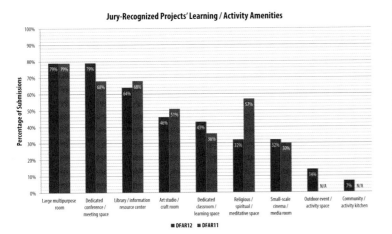
Asbury Place at Arbor Acres
Atria Valley View

Armed Forces Retirement Home

The Village at Orchard Ridge

Armed Forces Retirement Home
Laclede Groves

Armed Forces Retirement Home

Sixty-five percent of jury-recognized DFAR12 projects described fitness / wellness amenities, including: dedicated fitness equipment rooms, dedicated exercise classrooms, dedicated rehab / therapy gyms, swimming pools / aquatics facilities, salons, and massage / aromatherapy rooms.

Fifty-three percent of jury-recognized DFAR12 projects described outdoor amenities, including courtyards / gardens and resident-maintained gardening spaces.

Jury-Recognized Projects' Fitness / Wellness Amenities

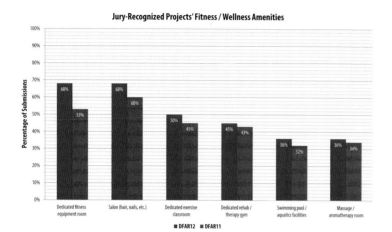

Jury-Recognized Projects' Outdoor Amenities

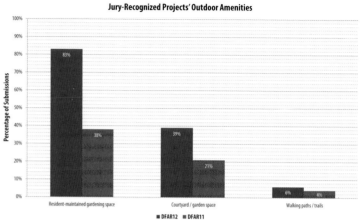

FITNESS / WELLNESS AMENITY SPACES

Asbury Place at Arbor Acres

Asbury Place at Arbor Acres

The Summit at Central Park

The Mather

The Mather

The Deupree House and Nursing Cottages

Moorings Park

OUTDOOR AMENITY SPACES

Moorings Park

Good Shepherd Cottage, Santa Teresita, Inc.

Tohono O'odham Elder Home

Moorings Park

Atria Valley View

The Mather

White Oak Cottages at Fox Hill Village

Connecting to the Greater Community

At only 29% of the jury-recognized DFAR12 projects, fewer submissions placed an emphasis on connecting to the greater community, compared to DFAR11 (at 42%). However, the projects that do focus on being a part of and / or taking advantage of the surrounding neighborhood do so through: close proximity to area services and amenities, easy access to public transit, providing programming to members of the greater community, offering mixed-use developments, and / or being embedded within existing neighborhoods.

Three projects also described creating partnerships with other service providers / organizations: Marian's House worked with the Alzheimer's Association and other senior care agencies when developing their dementia training / resource center; the Mary Helen Rogers Senior Community was planned in conjunction with another senior living building, located about a block away, to offer shared programming; and Worman's Mill Village Center is creating a town center for the surrounding naturally occurring retirement community and will provide dining, retail, and other services for anyone living nearby.

Perhaps not surprisingly, 70% of the projects that connect to the greater community are located in urban settings; the remaining 30% are suburban. Many additional submissions offer community connectivity through conscientious siting: out of all of the DFAR12 submissions, 69% have sites within 1,000 feet of public transportation, such as a bus stop or rapid transit line; and 52% are within 1,000 feet of everyday shopping and / or medical services.

DFAR12 projects recognized by the jury that described connecting to the greater community include:

- Brandman Centers for Senior
- Marian's House
- Mary Helen Rogers Senior Community
- Mather More Than a Cafe
- Moorings Park
- Rydal Park Repositioning
- The Summit at Central Park
- Sun City Tower Kobe
- The Townhomes on Hendricks Place
- Worman's Mill Village Center

Insights and Innovations

Two projects stood out for the innovative way they are delivering services to the greater community: Mather More Than a Cafe and Marian's House.

The Mather More Than a Cafe project consists of 4 decentralized programs, located in several Chicago neighborhoods. "The cafes serve as neighborhood-based administrative outposts as well as senior services centers. Along with the social component of the cafe, the senior services provided include computer classes, medical assistance, financial counseling, and exercise classes." The cafes encourage healthy eating, socialization, and are a place to find support so that people who are aging-in-place can remain in their homes.

Marian's House is a guesthouse for people with dementia who are living at home with a caregiver. The building is embedded in an existing residential neighborhood and looks like any other house along the street. However, it offers a dementia day center, an on-site caregiver's suite, and several bedrooms that allow for respite care (or, when not in use for overnight stays by people with dementia, can act as guest bedrooms for the caregiver's suite). In addition to allowing for one-on-one interaction and specialized group activities, the spaces in Marian's House also double as an after-hours resource center, providing training and support for family caregivers.

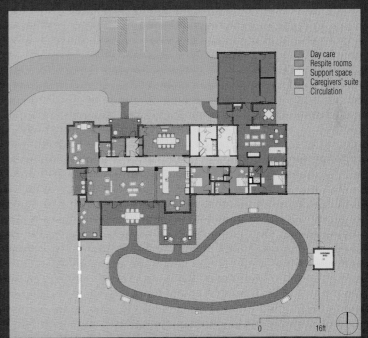

Day care
Respite rooms
Support space
Caregivers' suite
Circulation

Marian's House is specially designed for both one-on-one interaction and group activities. Day center spaces are designed to double as an evening resource center for classes and discussion groups.

Moorings Park

"The Center for Healthy Living will be open to the greater community for a monthly membership fee."

Sun City Tower Kobe

The project offers an "urban solution that fosters community, internally and externally. Integration into the surrounding community and sustainable transport were very important. This is a high-density project on a transit hub including two city bus lines; [it is also] conveniently [close] to rail and taxi. The provider offers hourly daytime shuttles to cultural and commercial areas, and the nearby train station."

The Townhomes on Hendricks Place

"The neighborhood of 12 attached, two-story cottage-style townhomes offers residents the opportunity to live, work and play within blocks of their new homes … An interconnecting sidewalk network provides residents with direct pedestrian access to the Center Green and to Lititz Borough's sidewalk and trail network. The townhomes are in close proximity to the Main Street shops and restaurants, Lititz Springs Park, farmers' markets and other amenities including physicians' and dental offices each located less than a block away … the townhomes continue the community's practice of seamlessly blending into the town, rather than trying to recreate the small town feel on a separate campus … The goal of strengthening connections to the town rather than creating the more typical inward-focused campus resulted in a number of measures to blend the townhomes into the existing context."

Promoting a Sense of Community

When senior living projects provide spaces that encourage residents to leave their private homes and interact with others, it encourages relationships to form and promotes a sense of community. Social interactions among residents help minimize isolation, improve quality of life, and even foster a sense of security as residents look out for each other. In fact, research has shown that social activities and productive engagement are as influential to elder survival as physical fitness activities.[3]

Among the DFAR12 submissions, 26% of the jury-recognized projects described ways in which their project improved or supported the sense of community. Though slightly less than DFAR11 (at 33%), this cycle's projects included similar features to bring people together. A sense of community is promoted by common spaces that encourage socialization—both informal / spontaneous social interaction spaces (e.g., residents running into each other in the lobby or at the mailboxes), as well as formal / planned social interaction spaces (e.g., the interactions that occur in an activity room or theater). Also described were communal dining venues, wide hallways with places to sit and chat, spaces that encourage and support visitors, and providing a circulation system that promotes socialization, with short walking distances and ease of access to common areas to encourage use.

DFAR12 projects recognized by the jury that described promoting a sense of community include:

- Cosby Spear Highrise
- Good Shepherd Cottage, Santa Teresita, Inc.
- Haven Hospice Custead Care Center
- Laclede Groves
- Mather More Than a Cafe
- Rose Villa Pocket Neighborhoods & Main Street
- Rydal Park Repositioning
- Sharon Towers Dining Renovation
- Sun City Tower Kobe

Cosby Spear Highrise

Through the new design, residents "are finding increased interaction with family, friends, and service providers. Now fully operational, the new open social spaces and programming are bringing residents out of their [private residential] units and allowing them to engage as never before ... Such openness increased social interaction among residents and adds to the value of the programming."

Spaces that encourage residents to interact outside their private home, like this cafe in the Cosby Spear Highrise project, promote social interactions and a sense of community.

Good Shepherd Cottage, Santa Teresita, Inc.

"The creation of engaging space addresses the common challenge of isolation in the elderly. The building provides a vibrant and engaging lifestyle by focusing on direct access to social areas that have abundant natural light and multiple connections to the outdoors. The floor plan, with a central communal living room, provides options for both group and private activities. The patios and outdoor gardens on the first floor become places for residents to interact ... A natural flow between indoor and outdoor space and open relationships with surrounding campus buildings creates a sense of interconnectivity."

Haven Hospice Custead Care Center

"Multiple family members often participate in the hospice experience together. They are joined together during this difficult time and find themselves sharing a similar experience with other patient's families at the same time. The building was designed with this phenomenon in mind. Four distinct yet centrally located living rooms create casual settings where related and 'unrelated' families can sit, chat, or help console one another. A community dining area allows social interaction between family members and staff. All can share the family kitchen and children's play area. And of course the outdoor spaces, whether enclosed porches or landscaped courtyards, are common destinations that can be shared as well."

Mather More Than a Cafe

To help residents hear one another in the cafes "the acoustic environment was improved to eliminate the echoes and background noise that dominates the larger regional centers." In addition to providing good acoustics that allow for conversations, "a variety of seating options were included on the periphery for those preferring to talk with staff at the lunch counters or observe from a distance," thereby recognizing people's varying needs for interaction versus privacy outside one's home.

The dining spaces in the Mather More Than a Cafe projects have good acoustics, making it easier to hear conversations. Poor acoustical design (a common problem in dining settings) can make it difficult for older adults to hear and be heard, and can potentially contribute to social discomfort, fear, embarrassment, depression, or isolation. On the other hand, spaces that support conversation promote a sense of community.

Rose Villa Pocket Neighborhoods & Main Street

"Creating a smaller 'community within a community' resulted in the introduction of pocket neighborhoods. Each pocket neighborhood consists of 7 cottage homes organized around an intimate garden setting that promotes a close-knit sense of community and neighborliness through an increased level of contact. Neighbors are naturally acquainted through the daily flow of life, by the simple fact of shared space and small-scale living. The courtyard space provides a natural setting for outdoor picnics and group gatherings."

At Rose Villa Pocket Neighborhoods & Main Street, the sense of community is supported by the day-to-day interactions that occur between people. Residents share common courtyards and paths, which increase the likelihood of running into one's neighbors.

Fitting the Local Context

For this cycle, fewer projects—26% of the jury-recognized DFAR12 projects—described how they fit the local context (compared to 54% of DFAR11 projects recognized by the jury). Of those submissions that do respond to their surroundings, half of the projects implemented a design that blends into the surrounding neighborhood. The other half described their adoption of the local vernacular architectural style.

DFAR12 projects recognized by the jury that described how they fit the local context include:

- Asbury Place at Arbor Acres
- Haven Hospice Custead Care Center
- Legacy Place
- Marian's House
- Mary Helen Rogers Senior Community
- The Mather
- The Townhomes on Hendricks Place
- The Village at Orchard Ridge
- Worman's Mill Village Center

In Their Own Words

Marian's House

The project aimed to "create a daytime home for people with dementia that fits into the surrounding community. The house looks like the houses around it, with the narrow side turned to the street to visually reduce its larger size for passersby; it also sits back from the street abiding by the neighborhood's setback restrictions. The residential scale of materials, massing, and roofs allow this large house to feel homelike."

Marian's House (pictured to the left) had a goal of fitting into the surrounding neighborhood. Through careful siting, massing, and use of materials, this dementia day center does not stand out from the single-family homes around it.

The Townhomes on Hendricks Place

"The townhomes are designed to architecturally emulate the character of their surroundings ... [The project] complements the historical context of the surrounding downtown."

Mary Helen Rogers Senior Community

"For an affordable senior building in an area of high-end condominiums and market rate developments it was important that this project blend with the surrounding neighborhood and not stand out as a stigmatized low-income project. As such, it was designed with a contemporary flair that embodies the urban feel of the area and uses color and materials, such as the stone at the ground floor, which enriches the look and sophistication of the building, all within a very limited budget."

The Village at Orchard Ridge

"Historic Old Town Winchester is a unique highlight of the region and serves as the design inspiration for the town center which features a clock tower, chapel, and Village Green featuring fountains, gardens and walking paths. Varied facade treatments and awnings reflect the vernacular of neighboring towns. Regional products, including Virginia brick, help to keep the project in context with Western Virginia."

From Florida Cracker style to Virginian Colonial, embodied here by The Village at Orchard Ridge, several projects aimed to fit the local context by adopting the region's vernacular architectural style.

Worman's Mill Village Center

"To reinforce the Village Center concept, the buildings were designed to resemble the texture, scale, style, and materials of the historic downtown of the Middle Atlantic city in which this community is located."

Fitting the surrounding context applies not only to suburban developments but to urban projects as well. The Mary Helen Rogers Senior Community achieved this by creating a contemporary facade that "embodies the urban feel of the neighborhood."

The aesthetic of Worman's Mill Village Center is based on the historic downtowns of the mid-Atlantic region where this project is located.

Flexibility

Twenty-one percent of the jury-recognized DFAR12 projects described ways in which their submission incorporated built-in flexibility—a new theme (not seen to a great extent in the analysis for DFAR11). Projects described how they were designed to: support aging-in-place, with features such as extra wall blocking in shower areas for future grab bar installation; accommodate different levels of care in one setting for if / when the market shifts (e.g., switching from Assisted Living to Skilled Nursing); allow for an easy remodel that would combine two smaller residential units into one larger unit, or to have one larger unit split into two smaller units to address market demand; offer flexible commons spaces that serve different users / purposes depending on the time of day and on the program / building occupants' needs; and consider the future expansion of the project, minimizing the need for moving or replacing major equipment and / or systems.

DFAR12 projects recognized by the jury that described a theme of flexibility include:

- Asbury Place at Arbor Acres
- Good Shepherd Cottage, Santa Teresita, Inc.
- The Friendship House at Royal Oaks
- Marian's House
- The Mather
- Moorings Park
- Sharon Towers Dining Renovation
- The Townhomes on Hendricks Place

Insights and Innovations

Taking the idea of flexibility to a new level, Moorings Park offers Independent Living apartments that "were designed to be completely customized by the owner—essentially blank slates to be configured and finished to suit the resident's lifestyle." Apartments can be personalized to accommodate such features as a large space for entertaining guests, or a high-end kitchen for cooking. An artist can devote floor area to a studio; an athlete can have space for exercising. Many options abound and residents are able to "work backwards from their price point, matching lifestyle and entrance fee with square footage and interior design choices."

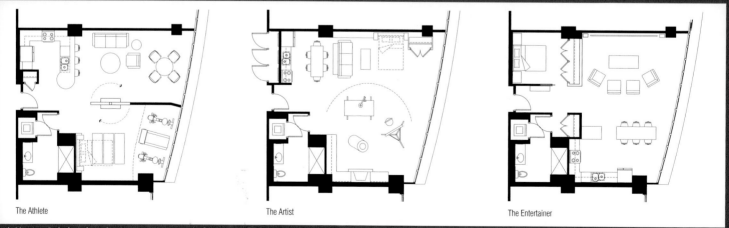

The Athlete   The Artist   The Entertainer

At Moorings Park, the Independent Living apartments can be fully customized to accommodate the interests of the resident. Interior settings can support a person's lifestyle, from providing a great kitchen and a space to entertain, to creating an artist's studio, or fitness space.

Asbury Place at Arbor Acres

The project built in "flexibility so that the two-bedroom units could be converted into a studio and one-bedroom unit in the future if needed."

Two-bedroom residence

Unit plan to convert two-bedroom residence to two studio residences

Several projects integrate built-in flexibility—from accommodating a change in the level of care provided within the setting, to the design of the residential units, like these at Asbury Place at Arbor Acres, which can easily convert to larger or smaller apartments, depending on market demands.

Good Shepherd Cottage, Santa Teresita, Inc.

"In order to allow for future flexibility as the master plan is built out, the original design intent of the Cottage is that it can be used as Memory Care, Skilled Nursing, or Assisted Living."

Marian's House

"Some [of the] daycare spaces are designed [to] double as an evening resource center for classes and discussion groups. Media and technology have been integrated for participant use and for evening presentations and training videos / presentations. There is [also] flexibility of use with two respite bedrooms, which can be open to either the caregiver as private guest rooms or open to the daycare portion of the home when residents stay over."

The Mather

"We have unique 'flex' spaces that can be sub-divided—using moveable glass partitions with curtains or large sliding doors—to serve as meeting venues, private dining rooms or the location of a bridge tournament or a game of Mahjong."

Sharon Towers Dining Renovation

"The project required the addition of multiple, equipment-intensive programs within a limited space while planning for a future expansion … [The project was planned] for future service area expansion without moving major equipment such as hoods and washing equipment. The 'Center Stage', buffet cabinet work and equipment is planned so that it can be easily relocated with the future expansion without major rework."

The Townhomes on Hendricks Place

"While one of the primary design goals was to accommodate aging in place, those accommodations could not be at the expense of the residential aesthetic. Prospective residents were clear that they did not wish to live in a home where accessibility features were apparent. Therefore, wider doorways and similar measures, such as extra blocking in showers, allow for future accommodations, when needed by the residents living in the home."

Holistic Wellness

According to the *National Whole-Person Wellness Survey*, there are 7 dimensions of wellness.[4]

Dimensions of Wellness	
Physical	Promotes involvement in physical activities for cardiovascular endurance, muscular strengthening, and flexibility. Advocates healthy lifestyle habits, encourages personal safety, and appropriate use of the healthcare system.
Social	Emphasizes creating / maintaining healthy relationships by talking, sharing interests, and actively participating in social events.
Intellectual	Encourages individuals to expand their knowledge and skill base through a variety of resources and cultural activities.
Emotional	Involves the capacity to manage feelings and behaviors, recognize and express feelings, control stress, problem solve, and manage success and failure.
Spiritual	Includes seeking meaning and purpose, demonstrating values through behaviors, such as meditation, prayer, and contemplation of life / death, as well as appreciating beauty, nature, and life.
Vocational (Occupational)	Emphasizes the process of determining and achieving personal and occupational interests through meaningful activities including lifespan occupations, learning new skills, volunteering, and developing new interests or hobbies.
Environmental	Focuses on protecting and improving their personal environment and the environment at large for health and safety benefits for themselves and the generations that follow.

Fifteen percent of the jury-recognized DFAR12 projects described approaches and / or community features that support holistic wellness (similar to DFAR11's 17%). Wellness-related features described include: biodynamic farming on-site, gardens and paths that encourage walking and connecting to nature, medical clinics and therapy spaces, fitness / spa amenities, educational settings, spaces that support group gatherings and encourage a sense of community, dining venues that support healthy eating, and ecologically sustainable design practices (as previously described).

DFAR12 projects recognized by the jury that discussed providing environments for holistic wellness include:

- Asbury Place at Arbor Acres
- Camphill Ghent
- Moorings Park
- Orchard Cove
- The Summit at Central Park

In Their Own Words

Orchard Cove

"The new fitness / wellness center has become one of the new hubs of the community … The space is designed for residents to exercise [and] fosters a lifestyle geared towards wellness."

Moorings Park

"The Center for Healthy Living offers concierge medical services and amenities that include a spa, exercise studios, fitness / weight rooms, and a rehabilitation center. To encourage wellness dimensions beyond the physical, the Center also offers a meditation room, Zen garden, creative arts studios, and [a] lecture space for visiting speakers. Wellness programs are customized to fit each resident's specific desires."

At Moorings Park, the concept of whole-person wellness heavily influenced the design. There are "five areas of core wellness activities—a medical clinic, physical therapy, fitness, comprehensive spa, education and social interaction" spaces. The Center for Healthy Living even includes a wellness store.

Endnotes

1 Gabriel, Z., & Bowling, A. (2004). Quality of life from the perspective of older people. *Aging & Society, 24*, 675-691.

2 The Advancing Excellence in America's Nursing Homes Campaign. Retrieved March 17, 2014 from <http://www.nhqualitycampaign.org/star_index.aspx?controls=personcenteredcareexploregoal>

3 Glass, T. A., Mendes de Leon, C., Marottoli, R. A., & Berkman, L. F. (1999). Population-based study of social and productive activities as predictors of survival among elderly Americans. *BMJ, 319*, 478-483.

4 Mather LifeWays, Dorsky Hodgson Parrish Yue, and Ziegler Capital Markets Group. (2006). *The National Whole-Person Wellness Survey*. Page 5.

Insights and Innovations

Holistic wellness is a personal objective for many people, with multiple senior living projects providing spaces and programming to support this goal. One project, in particular, was designed to a philosophy that takes holistic wellness to another level: Camphill Ghent was designed under the community's guiding philosophy of anthroposophy, which is dedicated to supporting the potential of all people regardless of physical or other disabilities. Grounded in the teachings of Rudolf Steiner, anthroposophy is based on the idea that inner development can positively change oneself and the greater world around us.

At Camphill Ghent "the Steiner principles affected the overall building geometry, creating many irregular angles in building form and corridor configuration. As a result, the design avoided flat ceilings and right angles where possible to create the sense of a living environment as opposed to a closed box." The buildings also "encourage movement and balance and the activity spaces are light-filled. The design enlivens surfaces with different textures, colors evoke certain emotions, and the design integrates color in an anthroposophic way: blue / violet evokes reverential feelings, green evokes new life, yellow / orange: light and brightness, red / blue: deep emotions / contemplation."

Along with community leaders, the designers of Camphill Ghent envisioned a nurturing, supportive residence for developmentally disabled seniors based on the philosophy of Anthroposophy.
Photography: Sarah Mechling / Perkins Eastman

Project Data

Armed Forces Retirement Home

Client / Owner / Provider: Armed Forces Retirement Home
Architect: SFCS Inc.
Architect of Record: URS Corporation
General Prime Contractor: Yates Construction
Interior Designer: SFCS Inc.
Landscape Architect: RCI Landscaping
Structural Engineer: URS Corporation
Mechanical Engineer: URS Corporation
Electrical Engineer: URS Corporation
Civil Engineer: URS Corporation
Environmental Gerontologist: Lori Hiatt, PhD

Building Data

Independent living: Total GSF: 352,800
Independent living: Total NSF of residential spaces: 220,500
Independent living: Total NSF of common spaces: 160,000
Assisted living: Total GSF: 43,200
Assisted living: Total NSF of residential spaces: 27,000
Assisted living: Total NSF of common spaces: 18,400
Assisted living—dementia / memory support: Total GSF: 16,500
Assisted living—dementia / memory support: Total NSF of residential spaces: 11,900
Assisted living—dementia / memory support: Total NSF of common spaces: 8,600
Long-term skilled nursing: Total GSF: 17,900
Long-term skilled nursing: Total NSF of residential spaces: 12,200
Long-term skilled nursing: Total NSF of common spaces: 8,680
Skilled nursing—dementia / memory support: Total GSF: 16,800
Skilled nursing—dementia / memory support: Total NSF of residential spaces: 11,450
Skilled nursing—dementia / memory support: Total NSF of common spaces: 8,500

Independent Living

Unit type	Number of units	Size range (NSF)	Typical size (NSF)
Studio	490	-	450
Total (all units)	490		

Accessible independent living units (%): 100

Assisted Living

Unit type	Number of units	Size range (NSF)	Typical size (NSF)
Studio	60	-	450
Total (all units)	60		

Accessible assisted living units (%): 100

Assisted Living—Dementia / Memory Support

Unit type	Number of units	Size range (NSF)	Typical size (NSF)
Private room*	24	-	380
Total (all units)	24		

*single occupant

Long-Term Skilled Nursing

Unit type	Number of units	Size range (NSF)	Typical size (NSF)
Private room*	24	-	380
Total (all units)	24		

*single occupant

Skilled Nursing—Dementia / Memory Support

Unit type	Number of units	Size range (NSF)	Typical size (NSF)
Private room*	24	-	380
Total (all units)	24		

*single occupant

Project Costs (actual or estimated if the project is yet to be built; not including FF&E, site, or soft costs)

Independent living: Total cost for new construction ($): 69,500,000
Assisted living: Total cost for new construction ($): 17,400,000
Assisted living—dementia / memory support: Total cost for new construction ($): 6,700,000
Long-term skilled nursing: Total cost for new construction ($): 6,900,000
Skilled nursing—dementia / memory support: Total cost for new construction ($): 7,100,000

Project Funding Sources

Public-private sector funding (%): 100

Gender Breakdown of the Residents

Women (%): 10
Men (%): 90

Status of the Residents

Single (living alone) (%): 97
Living with a spouse / domestic partner (%): 3

Source of Resident Payments

Private payment (%): 100

Average Age of the Residents

Independent living: Average age designed to support: 81
Independent living: Average entry age: 81
Assisted living: Average age designed to support: 81
Assisted living: Average entry age: 84
Long-term skilled nursing: Average age designed to support: 81
Long-term skilled nursing: Average entry age: 88

Asbury Place at Arbor Acres

Client / Owner / Provider: Arbor Acres United Methodist Retirement Community

Architect: RLPS Architects

Local Liaison and Construction Administration Support: LAMBERT Architecture + Interiors

General Prime Contractor: Landmark Builders of the Triad, Inc.

Interior Designer: Interior Solutions, Inc.

Structural Engineer: MacIntosh Engineering

Mechanical Engineer: Reese Engineering, Inc.

Electrical Engineer: Reese Engineering, Inc.

Civil Engineer: Allied Civil Engineering & Land Surveying

Building Data
Assisted living: Total GSF: 117,277
Assisted living: Total NSF of residential spaces: 34,944
Assisted living: Total NSF of common spaces: 14,483

Assisted Living			
Unit type	Number of units	Size range (NSF)	Typical size (NSF)
Studio	12	476	476
One-bedroom	42	570	570
Two-bedroom	6	882	882
Total (all units)	60		

Accessible assisted living units (%): 100

Project Costs (actual or estimated if the project is yet to be built; not including FF&E, site, or soft costs)
Assisted living: Total cost for new construction ($): 23,214,665

Project Funding Sources
Non-taxable bond offering funding (%): 94
Other funding source (%): 6

Gender Breakdown of the Residents
Women (%): 77
Men (%): 23

Status of the Residents
Single (living alone) (%): 91
Living with a spouse / domestic partner (%): 9

Source of Resident Payments
Private payment (%): 100

Average Age of the Residents
Assisted living: Average age designed to support: 90
Assisted living: Average entry age: 88

Atria Valley View

Client / Owner / Provider: Atria Senior Living Group

Prime Architect: GGLO

General Prime Contractor: Draeger Construction

Interior Designer: GGLO

Landscape Architect: GGLO

Structural Engineer: KPFF

Mechanical Engineer: Interface Engineering

Electrical Engineer: Interface Engineering

Civil Engineer: KPFF

Building Data
Assisted living: Total GSF: 98,658
Assisted living: Total NSF of residential spaces: 59,982
Assisted living: Total NSF of common spaces: 38,676

Assisted Living			
Unit type	Number of units	Size range (NSF)	Typical size (NSF)
Studio	112	365–503	503
One-bedroom	13	545–556	545
Total (all units)	125		

Accessible assisted living units (%): 11
Other assisted living units (%): 89

Project Costs (actual or estimated if the project is yet to be built; not including FF&E, site, or soft costs)
Assisted living: Total cost for addition(s) ($): 1,500,000
Assisted living: Total cost for renovation(s) / modernization(s) ($): 13,500,000

Project Funding Sources
Public-private sector funding (%): 100

Gender Breakdown of the Residents
Women (%): 76
Men (%): 24

Status of the Residents
Single (living alone) (%): 94
Living with a spouse / domestic partner (%): 6

Source of Resident Payments
Private payment (%): 80
Other payment source (%): 20

Average Age of the Residents
Assisted living: Average age designed to support: 88
Assisted living: Average entry age: 85

Brandman Centers for Senior Care

Client / Owner / Provider: Los Angeles Jewish Home

Architect: GMPA Architects, Inc.

General Prime Contractor: PNG General Contractor

Interior Designer: Wolcott Interiors

Landscape Architect: Ahbe Landscape Architects

Structural Engineer: MHP Structural Engineers

Mechanical Engineer: Davidovich & Associates

Electrical Engineer: Davidovich & Associates

Construction Management: Orgel Construction Management

Project Funding Sources
Other funding source (%): 100

Gender Breakdown of the Residents
Women (%): 68
Men (%): 32

Source of Resident Payments
Private payment (including philanthropic support) (%): 5
Medicaid / Medicare payment (%): 95

Camphill Ghent

Client / Owner / Provider: Camphill Village USA, Inc.

Architect: Perkins Eastman

General Prime Contractor: Lecesse Construction

Interior Designer: Perkins Eastman

Landscape Architect: Dirtworks, PC

Structural Engineer: Jensen / BRV Engineering, PLLC

Mechanical Engineer: Kohler Ronan, LLC

Electrical Engineer: Kohler Ronan, LLC

Civil Engineer: Crawford & Associates, PC

Building Data
Independent living: Total GSF: 47,850
Independent living: Total NSF of residential spaces: 32,315
Independent living: Total NSF of common spaces: 12,400
Assisted living: Total GSF: 30,860
Assisted living: Total NSF of residential spaces: 8,700
Assisted living: Total NSF of common spaces: 11,080
Assisted living—dementia / memory support: Total GSF: 5,490
Assisted living—dementia / memory support: Total NSF of residential spaces: 2,100
Assisted living—dementia / memory support: Total NSF of common spaces: 1,690

Independent Living

Unit type	Number of units	Size range (NSF)	Typical size (NSF)
Studio	12	335–445	420
One-bedroom	9	550–750	600
Two-bedroom	7	760–1485	1485
Two-bedroom plus den	2	940	940
Three-bedroom+	4	1485	1485
Total (all units)	34		

Accessible independent living units (%): 80
Adaptable independent living units (%): 20

Assisted Living

Unit type	Number of units	Size range (NSF)	Typical size (NSF)
Studio	29	300	300
Total (all units)	29		

Accessible assisted living units (%): 100

Assisted Living—Dementia / Memory Support

Unit type	Number of units	Size range (NSF)	Typical size (NSF)
Private room*	7	300	300
Total (all units)	7		

*single occupant

Project Costs (actual or estimated if the project is yet to be built; not including FF&E, site, or soft costs)
Independent living: Total cost for new construction ($): 6,890,800
Assisted living: Total cost for new construction ($): 4,443,850
Assisted living—dementia / memory support: Total cost for new construction ($): 790,560

Project Funding Sources
Conventional / private funding (%): 25
Public sector funding (%): 75

Gender Breakdown of the Residents
Women (%): 71
Men (%): 29

Status of the Residents
Single (living alone) (%): 85
Living with a spouse / domestic partner (%): 12
Living with a friend / family member (e.g., sibling) (%): 3

Source of Resident Payments
Private payment (%): 10
Medicaid / Medicare payment (%): 66
Government subsidy payment (%): 20
Other payment source (including reduced rental rate from Camphill and family members) (%): 4

Average Age of the Residents

Independent living: Average age designed to support: 75

Independent living: Average entry age: 75

Assisted living: Average age designed to support: 82

Assisted living: Average entry age: 80

Assisted living—dementia / memory support: Average age designed to support: 75

Cohen Rosen House

Client / Owner / Provider: Hebrew Home of Greater Washington

Architect: THW Design

General Prime Contractor: Lend Lease

Interior Designer: THW Interiors

Landscape Architect: THW Design

Structural Engineer: Starzer Brady Fagan Associates Inc

Mechanical Engineer: Barrett Woodyard & Associates

Electrical Engineer: Barrett Woodyard & Associates

Civil Engineer: Site Solutions

Building Data

Assisted living—dementia / memory support: Total GSF: 16,361

Assisted living—dementia / memory support: Total NSF of residential spaces: 5,544

Assisted living—dementia / memory support: Total NSF of common spaces: 10,817

Assisted Living—Dementia / Memory Support			
Unit type	Number of units	Size range (NSF)	Typical size (NSF)
Private room*	18	308	308
Total (all units)	18		

*single occupant

Project Costs (actual or estimated if the project is yet to be built; not including FF&E, site, or soft costs)

Assisted living—dementia / memory support: Total cost for new construction ($): 5,300,000

Project Funding Sources

Non-taxable bond offering funding (%): 75

Other funding source (%): 25

Gender Breakdown of the Residents

Women (%): 60

Men (%): 40

Status of the Residents

Single (living alone) (%): 100

Source of Resident Payments

Private payment (%): 100

Average Age of the Residents

Assisted living—dementia / memory support: Average age designed to support: 85

Assisted living—dementia / memory support: Average entry age: 85

Cosby Spear Highrise

Client / Owner / Provider: Atlanta Housing Authority

Architect: THW Design

General Prime Contractor: Choate

Interior Designer: THW Interiors

Landscape Architect: THW Design

Structural Engineer: HESM&A

Mechanical Engineer: Pruitt Eberly Stone

Electrical Engineer: Pruitt Eberly Stone

Civil Engineer: Travis Pruitt & Associates Inc

Building Data

Independent living: Total GSF: 127,300

Independent living: Total NSF of common spaces: 88,128

Independent Living			
Unit type	Number of units	Size range (NSF)	Typical size (NSF)
Studio	166	400	400
One-bedroom	114	525	525
Two-bedroom	2	525	525
Total (all units)	282		

Accessible independent living units (%): 6

Adaptable independent living units (%): 2

Other independent living units (%): 92

Project Funding Sources

Public sector funding (%): 100

Gender Breakdown of the Residents

Women (%): 60

Men (%): 40

Status of the Residents

Single (living alone) (%): 90

Living with a spouse / domestic partner (%): 5

Living with an in-home caregiver (%): 5

Source of Resident Payments

Private payment (%): 100

Average Age of the Residents

Independent living: Average age designed to support: 55

Independent living: Average entry age: 55

Creekside Homes at Givens Estates

Client / Owner / Provider: Givens Estates

Architect: RLPS Architects

General Prime Contractor: Landmark Builders of the Triad, Inc.

Interior Designer: RLPS Interiors

Structural Engineer: MacIntosh Engineering

Mechanical Engineer: Reese Engineering, Inc.

Electrical Engineer: Reese Engineering, Inc.

Civil Engineer: William G. Lapsley & Associates, P.A.

Development Consultant: Highland Farms

Building Data
Independent living: Total GSF: 54,260
Independent living: Total NSF of residential spaces: 36,288
Independent living: Total NSF of common spaces: 1,340

Independent Living			
Unit type	Number of units	Size range (NSF)	Typical size (NSF)
One-bedroom plus den	12	1402	1402
Two-bedroom plus den	12	1544–1700	1623
Total (all units)	24		

Accessible independent living units (%): 8
Adaptable independent living units (%): 92

Project Costs (actual or estimated if the project is yet to be built; not including FF&E, site, or soft costs)
Independent living: Total cost for new construction ($): 7,308,812

Project Funding Sources
Conventional / private funding (%): 100

Average Age of the Residents
Independent living: Average age designed to support: 78

The Deupree House and Nursing Cottages

Client / Owner / Provider: Episcopal Retirement Homes, Inc. (ERH)

Architect: SFCS Inc.

General Prime Contractor: Ridge Stone Builders & Developers

Interior Designer: Design Collective, Inc

Landscape Architect: KKG Studios

Structural Engineer: SFCS Inc.

Mechanical Engineer: SFCS Inc.

Electrical Engineer: SFCS Inc.

Civil Engineer: Bayer Becker

Planner for Culture Change: Steve Shields

Building Data
Independent living: Total GSF: 151,000
Independent living: Total NSF of residential spaces: 117,970
Independent living: Total NSF of common spaces: 16,347
Long-term skilled nursing: Total GSF: 22,160
Long-term skilled nursing: Total NSF of residential spaces: 15,283

Independent Living			
Unit type	Number of units	Size range (NSF)	Typical size (NSF)
One-bedroom plus den	8	1291	1291
Two-bedroom	28	1442–1525	1525
Two-bedroom plus den	24	1694	1694
Total (all units)	60		

Adaptable independent living units (%): 100

Long-Term Skilled Nursing			
Unit type	Number of units	Size range (NSF)	Typical size (NSF)
Private room*	24	350	350
Total (all units)	24		

*single occupant

Project Costs (actual or estimated if the project is yet to be built; not including FF&E, site, or soft costs)
Independent living: Total cost for new construction ($): 19,200,000
Long-term skilled nursing: Total cost for new construction ($): 3,500,000

Project Funding Sources
Conventional / private funding (%): 10
Non-taxable bond offering funding (%): 90

Gender Breakdown of the Residents
Women (%): 65
Men (%): 35

Status of the Residents
Single (living alone) (%): 62
Living with a spouse / domestic partner (%): 38

Source of Resident Payments
Private payment (%): 92
Medicaid / Medicare payment (%): 8

Average Age of the Residents
Independent living: Average age designed to support: 80
Independent living: Average entry age: 82
Long-term skilled nursing: Average age designed to support: 87
Long-term skilled nursing: Average entry age: 88

The Friendship House at Royal Oaks

Client / Owner / Provider: Royal Oaks Retirement Community

Architect: Todd & Associates, Inc.

General Prime Contractor: Sundt Construction

Interior Designer: Thoma-Holec Design

Landscape Architect: Todd & Associates, Inc.

Structural Engineer: Bakkum Noelke

Mechanical / Plumbing / Electrical Engineer: LSW Engineers Arizona, Inc.

Civil Engineer: Site Consultants, Inc.

Kitchen Consultant: Arizona Restauraunt Supply

Building Data

Assisted living—dementia / memory support: Total GSF: 59,038

Assisted living—dementia / memory support: Total NSF of residential spaces: 20,084

Assisted living—dementia / memory support: Total NSF of common spaces: 22,850

Assisted Living—Dementia / Memory Support			
Unit type	Number of units	Size range (NSF)	Typical size (NSF)
Private room*	56	323	323
Total (all units)	56		

*single occupant

Accessible assisted living units (%): 100

Project Costs (actual or estimated if the project is yet to be built; not including FF&E, site, or soft costs)

Assisted living—dementia / memory support: Total cost for new construction ($): 12,573,332 (est.)

Assisted living—dementia / memory support: Total cost for renovation(s) / modernization(s) ($): 12,573,332 (est.)

Project Funding Sources

Conventional / private funding (%): 100

Gender Breakdown of the Residents

Women (%): 70

Men (%): 30

Status of the Residents

Single (living alone) (%): 100

Source of Resident Payments

Private payment (%): 100

Average Age of the Residents

Assisted living—dementia / memory support: Average age designed to support: 92

Good Shepherd Cottage, Santa Teresita, Inc.

Client / Owner / Provider: Carmelite Sisters

Architect: SmithGroupJJR

General Prime Contractor: Slater Builders

Interior Designer: SmithGroupJJR

Landscape Architect: SiteScapes

Structural Engineer: Vinci & Associates

Mechanical Engineer: M-E Engineers

Electrical Engineer: M-E Engineers

Civil Engineer: Psomas

Acoustical Consultant: Charles M. Salter Associates

Building Data

Assisted living: Total GSF: 19,704

Assisted living: Total NSF of residential spaces: 11,840

Assisted living: Total NSF of common spaces: 2,944

Assisted Living			
Unit type	Number of units	Size range (NSF)	Typical size (NSF)
Studio	14	325–345	325
One-bedroom	4	506	506
Two-bedroom	2	600	600
Total (all units)	20		

Adaptable assisted living units (%): 100

Project Costs (actual or estimated if the project is yet to be built; not including FF&E, site, or soft costs)

Assisted living: Total cost for new construction ($): 5,000,000

Project Funding Sources

Conventional / private funding (%): 100

Gender Breakdown of the Residents

Women (%): 80

Men (%): 20

Status of the Residents

Single (living alone) (%): 94

Living with a spouse / domestic partner (%): 6

Source of Resident Payments

Private payment (%): 100

Average Age of the Residents

Assisted living: Average age designed to support: 85

Assisted living: Average entry age: 85

Haven Hospice Custead Care Center

Client / Owner / Provider: Haven Hospice
Architect: AG Architecture
General Prime Contractor: Elkins Constructors
Interior Designer: Bridget Bohacz & Associates, Inc.
Landscape Architect: Prosser Hallock
Structural Engineer: DDA Engineers, P.A.
Mechanical Engineer: AG Architecture
Electrical Engineer: AG Architecture
Civil Engineer: Prosser Hallock

Building Data
Hospice: Total GSF: 29,276
Hospice: Total NSF of residential spaces: 6,558 (patient rooms)
Hospice: Total NSF of common spaces: 13,491

Hospice			
Unit type	Number of units	Size range (NSF)	Typical size (NSF)
Private room*	18	352–463	364
Total (all units)	18		

*single occupant

Project Costs (actual or estimated if the project is yet to be built; not including FF&E, site, or soft costs)
Hospice: Total cost for new construction ($): 6,200,000

Project Funding Sources
Non-taxable bond offering funding (%): 100

Gender Breakdown of the Residents
Women (%): 60
Men (%): 40

Status of the Residents
Single (living alone) (%): 100

Source of Resident Payments
Private payment (%): 10
Medicaid / Medicare payment (%): 90

Average Age of the Residents
Hospice: Average entry age: 78

Laclede Groves

Client / Owner / Provider: Lutheran Senior Services
Architect: Perkins Eastman
General Prime Contractor: Paric Corporation
Interior Designer: Perkins Eastman
Structural Engineer: SSE, Inc.

Mechanical Engineer: Tennill & Associates (MEP Design-Build)
Electrical Engineer: Tennill & Associates
Civil Engineer: BAX Engineering Company

Building Data
Independent living: Total GSF: 197,760
Independent living: Total NSF of residential spaces: 135,760
Independent living: Total NSF of common spaces: 22,870
Long-term skilled nursing: Total GSF: 56,500
Long-term skilled nursing: Total NSF of residential spaces: 22,975
Long-term skilled nursing: Total NSF of common spaces: 28,660
Short-term rehab: Total GSF: 13,600
Short-term rehab: Total NSF of residential spaces: 8,450
Short-term rehab: Total NSF of common spaces: 7,690

Independent Living			
Unit type	Number of units	Size range (NSF)	Typical size (NSF)
One-bedroom plus den	15	945	945
Two-bedroom	33	1050–1270	1270
Two-bedroom plus den	32	1345	1345
Total (all units)	80		

Accessible independent living units (%): 3
Adaptable independent living units (%): 97

Long-Term Skilled Nursing			
Unit type	Number of units	Size range (NSF)	Typical size (NSF)
Private room*	84	200–288	236
Semi-private room**	12	270	270
Total (all units)	96		

*single occupant
**two occupants with separate bed areas but a shared bathroom

Short-Term Rehab			
Unit type	Number of units	Size range (NSF)	Typical size (NSF)
Private room*	36	200–288	236
Total (all units)	36		

*single occupant

Project Costs (actual or estimated if the project is yet to be built; not including FF&E, site, or soft costs)
Independent living: Total cost for new construction ($): 24,500,000
Long-term skilled nursing: Total cost for new construction ($): 6,100,000
Long-term skilled nursing: Total cost for addition(s) ($): 4,300,000
Long-term skilled nursing: Total cost for renovation(s) / modernization(s) ($): 1,800,000
Short-term rehab: Total cost for new construction ($): 2,435,000
Short-term rehab: Total cost for addition(s) ($): 2,152,000
Short-term rehab: Total cost for renovation(s) / modernization(s) ($): 223,000

Project Funding Sources
Conventional / private funding (%): 25
Non-taxable bond offering funding (%): 75

Gender Breakdown of the Residents
Women (%): 70
Men (%): 30

Status of the Residents
Single (living alone) (%): 67
Living with a spouse / domestic partner (%): 33

Source of Resident Payments
Private payment (%): 90
Medicaid / Medicare payment (%): 9
Other payment source (including managed care) (%): 1

Average Age of the Residents
Independent living: Average entry age: 85
Independent living: Average age designed to support: 62
Long-term skilled nursing: Average age designed to support: 62
Long-term skilled nursing: Average entry age: 87
Short-term rehab: Average age designed to support: 62

Legacy Place

Client / Owner / Provider: Jah-Jireh Homes of America
Architect: RLPS Architects
General Prime Contractor: Horst Construction / Ruhmel Contracting, Inc.
Interior Designer: RLPS Interiors
Structural Engineer: Zug & Associates, Ltd.
Mechanical Engineer: Moore Engineering Company
Electrical Engineer: Moore Engineering Company
Civil Engineer: Ott Consulting, Inc.
Dining / Food Service: SCOPOS Hospitality Group
Owner's Consultant: PHI National

Building Data
Assisted living: Total GSF: 17,905
Assisted living: Total NSF of residential spaces: 8,689
Assisted living: Total NSF of common spaces: 4,168
Assisted living—dementia / memory support: Total GSF: 18,269
Assisted living—dementia / memory support: Total NSF of residential spaces: 4,103
Assisted living—dementia / memory support: Total NSF of common spaces: 1,992

Assisted Living			
Unit type	Number of units	Size range (NSF)	Typical size (NSF)
Studio	16	350–441	404
One-bedroom	4	567	567
Total (all units)	20		

Accessible assisted living units (%): 100

Assisted Living—Dementia / Memory Support			
Unit type	Number of units	Size range (NSF)	Typical size (NSF)
Private room*	12	320–350	341
Total (all units)	12		

*single occupant

Project Costs (actual or estimated if the project is yet to be built; not including FF&E, site, or soft costs)
Assisted living: Total cost for new construction ($): 3,058,100
Assisted living—dementia / memory support: Total cost for new construction ($): 2,173,300

Project Funding Sources
Conventional / private funding (%): 100

Source of Resident Payments
Private payment (%): 100

Average Age of the Residents
Assisted living: Average age designed to support: 87
Assisted living—dementia / memory support: Average age designed to support: 82

Marian's House

Client / Owner / Provider: Jewish Senior Life
Architect: Perkins Eastman
General Prime Contractor: Lecesse Construction
Interior Designer: Perkins Eastman
Landscape Architect: BME / Dirtworks
Structural Engineer: Jensen BRV
Mechanical Engineer: Kennedy Mechanical (Design-Build)
Electrical Engineer: Radec Corporation (Design-Build)
Civil Engineer: BME

Building Data
Assisted living—dementia / memory support: Total GSF: 3,447
Assisted living—dementia / memory support: Total NSF of residential spaces: 382
Assisted living—dementia / memory support: Total NSF of common spaces: 2,720

Assisted Living—Dementia / Memory Support			
Unit type	Number of units	Size range (NSF)	Typical size (NSF)
Private room*	2	191	191
Total (all units)	2		

*single occupant

Project Costs (actual or estimated if the project is yet to be built; not including FF&E, site, or soft costs)
Assisted living—dementia / memory support: Total cost for new construction ($): 971,936

Project Funding Sources
Conventional / private funding (%): 100

Gender Breakdown of the Residents
Women (%): 16
Men (%): 84

Status of the Residents
Living with a spouse / domestic partner (%): 84
Living with a friend / family member (e.g., sibling) (%): 16

Source of Resident Payments
Private payment (%): 100

Average Age of the Residents
Assisted living—dementia / memory support: Average age designed to support: 84
Assisted living—dementia / memory support: Average entry age: 74

Mary Helen Rogers Senior Community

Client / Owner / Provider: Chinatown Community Development Center & UrbanCore
Architect: HKIT Architects
General Prime Contractor: Cahill Contractors, Inc.
Landscape Architect: Royston Hanamoto Alley & Abey (RHAA)
Structural Engineer: Structural Design Engineers
Mechanical Engineer: Tommy Siu & Associates
Electrical Engineer: F.W. Associates
Civil Engineer: Telamon Engineering Consultants

Building Data
Independent living: Total GSF: 95,000
Independent living: Total NSF of residential spaces: 84,041
Independent living: Total NSF of common spaces: 10,959

Independent Living			
Unit type	Number of units	Size range (NSF)	Typical size (NSF)
Studio	28	344–404	374
One-bedroom	72	518–582	550
Total (all units)	100		

Accessible independent living units (%): 7
Adaptable independent living units (%): 93

Project Costs (actual or estimated if the project is yet to be built; not including FF&E, site, or soft costs)
Independent living: Total cost for new construction ($): 31,600,000

Project Funding Sources
Public sector funding (%): 100

Gender Breakdown of the Residents
Women (%): 75
Men (%): 25

Status of the Residents
Single (living alone) (%): 60
Living with a spouse / domestic partner (%): 40

Source of Resident Payments
Government subsidy payment (%): 100

Average Age of the Residents
Independent living: Average age designed to support: 75
Independent living: Average entry age: 70

The Mather

Client / Owner / Provider: Mather LifeWays
Architect: Solomon Cordwell Buenz
Design Architect: Solomon Cordwell Buenz
General Prime Contractor: Phase I & II: Power Construction Company
Interior Designer: Phase I & II: Interior Design Associates, Inc.
Landscape Architect: Phase I & II: Daniel Weinbach and Partners, Ltd.
Structural Engineer: Phase I & II: Halvorson + Partners
Mechanical Engineer: Environmental Systems Design; Affiliated Eng. Inc.
Electrical Engineer: Environmental Systems Design; Affiliated Eng. Inc.
Civil Engineer: Phase I & II: Spaceco, Inc.
Other Consultants: Robert Pacifico; Shiner + Assc; Innovative Aquatic

Building Data
Independent living: Total GSF: 477,727
Independent living: Total NSF of residential spaces: 397,298
Independent living: Total NSF of common spaces: 38,796
Assisted living: Total GSF: 11,062
Assisted living: Total NSF of residential spaces: 7,557
Assisted living: Total NSF of common spaces: 3,505
Assisted living—dementia / memory support: Total GSF: 8,168
Assisted living—dementia / memory support: Total NSF of residential spaces: 3,629
Assisted living—dementia / memory support: Total NSF of common spaces: 4,539
Long-term skilled nursing: Total GSF: 24,794
Long-term skilled nursing: Total NSF of residential spaces: 10,695
Long-term skilled nursing: Total NSF of common spaces: 14,099

Independent Living			
Unit type	Number of units	Size range (NSF)	Typical size (NSF)
One-bedroom	68	830–1155	956
One-bedroom plus den	13	966–1160	1092
Two-bedroom	71	1185–1750	1389
Two-bedroom plus den	87	1366–2635	1714
Three-bedroom+	1	2570	2570
Total (all units)	240		

Adaptable independent living units (%): 100

Assisted Living			
Unit type	Number of units	Size range (NSF)	Typical size (NSF)
Studio	1	485	485
One-bedroom	8	574–838	720
Two-bedroom	1	1315	1315
Total (all units)	10		

Accessible assisted living units (%): 100

Assisted Living—Dementia / Memory Support			
Unit type	Number of units	Size range (NSF)	Typical size (NSF)
Private room*	12	272–343	302
Total (all units)	12		

*single occupant

Long-Term Skilled Nursing

Unit type	Number of units	Size range (NSF)	Typical size (NSF)
Private room*	33	253–494	294
Semi-private room**	2	491–499	495
Total (all units)	35		

*single occupant
**two occupants with separate bed areas but a shared bathroom

Project Costs (actual or estimated if the project is yet to be built; not including FF&E, site, or soft costs)

Independent living: Total cost for new construction ($): 132,854,231

Assisted living: Total cost for new construction ($): 2,319,224

Assisted living—dementia / memory support: Total cost for new construction ($): 1,712,477

Long-term skilled nursing: Total cost for new construction ($): 5,198,231

Project Funding Sources

Conventional / private funding (%): 100

Gender Breakdown of the Residents

Women (%): 64

Men (%): 36

Status of the Residents

Single (living alone) (%): 55

Living with a spouse / domestic partner (%): 45

Source of Resident Payments

Private payment* (%): 97

Medicaid / Medicare payment (%): 3

* The Mather is a repositioning project which combined two separate communities, Mather Gardens ("originally" The Mather Home, completed in 1952) and Mather Place at The Georgian, for which Mather LifeWays assumed sponsorship in 1992. Residents of these communities were relocated to The Mather at no additional cost. New entrance fees for these residents were funded by Mather Foundation. In addition, Mather LifeWays provides an ongoing financial assistance program, known as Alonzo's Wish, to new residents of the community. Mather LifeWays has committed to provide a minimum of $30 million in financial assistance during the first 10 years of operations.

Average Age of the Residents

Independent living: Average age designed to support: 83

Independent living: Average entry age: 79

Assisted living: Average age designed to support: 87

Assisted living: Average entry age: 85

Assisted living—dementia / memory support: Average age designed to support: 87

Assisted living—dementia / memory support: Average entry age: 85

Long-term skilled nursing: Average age designed to support: 88

Long-term skilled nursing: Average entry age: 85

Mather More Than a Cafe

Client / Owner / Provider: Mather LifeWays

Architect: Wheeler Kearns Architects

Project Funding Sources

Conventional / private funding (%): 100

Gender Breakdown of the Residents

Women (%): 60

Men (%): 40

Status of the Residents

Single (living alone) (%): 60

Living with a spouse / domestic partner (%): 40

Source of Resident Payments

Private payment (%): 100

Average Age of the Residents

Independent living: Average age designed to support: 100

Independent living: Average entry age: 66

Merritt Crossing

Client / Owner / Provider: Sattelite Affordable Housing Associates

Architect: Leddy Maytum Stacy Architects

General Prime Contractor: Nibbi Brothers General Contractors

Structural Engineer: KPFF San Francisco

Mechanical Engineer: MHC Engineers

Electrical Engineer: C&N Engineers

Civil Engineer: Luk & Associates

Lighting Consultant: Architectural Lighting Design

Building Data

Independent living: Total GSF: 62,000

Independent living: Total NSF of residential spaces: 52,000

Independent living: Total NSF of common spaces: 5,500

Independent Living

Unit type	Number of units	Size range (NSF)	Typical size (NSF)
Studio	5	450	450
One-bedroom	55	528–540	530
Two-bedroom	10	750	750
Total (all units)	70		

Accessible independent living units (%): 10

Project Costs (actual or estimated if the project is yet to be built; not including FF&E, site, or soft costs)

Independent living: Total cost for new construction ($): 18,600,000

Gender Breakdown of the Residents

Women (%): 49

Men (%): 51

Status of the Residents

Single (living alone) (%): 35

Living with a spouse / domestic partner (%): 20

Living with a friend / family member (e.g., sibling) (%): 40

Living with an in-home caregiver (%): 5

Source of Resident Payments

Private payment (%): 4

Medicaid / Medicare payment (%): 48

Government subsidy payment (%): 48

Average Age of the Residents

Independent living: Average age designed to support: 70
Independent living: Average entry age: 60

Moorings Park

Client / Owner / Provider: Moorings Park
Architect: Perkins Eastman
Architect of Record: Burt Hill / Pollock Krieg Architects, Inc.
General Prime Contractor: Manhattan Construction
Interior Designer: Wegman Design Group
Landscape Architect: JRL Design
Structural Engineer: Liebl & Barrow Engineering
Mechanical Engineer: TLC Engineering for Architecture
Electrical Engineer: TLC Engineering for Architecture
Civil Engineer: Davidson Engineering Inc.

Building Data

Independent living: Total GSF: 96,000
Independent living: Total NSF of residential spaces: 78,000
Independent living: Total NSF of common spaces: 18,000

Independent Living			
Unit type	Number of units	Size range (NSF)	Typical size (NSF)
Two-bedroom plus den	25	1800–3500	2800
Three-bedroom+	4	3500–5500	4000
Total (all units)	29		

Accessible independent living units (%): 25
Adaptable independent living units (%): 75

Project Costs (actual or estimated if the project is yet to be built; not including FF&E, site, or soft costs)

Independent living: Total cost for new construction ($): 25,100,000

Project Funding Sources

Conventional / private funding (%): 100

Gender Breakdown of the Residents

Women (%): 50
Men (%): 50

Status of the Residents

Living with a spouse / domestic partner (%): 100

Source of Resident Payments

Private payment (%): 100

Average Age of the Residents

Independent living: Average age designed to support: 79
Independent living: Average entry age: 85

Orchard Cove

Client / Owner / Provider: Hebrew Senior Life
Architect: DiMella Shaffer
General Prime Contractor: Commodore Builders
Interior Designer: DiMella Shaffer
Mechanical Engineer: AKF Group
Electrical Engineer: AKF Group
Lighting Designer: Collaborative Lighting, LLC

Project Funding Sources

Conventional / private funding (%): 60
Non-taxable bond offering funding (%): 40

Gender Breakdown of the Residents

Women (%): 80
Men (%): 20

Status of the Residents

Single (living alone) (%): 82
Living with a spouse / domestic partner (%): 13
Living with an in-home caregiver (%): 5

Source of Resident Payments

Private payment (%): 100

Average Age of the Residents

Independent living: Average age designed to support: 85
Independent living: Average entry age: 85

Rockhill Mennonite Community

Client / Owner / Provider: Rockhill Mennonite Community
Architect: SFCS Inc.
General Prime Contractor: Wholsen Construction Company
Interior Designer: SFCS Inc.
Landscape Architect: KCBA
Structural Engineer: SFCS Inc.
Mechanical Engineer: SFCS Inc.
Electrical Engineer: SFCS Inc.
Civil Engineer: Gilmore & Associates
Environmental Gerontologist: Lori Hiatt, PhD

Building Data

Assisted living: Total GSF: 19,910
Assisted living: Total NSF of residential spaces: 9,700
Assisted living: Total NSF of common spaces: 6,400

Assisted Living			
Unit type	Number of units	Size range (NSF)	Typical size (NSF)
Studio	20	-	385
Total (all units)	20		

Accessible assisted living units (%): 100

Project Costs (actual or estimated if the project is yet to be built; not including FF&E, site, or soft costs)
Assisted living: Total cost for addition(s) ($): 5,200,000

Project Funding Sources
Conventional / private funding (%): 100

Gender Breakdown of the Residents
Women (%): 86
Men (%): 14

Status of the Residents
Single (living alone) (%): 90
Living with a spouse / domestic partner (%): 10

Source of Resident Payments
Private payment (%): 100

Average Age of the Residents
Assisted living: Average age designed to support: 88
Assisted living: Average entry age: 87

Rose Villa Pocket Neighborhoods & Main Street

Client / Owner / Provider: Rose Villa
Architect: RLPS Architects
Collaborating Architect & Acoustical Consultant: Myhre Group Architects
General Prime Contractor: R&H Construction Company
Landscape Architect: Macdonald Enviornmental Planning
Structural Engineer: Lewis & VanVleet
Mechanical Engineer: Reese Engineering, Inc.
Electrical Engineer: Reese Engineering, Inc.
Civil Engineer: MGH Associates, Inc.
Development Consultant: Witz Company
Food Service: JEM Associates
IT: DaVinci Digital
Pool Design: Water Technology, Inc.

Building Data
Independent living: Total GSF: 128,263
Independent living: Total NSF of residential spaces: 77,930
Independent living: Total NSF of common spaces: 21,203

Independent Living			
Unit type	Number of units	Size range (NSF)	Typical size (NSF)
One-bedroom	17	813–846	813
One-bedroom plus den	47	864–1137	996
Two-bedroom	12	1222–1552	1222
Total (all units)	76		

Accessible independent living units (%): 2
Adaptable independent living units (%): 98

Project Costs (actual or estimated if the project is yet to be built; not including FF&E, site, or soft costs)
Independent living: Total cost for new construction ($): 30,000,000

Project Funding Sources
Non-taxable bond offering funding (%): 100

Average Age of the Residents
Independent living: Average age designed to support: 85

Rydal Park Repositioning

Client / Owner / Provider: Presby's Inspired Life
Architect: Stewart & Conners Architects, PLLC
General Prime Contractor: Whiting-Turner
Interior Designer: Interior Design Associates
Landscape Architect: McKloskey & Faber, PC
Structural Engineer: WK Dickson
Mechanical Engineer: Moore Engineering
Electrical Engineer: Moore Engineering
Civil Engineer: Charles E Shoemaker, Inc.

Building Data
Independent living: Total GSF: 48,596
Independent living: Total NSF of residential spaces: 24,936
Independent living: Total NSF of common spaces: 23,660
Assisted living: Total GSF: 28,784
Assisted living: Total NSF of residential spaces: 15,732
Assisted living: Total NSF of common spaces: 13,052
Assisted living—dementia / memory support: Total GSF: 14,392
Assisted living—dementia / memory support: Total NSF of residential spaces: 7,866
Assisted living—dementia / memory support: Total NSF of common spaces: 6,526
Long-term skilled nursing: Total GSF: 31,600
Long-term skilled nursing: Total NSF of residential spaces: 16,858
Long-term skilled nursing: Total NSF of common spaces: 14,742
Skilled nursing—dementia / memory support: Total GSF: 23,839
Skilled nursing—dementia / memory support: Total NSF of residential spaces: 8,652
Skilled nursing—dementia / memory support: Total NSF of common spaces: 15,187
Short-term rehab: Total GSF: 33,045
Short-term rehab: Total NSF of residential spaces: 16,858
Short-term rehab: Total NSF of common spaces: 16,187

Independent Living			
Unit type	Number of units	Size range (NSF)	Typical size (NSF)
One-bedroom	9	-	1000
Two-bedroom	9	-	1350
Total (all units)	18		

Accessible independent living units (%): 11
Adaptable independent living units (%): 89

Assisted Living

Unit type	Number of units	Size range (NSF)	Typical size (NSF)
Studio	3	-	314
One-bedroom	17	612–936	630
One-bedroom plus den	12		434
Total (all units)	32		

Accessible assisted living units (%): 10
Adaptable assisted living units (%): 90

Assisted Living—Dementia / Memory Support

Unit type	Number of units	Size range (NSF)	Typical size (NSF)
Private room*	14	300–425	425
Semi-private room**	4	-	600
Total (all units)	18		

*single occupant
**two occupants with separate bed areas but a shared bathroom

Long-Term Skilled Nursing

Unit type	Number of units	Size range (NSF)	Typical size (NSF)
Private room*	45	310–519	330
Total (all units)	45		

*single occupant

Skilled Nursing—Dementia / Memory Support

Unit type	Number of units	Size range (NSF)	Typical size (NSF)
Private room*	24	300–330	310
Total (all units)	24		

*single occupant

Short-Term Rehab

Unit type	Number of units	Size range (NSF)	Typical size (NSF)
Private room*	45	310–519	330
Total (all units)	45		

*single occupant

Project Costs (actual or estimated if the project is yet to be built; not including FF&E, site, or soft costs)
Independent living: Total cost for addition(s) ($): 108,000
Independent living: Total cost for renovation(s) / modernization(s) ($): 4,864,992
Assisted living: Total cost for renovation(s) / modernization(s) ($): 2,619,344
Assisted living—dementia / memory support: Total cost for renovation(s) / modernization(s) ($): 1,309,672
Long-term skilled nursing: Total cost for new construction ($): 6,699,200
Skilled nursing—dementia / memory support: Total cost for new construction ($): 5,053,868
Short-term rehab: Total cost for new construction ($): 7,005,540

Project Funding Sources
Non-taxable bond offering funding (%): 84
Other funding source (%): 16

Gender Breakdown of the Residents
Women (%): 72
Men (%): 28

Status of the Residents
Single (living alone) (%): 86
Living with a spouse / domestic partner (%): 14

Source of Resident Payments
Private payment (%): 90
Medicaid / Medicare payment (%): 10

Average Age of the Residents
Independent living: Average age designed to support: 78
Independent living: Average entry age: 80
Assisted living: Average age designed to support: 84
Assisted living: Average entry age: 89
Assisted living—dementia / memory support: Average age designed to support: 84
Assisted living—dementia / memory support: Average entry age: 89
Long-term skilled nursing: Average age designed to support: 86
Long-term skilled nursing: Average entry age: 88
Skilled nursing—dementia / memory support: Average age designed to support: 86
Skilled nursing—dementia / memory support: Average entry age: 90
Short-term rehab: Average age designed to support: 82
Short-term rehab: Average entry age: 82

St. Ignatius Nursing & Rehab Center

Client / Owner / Provider: Felician Franciscan Sisters
Architect: Lenhardt Rodgers Architecture + Interiors
General Prime Contractor: Berks Ridge
Interior Designer: Lenhardt Rodgers Architecture + Interiors
Landscape Architect: Design for Generations
Structural Engineer: MacIntosh Engineering
Mechanical Engineer: Moore Engineering Company
Electrical Engineer: Moore Engineering Company
Civil Engineer: CE Shoemaker

Building Data
Short-term rehab: Total GSF: 6,388
Short-term rehab: Total NSF of residential spaces: 3,227
Short-term rehab: Total NSF of common spaces: 2,466

Short-Term Rehab

Unit type	Number of units	Size range (NSF)	Typical size (NSF)
Private room*	1	138–138	138
Semi-private room**	21	83–102	91
Total (all units)	22		

*single occupant
**two occupants with separate bed areas but a shared bathroom

Project Costs (actual or estimated if the project is yet to be built; not including FF&E, site, or soft costs)
Short-term rehab: Total cost for renovation(s) / modernization(s) ($): 1,296,000

Project Funding Sources
Conventional / private funding (%): 67
Other funding source (%): 33

Gender Breakdown of the Residents
Women (%): 55
Men (%): 45

Status of the Residents
Single (living alone) (%): 100

Source of Resident Payments
Medicaid / Medicare payment (%): 32
Other payment source* (%): 68
 * LIFE (%): 22.6; BRAVO (%) 22.6; other (United Health, Health Partners, Evercare, Blue Cross) (%): 22.8

Average Age of the Residents
Short-term rehab: Average age designed to support: 65
Short-term rehab: Average entry age: 80

Sharon Towers Dining Renovation

Client / Owner / Provider: Sharon Towers
Architect: Stewart & Conners Architects, PLLC
General Prime Contractor: Omega
Interior Designer: Interior Design Associates
Mechanical Engineer: Teeter Engineering
Electrical Engineer: Teeter Engineering

Project Funding Sources
Conventional / private funding (%): 100

Gender Breakdown of the Residents
Women (%): 72
Men (%): 28

Status of the Residents
Single (living alone) (%): 87
Living with a spouse / domestic partner (%): 13

Source of Resident Payments
Private payment (%): 100

Average Age of the Residents
Independent living: Average age designed to support: 85
Independent living: Average entry age: 79
Assisted living: Average age designed to support: 88
Assisted living: Average entry age: 82
Long-term skilled nursing: Average age designed to support: 90
Long-term skilled nursing: Average entry age: 82

The Summit at Central Park

Client / Owner / Provider: City of Grand Prairie, Parks Department
Architect: Brinkley Sargent Architects
General Prime Contractor: Manhattan Construction Co.
Interior Designer: Brinkley Sargent Architects
Landscape Architect: MESA Design Associates
Structural Engineer: Structural Engenuity
Mechanical Engineer: M-E Engineers
Electrical Engineer: M-E Engineers
Civil Engineer: Halff Associates
Aquatics Engineer: Counsilman-Hunsaker

Project Funding Sources
Public sector funding (%): 100

Sun City Tower Kobe

Client / Owner / Provider: Half Century More
Design Architect: BAR Architects
Architect of Record: Asai Architectural Research
Interior Designer: BAMO
Landscape Architect: SWA Group
Project Manager: M.D. Associates, Inc.

Building Data
Independent living: Total GSF: 534,000
Independent living: Total NSF of residential spaces: 303,000
Independent living: Total NSF of common spaces: 231,000
Long-term skilled nursing: Total GSF: 49,000
Long-term skilled nursing: Total NSF of residential spaces: 23,000
Long-term skilled nursing: Total NSF of common spaces: 26,000

Independent Living			
Unit type	Number of units	Size range (NSF)	Typical size (NSF)
One-bedroom	240	440–500	460
One-bedroom plus den	78	501–600	555
Two-bedroom	140	601–880	710
Two-bedroom plus den	25	880+	910
Total (all units)	483		

Accessible independent living units (%): 100

Long-Term Skilled Nursing			
Unit type	Number of units	Size range (NSF)	Typical size (NSF)
Private room*	98	235	235
Total (all units)	98		

*single occupant

Project Costs (actual or estimated if the project is yet to be built; not including FF&E, site, or soft costs)
Independent living: Total cost for new construction ($): 114,000,000
Long-term skilled nursing: Total cost for new construction ($): 10,535,000

Project Funding Sources
Conventional / private funding (%): 100

Gender Breakdown of the Residents
Women (%): 70
Men (%): 30

Status of the Residents
Single (living alone) (%): 70
Living with a spouse / domestic partner (%): 30

Source of Resident Payments
Private payment (%): 100

Average Age of the Residents
Independent living: Average age designed to support: 75
Long-term skilled nursing: Average age designed to support: 75

Tohono O'odham Elder Home

Client / Owner / Provider: Tohono O'odham Nursing Authority
Architect: Lizard Rock Designs, LLC
Interior Designer: Interior Sanctuaries, LLC
Structural Engineer: Schneider & Associates
Mechanical Engineer: KC Mechanical
Electrical Engineer: Jeff Matthews
Civil Engineer: Cornerstone Engineering Group

Building Data
Assisted living: Total GSF: 8,000
Assisted living: Total NSF of residential spaces: 2,000
Assisted living: Total NSF of common spaces: 6,000

Assisted Living			
Unit type	Number of units	Size range (NSF)	Typical size (NSF)
Studio	12	115	115
Total (all units)	12		

Accessible assisted living units (%): 100

Project Costs (actual or estimated if the project is yet to be built; not including FF&E, site, or soft costs)
Assisted living: Total cost for new construction ($): 2,250,000

Project Funding Sources
Conventional / private funding (%): 100

Gender Breakdown of the Residents
Women (%): 40
Men (%): 60

Status of the Residents
Single (living alone) (%): 100

Source of Resident Payments
Private payment (%): 10
Medicaid / Medicare payment (%): 90

Average Age of the Residents
Assisted living: Average age designed to support: 70
Assisted living: Average entry age: 68

The Townhomes on Hendricks Place

Client / Owner / Provider: Moravian Manor
Architect: RLPS Architects
General Prime Contractor: Simeral Construction
Interior Designer: RLPS Interiors
Structural Engineer: Zug & Associates, Ltd.
Mechanical Engineer: Reese Engineering, Inc.
Electrical Engineer: Reese Engineering, Inc.
Civil Engineer: RGS Associates

Building Data
Independent living: Total GSF: 42,584
Independent living: Total NSF of residential spaces: 36,445
Independent living: Total NSF of common spaces: 0
Adaptable independent living units (%): 100

Independent Living			
Unit type	Number of units	Size range (NSF)	Typical size (NSF)
Two-bedroom plus den	12	2609–2833	2833
Total (all units)	12		

Project Costs (actual or estimated if the project is yet to be built; not including FF&E, site, or soft costs)
Independent living: Total cost for new construction ($): 4,429,267

Project Funding Sources
Conventional / private funding (%): 100

Gender Breakdown of the Residents
Women (%): 50
Men (%): 50

Status of the Residents
Living with a spouse / domestic partner (%): 100

Source of Resident Payments
Private payment (%): 100

Average Age of the Residents
Independent living: Average age designed to support: 75
Independent living: Average entry age: 73

The Village at Orchard Ridge

Client / Owner / Provider: National Lutheran Communities & Services
Architect: RLPS Architects
General Prime Contractor: Howard Shockey & Sons, Inc.
Interior Designer: RLPS Interiors / Partners in Planning
Structural Engineer: A.W. Lookup Corporation
Mechanical Engineer: Reese Engineering, Inc.
Electrical Engineer: Reese Engineering, Inc.
Civil Engineer: Greenway Engineering
Geotechnical Engineer: GeoConcepts Engineering, Inc.
Owner's Project Director: Arch Consultants, Ltd
Owner's Counsel: Lerch, Early & Brewer, Chtd.
Owner's Food Service Consultant: Dining Management Resources, Inc.

Building Data
Independent living: Total GSF: 377,771
Independent living: Total NSF of residential spaces: 266,966
Independent living: Total NSF of common spaces: 46,342
Assisted living—dementia / memory support: Total GSF: 13,562
Assisted living—dementia / memory support: Total NSF of residential spaces: 5,482
Assisted living—dementia / memory support: Total NSF of common spaces: 8,080
Long-term skilled nursing: Total GSF: 8,395
Long-term skilled nursing: Total NSF of residential spaces: 3,300
Long-term skilled nursing: Total NSF of common spaces: 5,095

Independent Living			
Unit type	Number of units	Size range (NSF)	Typical size (NSF)
One-bedroom	31	711–790	765
One-bedroom plus den	43	768–949	877
Two-bedroom	82	1170–2032	1502
Two-bedroom plus den	47	1479–2107	1779
Total (all units)	203		

Adaptable independent living units (%): 100

Assisted Living—Dementia / Memory Support			
Unit type	Number of units	Size range (NSF)	Typical size (NSF)
Private room*	14	274–281	277
Semi-private room**	2	516	516
Total (all units)	16		

*single occupant
**two occupants with separate bed areas but a shared bathroom

Long-Term Skilled Nursing			
Unit type	Number of units	Size range (NSF)	Typical size (NSF)
Private room*	10	274–347	301
Total (all units)	10		

*single occupant

Project Costs (actual or estimated if the project is yet to be built; not including FF&E, site, or soft costs)
Independent living: Total cost for new construction ($): 50,796,372
Assisted living—dementia / memory support: Total cost for new construction ($): 3,001,348
Long-term skilled nursing: Total cost for new construction ($): 1,839,536

Project Funding Sources
Conventional / private funding (%): 3
Non-taxable bond offering funding (%): 97

Gender Breakdown of the Residents
Women (%): 62
Men (%): 38

Status of the Residents
Single (living alone) (%): 66
Living with a spouse / domestic partner (%): 34

Source of Resident Payments
Private payment (%): 100

Average Age of the Residents
Independent living: Average age designed to support: 78
Independent living: Average entry age: 78
Assisted living—dementia / memory support: Average age designed to support: 82
Assisted living—dementia / memory support: Average entry age: 90
Long-term skilled nursing: Average age designed to support: 88

The Village at Rockville

Client / Owner / Provider: National Lutheran Communities & Services
Architect: RLPS Architects
General Prime Contractor: Whiting-Turner Contracting / Howard Shockey & Sons
Interior Designer: RLPS Interiors / Partners in Planning
Structural Engineer: A.W. Lookup Corporation
Mechanical Engineer: Reese Engineering, Inc.
Electrical Engineer: Reese Engineering, Inc.
Civil Engineer: Macris, Hendricks & Glascock
Fire Protection Engineer: The Protection Engineering Group, Inc.
Owner's Project Director: ARCH Consultants
Owner's Consultant: Lerch, Early & Brewer, Chtd.
Owner's Food Service Consutants: Dining Management Resources & Avalon Design LLC

Building Data
Assisted living: Total GSF: 13,205
Assisted living: Total NSF of residential spaces: 7,023
Assisted living: Total NSF of common spaces: 773
Long-term skilled nursing: Total GSF: 13,114
Long-term skilled nursing: Total NSF of residential spaces: 6,007
Long-term skilled nursing: Total NSF of common spaces: 773
Short-term rehab: Total GSF: 18,076
Short-term rehab: Total NSF of residential spaces: 6,187
Short-term rehab: Total NSF of common spaces: 2,670

Assisted Living

Unit type	Number of units	Size range (NSF)	Typical size (NSF)
Studio	16	323–458	375
One-bedroom	2	553	553
Total (all units)	18		

Accessible assisted living units (%): 100

Long-Term Skilled Nursing

Unit type	Number of units	Size range (NSF)	Typical size (NSF)
Private room*	32	180–308	180
Total (all units)	32		

*single occupant

Short-Term Rehab

Unit type	Number of units	Size range (NSF)	Typical size (NSF)
Private room*	33	180–308	180
Total (all units)	33		

*single occupant

Project Costs (actual or estimated if the project is yet to be built; not including FF&E, site, or soft costs)

Assisted living: Total cost for renovation(s) / modernization(s) ($): 2,840,000
Long-term skilled nursing: Total cost for renovation(s) / modernization(s) ($): 2,757,000
Short-term rehab: Total cost for renovation(s) / modernization(s) ($): 4,209,000

Project Funding Sources

Conventional / private funding (%): 100

Gender Breakdown of the Residents

Women (%): 82
Men (%): 18

Status of the Residents

Single (living alone) (%): 100

Source of Resident Payments

Private payment (%): 29
Medicaid / Medicare payment (%): 71

Average Age of the Residents

Assisted living: Average age designed to support: 88
Assisted living: Average entry age: 89
Long-term skilled nursing: Average age designed to support: 90
Long-term skilled nursing: Average entry age: 82
Short-term rehab: Average age designed to support: 85
Short-term rehab: Average entry age: 87

White Oak Cottages at Fox Hill Village

Client / Owner / Provider: White Oak Cottages
Architect: EGA PC
General Prime Contractor: Cutler Associates
Interior Designer: Siemasko and Verbridge
Landscape Architect: HBLA
Structural Engineer: Shelley Engineering
Mechanical Engineer: McGill Engineering
Electrical Engineer: Reno Engineering and Light Design
Civil Engineer: Norwood Engineering

Building Data

Assisted living—dementia / memory support: Total GSF: 17,050
Assisted living—dementia / memory support: Total NSF of residential spaces: 7,102
Assisted living—dementia / memory support: Total NSF of common spaces: 2,000

Assisted Living—Dementia / Memory Support

Unit type	Number of units	Size range (NSF)	Typical size (NSF)
Private room*	24	297–314	300
Total (all units)	24		

*single occupant

Project Costs (actual or estimated if the project is yet to be built; not including FF&E, site, or soft costs)

Assisted living—dementia / memory support: Total cost for new construction ($): 3,800,000

Project Funding Sources

Conventional / private funding (%): 100

Gender Breakdown of the Residents

Women (%): 80
Men (%): 20

Status of the Residents

Single (living alone) (%): 100

Source of Resident Payments

Private payment (%): 100

Average Age of the Residents

Assisted living—dementia / memory support: Average age designed to support: 85
Assisted living—dementia / memory support: Average entry age: 82

Worman's Mill Village Center

Client / Owner / Provider: The Wormald Companies
Architect: Brown Craig Turner
Structural Engineer: Structura Engineering
Mechanical Engineer: Century Engineering
Electrical Engineer: Century Engineering
Civil Engineer: Piedmont Engineering

Building Data

Independent living: Total GSF: 200
Independent living: Total NSF of residential spaces: 140,000
Independent living: Total NSF of common spaces: 10,000
Assisted living: Total GSF: 27,000
Assisted living: Total NSF of residential spaces: 10,800
Assisted living: Total NSF of common spaces: 7,200

Independent Living			
Unit type	Number of units	Size range (NSF)	Typical size (NSF)
One-bedroom	61	706–757	706
One-bedroom plus den	27	870–914	870
Two-bedroom	53	1096–1576	1096
Two-bedroom plus den	30	1221–1333	1333
Total (all units)	171		

Accessible independent living units (%): 5
Adaptable independent living units (%): 95

Assisted Living			
Unit type	Number of units	Size range (NSF)	Typical size (NSF)
Studio	36	280–320	300
Total (all units)	36		

Accessible assisted living units (%): 100

Project Costs (actual or estimated if the project is yet to be built; not including FF&E, site, or soft costs)

Independent living and assisted living: Total cost for new construction ($): 30,000,000

Project Funding Sources

Conventional / private funding (%): 50
Public sector funding (%): 50

Source of Resident Payments

Private payment (%): 100

Average Age of the Residents

Independent living: Average age designed to support: 75
Assisted living: Average age designed to support: 85
Assisted living—dementia / memory support: Average age designed to support: 85